Implementing SSH®
Strategies for Optimizing the Secure Shell

Implementing SSH®
Strategies for Optimizing
the Secure Shell

Himanshu Dwivedi

WILEY

Wiley Publishing, Inc.

Vice President and Executive Group Publisher: Richard Swadley
Vice President and Executive Publisher: Bob Ipsen
Vice President & Publisher: Joseph B. Wikert
Executive Editorial Director: Mary Bednarek
Executive Editor: Carol Long
Development Editor: Scott Amerman
Editorial Manager: Kathryn A. Malm
Production Editor: Felicia Robinson
Media Development Specialist: Travis Silvers
Permissions Editor: Laura Moss
Text Design & Composition: Wiley Composition Services

For general information on our other products and services please contact our Customer Care Department within the United States at (800) 762-2974, outside the United States at (317) 572-3993 or fax (317) 572-4002.

Library of Congress Control Number available from publisher.

ISBN: 0-471-45880-5

Printed in the United States of America

10 9 8 7 6 5 4 3 2 1

Dedication

This book is dedicated to my wife, Kusum. Without her, this book would not have been possible. Kusum, you are truly special to me.

I would like to especially thank my parents, Chandradhar and Prabha Dwivedi. Without their guidance, support, and inspiration, I would not be where I am today. Lastly, I would like to thank my brother and sister, Sudhanshu and Neeraja Dwivedi, from whom I have learned every important lesson in life. Without their influence and experiences, I could not have learned so much.

I thank you and love you all very much.

Contents

Acknowledgments

I would like to acknowledge and thank several people who have helped me throughout my career. The following people have supported me in numerous ways that have made me a better professional. To these people, I want to say thank you: Andy Hubbard, Ronnie Dinfotan, Amy Bergstrom, Tim Gartin, Troy Cardinal, Anthony Barkley, Jason Chan, Kevin Rich, Paul Nash, Nitra Lagrander, Sumit Kalra, Glen Joes, Joel Wallenstrom, Ted Barlow, Allen Dawson, Rob Helt, Larry Harvey, and jum4nj1. Also, special thanks to Mike Schiffman, Carol Long, and Scott Amerman, who were integral in getting this book established.

About the Author

Himanshu Dwivedi is a Managing Security Architect for @stake, the leading provider of digital security services. Himanshu has over nine years of experience in information security, with several years of technical security experience at Electronic Data Systems (EDS), Deloitte and Touche, and @stake. He holds a wide spectrum of security skills, specializing in the telecommunications industry. Also, he has worked with major organizations in the U.S., Europe, South America, and Asia, including some of the major software, manufacturing, and financial-based entities. Furthermore, Himanshu has various skills across multiple facets, including operating systems (Microsoft NT/2000, Linux RedHat/Caldera, OpenBSD); firewalls (Checkpoint Firewall-1, ipfilter, ipchains); Intrusion Detection Systems (ISS, Tripwire, Snort, and so on); Mainframe (OS/3900-RACF); protocols (SSH, SSL, and IPSEC); Storage Area Networks (EMC, Network Appliance, Brocade, Qlogic); storage protocols (Fibre Channel, iSCSI, Gigabit IP, and so on); network devices (Cisco, Nortel, Netscreen, and so on); and various other products and technologies. Himanshu is the leading instructor of several security-training classes offered throughout the U.S., including Cyber Attacks and Counter Measures, Storage Security, and Windows 2000 Security.

At @stake, Himanshu leads the Storage Center of Excellence (CoE), which focuses research and training around storage technology, including Network Attached Storage (NAS) and Storage Area Networks (SAN). He is considered an industry expert in the area of SAN security, specifically Fibre Channel Security. He has given numerous presentations and workshops regarding the security in SANs, including the BlackHat Security Conference, SNIA Security Summit, Storage Networking World, TechTarget's Storage Management Conference, StorageWorld, the Fibre Channel Conference, SAN-West, and SAN-East.

Himanshu currently has a patent pending on a storage design architecture that he co-developed with other @stake professionals. The patent is for a storage security design that can be implemented on enterprise storage products deployed in Fibre Channel storage networks. In addition, he has published two books on storage security: *The Complete Storage Reference* (McGraw-Hill/Osborne) and *Storage Security Handbook* (NeoScale Publishing). He has also published two papers. His first paper is "Securing Intellectual Property" (www.vsi.org/resources/specs/ippwp310.pdf), which provides recommendations on how to protect an organization's network from the inside out. His second paper is "Storage Security" (www.atstake.com/research/reports/index.html), which provides the best practices and recommendations for securing a SAN or a NAS storage network.

Author Accomplishments

Patents

- U.S. Patent Serial No. 10/198,728: Patent Pending for Design Architecture and Methods for Enterprise Storage Devices

Published Books

- *The Complete Storage Reference*, McGraw-Hill/Osborne (Chapter 25, "Security Considerations")
- *Storage Security Handbook*, NeoScale Publishing

Papers

- Storage Security
  (http://www.atstake.com/research/reports/index.html)
- Securing Intellectual Property
  (http://www.vsi.org/resources/specs/ippwp310.pdf)

Introduction

Secure Shell (SSH) is a utility that can be described in many different ways. It can be described as a protocol, an encryption tool, a client/server application, or a command interface. Along with its various descriptions, SSH provides various functions with a single package. SSH's diverse set of services and the ability to provide those services in a secure manner have allowed it to become a staple in many enterprise networks.

Most security professionals probably discovered SSH very early in their careers and have fallen in love with it ever since. SSH to the security professional is like a donut to Homer Simpson: a godsend. Professionals continually ask themselves if there is anything SSH can't do. For the security professional, SSH provides everything one could ask for, including a free car wash on weekends (well, that is what it seems like sometimes). One of the great things about SSH is that not only do security professionals use and love the utility, but non-security technical professionals and nontechnical professionals love it as well. Furthermore, SSH is compared with other security utilities in the industry, such as RSA SecureID tokens, it is evident that security professionals are the predominant end-users of these other utilities. SecureID tokens are not widely used by nontechnical personnel and are not deployed often in environments that are not closely affiliated with corporate security. On the other hand, SSH is deployed in many Unix workstations/servers, Windows workstations, and a variety of network devices such as Cisco routers and switches.

Some books on the market today cover SSH. Unlike most of them, this book does not cover the ins and outs of SSH as a protocol, the encryption modules used in SSH1 and SSH2, or the supported algorithms. Instead, it covers the ins and outs of implementing and optimizing SSH. Think of this book as a tactical guide to SSH: *Now that I understand SSH, how can I use it?* This book covers the *how can I use it* part. Covered in detail is how to install, implement, optimize, and support SSH in Unix, Windows, and network architecture environments.

What Secure Shell Is

What is Secure Shell? For the purposes of this book, Secure Shell is a *solution*, period! Most readers should have some knowledge of Secure Shell, having used it in a given capacity, read about it, or even deployed it in some manner. I do not explore the theoretical foundations of Secure Shell but rather its practical definition, simply stated as follows:

> **Secure Shell:** A well-balanced and flexible solution that can solve a variety of security and functionality issues within an organization

To expand the preceding definition, the following elements of SSH are explored during the course of this book, as are the following solutions SSH provides:

- Secure Management Solution
- Secure Proxy Solution
- Secure Telnet Solution
- Secure Remote Access Solution
- Secure "R" services Solution
- Secure File Transfer Solution
- Secure VPN Solution
- Secure Wireless (802.11) Solution
- Secure Backup Solution
- Secure Web Browsing Solution

Implementing and Optimizing SSH

The chapters that follow focus on the methods and options for implementing and optimizing Secure Shell. In addition to understanding this book's primary focus on implementation, it is important to understand that this book does not make recommendations regarding why or when to use SSH. It does, however, make recommendations regarding how to use it. It would not be in your best interest for me to say that SSH should be used in all situations where X and Y exist (where X and Y are specific problems in a given organization). Not only would that be a very risky alternative; it would make me irresponsible by portraying SSH as a silver bullet. There are no silver bullets in the world of security.

Once an organization has decided to implement SSH or is interested in learning more about how to optimize it, this book can provide step-by-step guidelines on how to implement SSH in a secure and stable manner. Furthermore, once an organization has decided that SSH might be one of few solutions to a particular problem, this book can describe the ways SSH can be optimized, helping the organization determine if SSH is the right solution.

In addition to describing the specific implementation steps for deploying SSH, this book discusses ways to optimize current implementations of SSH. Also, this book can be used by organizations that already have deployed SSH but are interested in learning additional ways to optimize the utility.

To add to the focus of implementation (and to avoid any confusion about this book being a primer on SSH), various chapters throughout the book offer several architectural examples that illustrate the methods for optimizing SSH. For example, the chapter concerning port forwarding has two to three real network architectures where there are problems in a given environment, concerning both security and functionality. The solutions that SSH can offer are discussed in detail in each example. Also, the methods for optimizing SSH, according to the issue discussed in each example, are described in detail in order to satisfy technical and business requirements.

Why More Secure Shell?

One of the many reasons why I wanted to write this book was to explain SSH usage. Despite the flexibility, advantages, features, and, most of all, security of SSH, few implementations of SSH take advantage of all its capabilities. Even the savviest Unix administrators, who have been exposed to SSH a lot longer than many Windows or Macintosh users have, may not know that there is a whole world to SSH besides encrypted Telnet. Features such as port-forwarding, secure e-mail, proxy, dynamic port forwarding, VPN, and so on are minor when it comes to deploying SSH; however, these features can significantly add to the value of an organization.

Another reason I wanted to write this book was to promote SSH's ease of use. Many administrators know that using SSH as a replacement for Telnet is quite easy; however, many administrators assume that using SSH as a security file transfer protocol, a port-forwarder, and a VPN solution is quite difficult. Furthermore, many administrators think there is an involved process to configuring an SSH server in order to get its full functionality. As I demonstrate in this book, the implementation of SSH as a server is not only quite easy, but most of the configuration required takes place on the client rather than the server.

Furthermore, many environments that deploy SSH still use Telnet, RSH, Rlogin, and FTP. While there may be problems with interoperability and SSH on various platforms and applications, a lot of organizations use SSH but leave FTP enabled for file transfer (or even worse, use SFTP for file transfer but leave Telnet enabled for command line execution). SSH not only can do both; it can do both with one daemon or service, eliminating the need to have two separate services running on a single machine.

This book provides a detailed guide, with screen shots and steps, for using SSH in a variety of ways. The goal of this book is to be an accessible reference used in data centers to deploy a range of services (from secure FTP to secure e-mail with Microsoft Exchange).

Best Practice Benefits for Security

What are the benefits of using SSH in any type of environment, and why is there a need for utilities like SSH? SSH offers many *best practices* in terms of security. Best practices are prerequisites in order to deploy an acceptable amount of security in a given entity. Four of the best practices that SSH offers are:

- **Authentication:** Two-factor authentication
- **Encryption:** Secure (encrypted) communication with 3DES or equivalent
- **Integrity:** MD5 and SHA1 hashing
- **Authorization:** IP/DNS filtering

SSH provides two-factor authentication by offering the use of public and private keys, in addition to a username and password, to authenticate two SSH servers. In addition to providing two-factor authentication, SSH offers safe and encrypted communication with a variety of encryption standards, including triple-DES (3DES), Blowfish, Two-fish, and so on. SSH also offers packet-level integrity by using MD5 and SHA1 hashing of each session. Lastly, SSH has the ability to permit or restrict nodes based on an IP address or hostname. These four best practices can help defend against many security attacks in sensitive networks that contain critical data.

Defenses

The primary purpose for deploying SSH is security. SSH defends against several attacks that plague IP (Internet Protocol) version 4 networks, including poor protocols with IPv4, such as Address Resolution Protocol (ARP), Initial Sequence Numbers (ISN), and various clear-text protocols, such as Telnet, RSH, Rlogin, FTP, POP3, IMAP, LDAP, and HTTP.

Because space is limited, *Implementing SSH* does not discuss in detail *all* types of attacks that SSH defends against. You should be aware of three critical types of security attacks against which SSH is quite effective. (Be aware that while SSH cannot prevent all of these attacks, it has safeguards in place that make it extremely difficult, if not well-nigh impossible, to execute them.) The three major types of security attacks are:

Man-in-the-Middle (MITM) attacks.   Man-in-the-Middle attacks occur against ARP in IPv4 networks. Such attacks allow an unauthorized entity to sniff the network even on a switched environment by capturing the communication between two trusted entities. SSH version 2 prevents attackers from gaining access to communication by fully encrypting it. The chances that an attacker can capture the communication between two entities are minimized, as the communication is in a form that is unreadable to the attacker.

Session hijacking.   Session-hijacking attacks occur against the ISN in the TCP header of a TCP/IP packet. An attacker can take advantage of the poor sequence numbers used by the ISN and hijack a session between two trusted entities. SSH can make it virtually impossible for an attacker to view, capture, or attempt to hijack the ISN altogether, although it cannot always make the ISN in a TCP header less predictable.

Sniffing.   Sniffing is the simple act of viewing the communication (packets) in a network. SSH provides a strong level of encryption that can protect weak protocols such as Telnet, RSH, Rlogin, FTP, POP3, IMAP, LDAP, and HTTP either by replacing them altogether (for Telnet, RSH, and Rlogin, for example) or by wrapping them within a tunnel (for POP3). This encryption prevents most, if not all, unauthorized users from sniffing the network.

How This Book Is Organized

This book is organized into three main parts: SSH Basics, Remote Access Solutions, and Protocol Replacement. Part One covers the basics of SSH. Chapter 1 gives a broad overview of SSH, which can be used as a refresher for professionals familiar with this utility. It also explores why SSH should be used and some of the major features that make it useful in a network environment.

Chapters 2 and 3 present the various SSH servers and clients that exist on the market today, both commercial and freely downloadable. SSH's features, functions, and capabilities often differ from each other, sometimes in extreme ways, depending on which client or server is used; therefore, these two chapters show the similarities and differences, and positives and negatives of some of the major SSH vendors in the market.

Chapter 4 delves into authentication, a process that covers everything from username and password to key-based authentication with digital certificates.

To round out Part One, Chapter 5 explores how SSH can be used on network devices such as routers, switches, firewalls, and other devices that are traditionally managed by Telnet. In addition, Chapter 5 covers management methods to be used with SSH.

Part Two shifts to the different remote access solutions available with SSH. Chapter 6 examines the basics of port forwarding, from theory and setup to configuration, and Chapter 7 discusses port forwarding in greater detail, explaining specifically how it functions as an enterprise-wide remote access solution.

Part Three provides a detailed discussion of protocol replacement with SSH. Chapter 8 describes the versatility of SSH. This chapter not only investigates how SSH can be used to replace insecure protocols such as RSH, Rlogin, and FTP but also shows how to use SSH as a secure file transfer solution, a secure chat server, and a server backup solution. Chapter 9 describes methods for using SSH with SOCKS proxies and dynamic port forwarding, plus ways in which SSH can be used as a secure Web and a secure wireless solution.

Chapter 10 presents three case studies involving remote access, secure wireless connectivity, and secure file transfer in mixed operating environments. Each case study describes a problem situation, presents several business requirements, and provides a solution involving SSH.

Who Should Read This Book

Implementing SSH is intended for professionals working in data centers. The material presented in the chapters that follow is essential, need-to-know information on how to implement SSH from small networks to enterprise networks. This book covers common "How-Tos," providing the necessary implementation steps and detailed descriptions of all the services SSH can provide to an environment. You are encouraged to use this book as a quick reference for how to do certain tasks. It is not necessarily meant to be read from start to finish; thus, individual chapters are self-supporting, without requiring any prior knowledge of the other chapters. For example, if you need or want to learn how to use SSH as a proxy service, you can simply go to Chapter 9, "Proxy Technologies in a Secure Web Environment," and begin reading. You do not have to have read Chapters 1 through 8 to understand the concepts discussed in Chapter 9.

Generally speaking, this book is for the following types of individuals:

- Anyone interested in learning how to implement SSH, including all of its capabilities and strengths
- Anyone interested in expanding his or her existing knowledge of SSH
- Anyone looking for new strategies in optimizing her or his current usage of SSH

Platforms

The platforms used in this book are OpenBSD 3.1, Linux RedHat 8.0, and Windows 2000 (Server or Professional), except where noted. Also, it is safe to assume that most flavors of Windows (NT4.0 to 2003 Server) and Unix (Linux, Solaris, HP-UX, and so on) will obtain similar results, if not the same results, as the platforms used in this book.

About the Web Site

To access the companion Web site for this book, please go to:

www.wiley.com/compbooks/dwivedi

The site will link you to the three primary vendors discussed throughout the book — OpenSSH, SSH Communications, and VanDyke Software — where you can download freeware or licensed commercial versions of SSH, as the case may be.

Also to be found on the site are links where you can find information on open source and commercial implementations for servers and clients discussed throughout the book.

Lastly, the site contains all the code used throughout the book. Readers will be able to cut and paste the code onto their own PCs to be used for various implementations.

Product Notes

SSH is an industry standard defined by the IETF's Secure Shell working group (www.ietf.org/html.charters/secsh-charter.html). In addition, SSH has many open source and commercial implementations for both SSH servers and SSH clients. In this book we will discuss, reference, or describe the following implementations of SSH:

- OpenSSH (www.openssh.org)
- OpenSSH—Win32 (http://lexa.mckenna.edu/sshwindows/)
- SSH Communications Commercial (www.ssh.com)
- VShell and Secure CRT (www.vandyke.com)
- Putty (www.putty.com)
- F-Secure (www.fsecure.com)
- Mindterm—SSH over Java with Web browsers (www.appgate.com/mindterm)
- WinSCP (http://winscp.vse.cz/eng)

SSH Basics

Overview of SSH

Secure Shell (SSH) is a program used to secure communication between two entities. SSH uses a client/server architecture, where SSH clients, available on all versions of Windows, different flavors of Unix, and various Macintosh operating systems, connect to SSH servers, which can be operating systems such as Sun Solaris or Microsoft Windows or devices such as a Cisco router. In its simplest sense, SSH is used to execute remote commands securely on another entity, often used as a replacement for Telnet and the Berkeley "R" protocols such as remote shell (RSH) and remote login (Rlogin), discussed further in Chapter 8. In addition to executing remote commands, SSH is used as a secure remote copy utility, replacing traditional protocols such as the File Transfer Protocol (FTP) and Remote Copy Protocol (RCP).

Despite the name *Secure Shell*, SSH is not a shell at all. Unlike other traditional shells found in different flavors of Unix, such as BASH, KORN, and C, SSH provides encryption between entities, not a shell interface between entities. The encryption methods and algorithms used for SSH are all based on industry standards such as 3DES, Blowfish, Twofish, and AES.

The paragraphs that follow discuss the basics of SSH: how it works, what it can be used for, and why it is tremendously flexible. This chapter is useful for readers who do not have experience with SSH or who have never been introduced to it aside from a casual reference. Advanced users may want to skip to the next chapter. Specifically, this chapter discusses the following topics:

- Differences between SSH1 and SSH2
- Uses of SSH
- Client/server architecture for SSH
- SSH's Encryption Architecture
- Basic miscues with SSH
- Types of SSH clients/servers
- Basic setup of SSH
- Summary of SSH's optimal uses

Differences between SSH1 and SSH2

SSH version 1 (SSH1) was the first iteration of SSH; however, SSH1 had several limitations, including the use of port forwarding, which led to the second iteration of SSH: SSH version 2 (SSH2). In addition to its limitations, SSH1 had several security issues associated with its cryptography, which also led to the establishment of SSH2.

The differences between SSH1 and SSH2 may seem minor to most end-users; however, the differences are quite significant. SSH1 and SSH2 are two different protocols. SSH2 was completely rewritten from scratch, giving it more security, performance, and flexibility than SSH1. Also, SSH1 and SSH2 encrypt communication differently, which mitigated several of the documented issues with SSH1's encryption methods. SSH1 is not being developed now, whereas SSH2 is becoming the standard when referring to SSH. There are still many implementations of SSH1, but the implementations are becoming fewer and more in favor of SSH2. For the purposes of this book, I do not refer to, use, or demonstrate the use of SSH1. I concentrate solely on the usage and optimization of SSH2. The following is a short list of the advantages of using SSH2 instead of SSH1:

- Significant improvements with security and speed
- Considerably greater flexibility with Secure File Transfer Protocol (SFTP)
- Interoperability with several different public key algorithms, including Diffie-Hellman (see http://www.rsasecurity.com/rsalabs/faq/3-6-1.html for more information on Diffie-Hellman)
- New architecture that requires far less code usage

Various Uses of SSH

SSH can be used in a variety of ways, depending on your network environment and business requirements. The flexibility that SSH provides in any type of dynamic or static environment gives it a significant advantage over other utilities in the industry, both security-focused utilities, such as IPSEC, and nonsecurity-focused utilities, such as FTP. SSH can be used for multiple users with just a single process (daemon) or service running on the server, with most of the configuration required on the client side. During the course of this book, I explore the various uses of SSH; however, I take the better half of this chapter to describe the different uses of SSH to illustrate its full capabilities:

- Security
- Remote command execution
- Remote file transfer
- Remote network access
- Secure management
- Proxy services

Security

The implementation of SSH in a trusted or nontrusted environment can protect against many of the security issues with Internet Protocol version 4 (IPv4). IPv4 has been plagued with security issues ranging from poor initial sequence numbers (ISN) in TCP header packets, which leads to session hijacking, to unauthenticated address resolution packets (ARPs) being distributed to the network. The use of SSH not only protects against the common LAN attacks described previously; it guards against the following types of attacks as well:

Spoofing of IP addresses. A remote device, usually an operating system, can change its IP address and pretend to be a different source, usually a trusted source.

Data modification. As data is passed through corporate networks and the Internet, any intermediary can modify the data while it is in transit.

ARP pollution. This occurs when incorrect ARP packets to redirect and capture sensitive data are distributed.

Session hijacking. This occurs when individuals guess or predict the ISN in TCP headers, gaining control of Telnet and RSH sessions.

Clear-text data. This occurs when critical or sensitive clear-text data, such as usernames, passwords, and commands, is intercepted.

The preceding list is not exhaustive, as SSH can protect against many other attacks, which may be direct or indirect. Another reason SSH is so popular is its ability to protect against network sniffing on both Local Area Networks (LANs) and Wide Area Networks (WANs). That feature allows network administrators and server administrators to manage and connect to remote systems without the risk of losing sensitive information to unauthorized users. Figure 1.1 shows a Telnet packet between two entities in clear-text:

Notice in Figure 1.1 that the username is in the clear-text, "kusum," and the password is also in the clear-text, "password." The session can be captured by any type of network sniffer, as long as the session is in clear-text. Some of the most common and vulnerable connections that often get targeted for sensitive information such as passwords are Telnet, FTP, POP3, SMTP, IMAP, SNMP, and HTTP. Figure 1.2 shows an SSH packet between the same two entities used in Figure 1.1.

Notice in Figure 1.2 that none of the information is in clear-text or comprehendible, thus being encrypted. This connection mirrors the Telnet connection (remote command line execution), but with significantly greater security over the password and the username "kusum."

SSH provides the following three key security features:

Encryption.   SSH encrypts all communication with a variety of cipher algorithms to choose from.

Two-factor authentication.   SSH can require a username/password or public key for authentication. In addition, these two options can be used together for two-factor authentication

Integrity.   SSH can create a digital signature of the data transferred from one entity to another, ensuring that the data has not been modified or tampered with in any way.

```
ýûⁿ ýýⁿ ýýⁿ ýýýûMicrosoft (R) Windows (TM) Version 5.00 (Build 2195)
Welcome to Microsoft Telnet Service
Telnet Server Build 5.00.99201.1

login:  ýýⁿ ýûⁿ ýûⁿ ýúⁿPⁿ ýóýûýýkkuussuumm

password:  p*a*s*s*w*o*r*d*
ýýⁿ ýûⁿ ýûⁿ ýóýúⁿANSIýóⁿ[1;1H*===================================================================
```

Figure 1.1   Telnet packet between two entities in clear-text.

```
SSH-2.0-OpenSSH_2.9p1
SSH-1.99-3.0.0 SSH Secure Shell for Windows
```

[binary/garbled SSH packet data]

Figure 1.2 Contents of SSH packet.

Remote Command Line Execution

SSH offers the ability to execute commands on a remote entity, which can be an operating system or a network device. In the Unix world, SSH gives the remote user the shell listed in the passwd file of the /etc directory; however, the communication is still encrypted over the wire. For example, based on the following Unix passwd file:

```
root:x:0:0:root:/root:/bin/bash
kusum:x:4:101:kusum:/home/kusum:/bin/bash
shreya:x:4:102:shreya:/home/shreya:/bin/bash
sudhanshu:x:4:103:sudhanshu:/home/sudhanshu:/bin/csh
sangeeta:x:4:104:sangeeta:/home/sangeeta:/bin/ksh
jignesh:x:4:105:jignesh:/home/jignesh:/bin/csh
kanchan:x:4:106:kanchan:/home/kanchan:/bin/bash
katie:x:4:107:katie:/home/katie:/bin/csh
amit:x:4:108:amit:/home/amit:/bin/bash
rohan:x:4:109:rohan:/home/rohan:/bin/sh
anand:x:4:110:anand:/home/anand:/bin/bash
amiee:x:4:111:amiee:/home/amiee:/bin/sh
neeraja:x:4:112:neeraja:/home/neeraja:/bin/sh
jum4nj1:x:4:113:jum4nj1:/home/jum4nj1:/sbin/nologin
```

root gets a bash shell, sudhanshu gets a C shell, neeraja gets a Korn shell, and the user jum4nj1 is not allowed to log in, since the shell allocated to jum4nj1's account is nologin, despite making a valid SSH connection. The SSH daemon running on the Unix server would query the information from the passwd file in order to process usernames for authentication. SSH does not use its own username and passwords for authentication; it uses the operating system's username and password information, which makes the process a lot easier to use. The result would be that valid accounts with an appropriate shell in the passwd file would be authenticated and given the correct shell, while being encrypted with SSH.

The process works a bit differently in the Windows world, but the result is still the same. Since Windows does not have different shell options, all SSH users would be given a command prompt (cmd.exe) or some form of the command prompt itself. Similar to the Unix world, SSH services in Windows use the existing password database (the SAM or ntds.dit files) for authentication.

Remote File Transfer

Remote file transfer is similar to remote command line execution. SSH offers the ability to retrieve and send files to and from a remote entity. Remote file transfer actually comes in two forms in the Unix world. SSH offers Secure Copy Protocol (SCP) in some installations of SSH1 and SSH2, or Secure File Transfer Protocol (SFTP), in most installations of SSH2. In the Windows world, only SFTP exists. Both SCP and SFTP provide similar, if not the same, function, which is to put and get files from a remote entity in a secure fashion. SFTP uses the existing SSH daemon on Unix and the existing SSH service on Windows. There is no extra step required to enable secure file transfer; it is automatically enabled on most versions of SSH2. Many SSH clients also come packaged with SCP or SFTP clients; therefore, the use and execution of the additional functionality is very straightforward. Furthermore, there are SCP/SFTP clients only, such as PuTTY, which are discussed in Chapter 3. But several installations of SSH clients have some type of file transfer utility included.

Similar to the Telnet session described previously, most SCP or SFTP installations are able to protect against the weaknesses of their counterpart: clear-text communication of FTP. Figure 1.3 shows an FTP packet between two entities in clear text.

```
220 Microsoft FTP Service
USER kusum
331 Password required for kusum.
PASS dwivedi
```

Figure 1.3 Contents of an FTP packet.

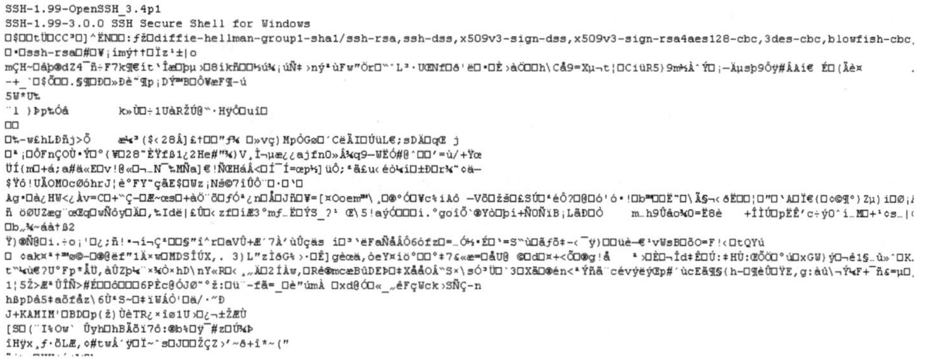

```
SSH-1.99-OpenSSH_3.4p1
SSH-1.99-3.0.0 SSH Secure Shell for Windows
□§□□t□CC²□}^ÈN□□:f£□diffie-hellman-group1-sha1/ssh-rsa,ssh-dss,x509v3-sign-dss,x509v3-sign-rsa4aes128-cbc,3des-cbc,blowfish-cbc
□·□ssh-rsa□#□¥¡imý††□Iz¹±¡o
mÇH–Ôáp@dZ4¯ñ−F7k¶¶it¹'Ì□pµ»□8ikÀ□□½ú¼¡úÑª»ný¹ùFw"Ör□¨`L³·Ù⊠Nf□á¹è□·□Ě>àC□□h\Cå9=Xµ¬t¡□CiuR5}9m»À¨ÝÔ¡-屶sp9Óý#Åài€·É□{Åè¤
−+·¨□$Ô□□.§¶□Ð□»Ðè¯¶p¡DÝ¯B□Ô¥¤F¶–ú
5Ý¨Ü½
¯1 }Þp¾Óá      k»Ù□÷1UàRŽÛ§¯·HÿÈ□uî□
□□
□t–¢£hLĐñj>Õ      ¬¼³(¢<28Å]£†□□"ſ¼·□»vç}Mþ0G¬□¨C鿿îî□ŮûL€;sDÀ□q挷j
□¹¡DÔFñçOÙ·Ÿ□°(¥□28¨£Ý£ø1¿2He#¨¥¾)V¸Î¬µ¬¿¿ajfn0»Å¾q9−WÉ0#0¨□□¹=ù/+Ý¤
Üí(m□+á;a#å«É□v!@«□¬¬_N¯¾MÑa]€!ÑÇH&å«□í¯í=œp¾]·üÔ;ªª&£u«é貶î□±Ð□r¾¨¢ª–
$Ýó!ÚÂOM□c@óhrJ¡è°FY¨ç¾£$□Wz¡Nª@7íÔÔ¨□·□¡□
Ag¹Ôá¿HW<¿Åv=C□+¨Ç–□Æ–œs□+àÔ¨õ□ƒÔª¿n□Å□JÀ□¥=[¤Ooem¶¨\,□®°ÔÙ¥c¾iÅö −Vš□ž§□£SÚ□ªéÔ¿□§□ó¹ó·!□b¨□□É¨□\Å§¬<δÉ□□¡□¨□¹A□Ï€(□○¶¶°)Žµ}î□□¡¸
ñ·ôøUŽæg¨œÆ□u¨Nôy□Å□,¾Idè¡£Û□«zf□í£3¨mƒ¸É□ÝS_?¹(¥\5!aý□□□i.°goî□·®Ýóⓤpi+ÑÔÑ±B¡LÅĐ□Ô      m.h9Úáo¾0=Éₘè      +ÎÎÚpÉÉ'c÷ý0¨i¸M□+¹cs¸¡(
□b¸¾–áá†â2
Ý}@ÑÈ□1¸+o¡¯Ù¿¡ñ¹+¬i¬Ç¨□□§¨í¹r□aVÛ+Æ¯7å¨ùÛ¢às·í□³¨eF¤Ñ&Å□5óƒ□¬.¸Ô¾¸É□¨=S¨ù□åƒ5ê−<¨¯ÿ}□□ù꬀¹v¥sB□ð0=F!<□¬QÝú
□·¢akפ¹#¨¾@−□@@éf¨1à×¾□MD5îÚX,¸3}L¨zïãG¼>¡ÔÉ]gꬢ,ôeÝ¥îô¨□□¹†7¼«æ=□Åû@·@□d□×+<Ô□@g¡Å      ·¹□É□–Îð¹É0Ú¹#HÙ¡@Ô□¨ûÔ×Gٷⓨ□·ýÔ−éî§_û»¨□K¸
t¨¾ûЀ?Ù¨Fp¹Åú,åÚžp¾¨¨×Ô¼hĐ\nÝ¾Rô¿¸¸Å□2Îåw,□R鬬mcæBûÐÉM□+XåÅôÀ¨S<¸sô¹Ù□¨30XÅ□@én<¹ÝñÁ¨cévýéý□p#¨ùcÉ¢q§(h–□¶êÙÙÝE,g:àü¸¬Ý¨F+¯ñ¢=µ□¸
1¡5ž>Æ¹ÛÎ»#£□□á□□□6PÉc@ôJó°¨ż¡□ù¨–ſâ=_Ðê¨úmå·□xd@ÇÔ«¸¸éFçWck>SÑÇ–n
hâpDá5¢aôƒår¡6Ù¹S–Ô¹±¥å0¹Ôã/¨¯Ð
J+KAHIN¨□B□□p(ż)Ûè TR¿ª¤ïø1U□¿¬±ŽèÙ
[S□(¨I¾0w¨·Ûÿh□hBåõï7ó:@b¾0y¨#z□Ü¾ð
îHÿx¸ƒ·ÔLÆ¸o#t¤Å¨ý□Î¬¨s□J□□Ž¿Z}'¬δ+î¨¬(¨
```

Figure 1.4 Contents of an SFTP packet.

Notice in Figure 1.3 that the FTP username (kusum) and password (dwivedi) is in clear-text, similar to the Telnet session described previously. Furthermore, since FTP provides remote file service, SCP and SFTP provide the same service with a significant amount of security. Also, with a single service, remote command line execution and secure file transfer can be provided, instead of enabling two different services such as Telnet and FTP. Figure 1.4 shows the same two entities but uses SFTP instead.

Notice in Figure 1.4 that none of the information is in clear-text and readable to anyone; thus, it is encrypted. In addition, Figure 1.5 shows the SFTP client interface, which is similar to many FTP interfaces.

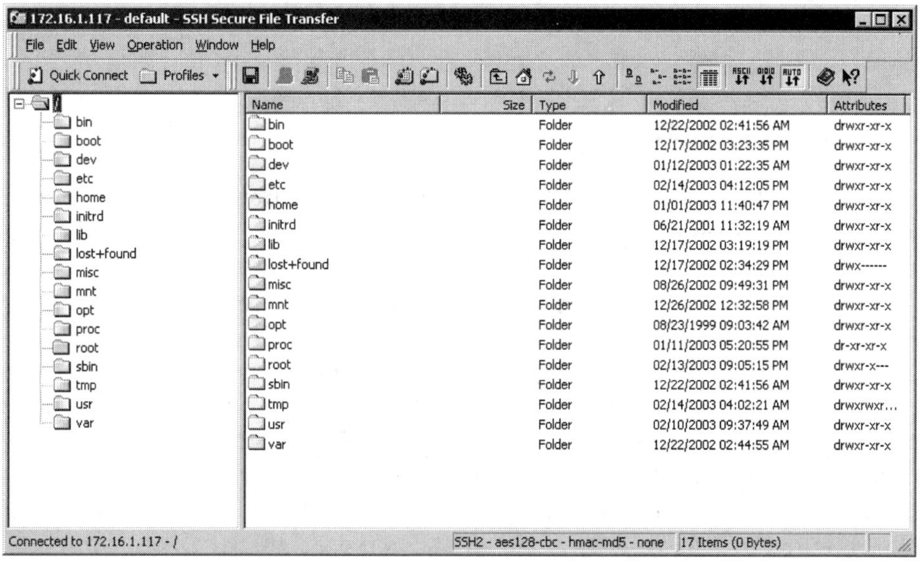

Figure 1.5 SFTP client for secure file transfer.

While SCP and SFTP are good replacements for FTP, in certain environments they also can replace other risky protocols such as Windows' Server Message Block (SMB) and Unix's Network File Server (NFS). Both SMB and NFS networking have had problems with security and continue to plague many networks today. The use of SFTP for a common file server can reduce or even eliminate reliance on SMB or NFS networking. Also, using a standard protocol such as SFTP, both Unix and Windows clients can access the same server, since both can communicate and use SSH but cannot necessarily communicate with SMB or NFS. Note that SSH can make the file-transfer process longer than FTP, NFS, or SMB; however, in many cases, the delay is minor.

Remote Network Access

In addition to providing remote command line and remote file transfer utilities, SSH can provide access to remote networks, creating something similar to a virtual private network (VPN). SSH can not only provide VPN functionally in the typical sense of the word (PPP over SSH), but can also provide services that many VPN users require, such as e-mail, file transfer, and Intranet services with port forwarding. Also, using SSH as a VPN solution is far less expensive than using a typical VPN solution. When considering any SOHO VPN appliance, a VPN card in a current network device, or any full-scale VPN server/ device, the cost of any such device is not any different from the cost of most other network devices, but far exceeds the cost of SSH server implementations.

SSH as a VPN solution not only provides access to services such as e-mail, internal file servers, and Intranet services, but with the use of advanced tunneling, it provides access to X11 services, remote applications, and remote tunneling.

Secure Management

Many networks today adhere to poor management practices, leaving their critical systems and devices vulnerable to management attacks. Many environments secure network devices and operating systems and create a properly segmented network perimeter, but then they connect to sensitive systems/ devices with poor management protocols over wide-open or nonexistent management networks. The clear-text protocols mentioned earlier, such as Telnet, FTP, and SNMP, are not the only poor management protocols in question, but many management applications have not secured their communication appropriately or have known issues identified with them. Older versions of certain management applications such as pcAnywhere, Virtual Network Computer (VNC), and Citrix have either had poor encrypted management protocols, which were reversed through engineering, or do not require any type of encrypted management for the sensitive communication. Furthermore, any attacker can download the client version of these applications and attempt to connect to the application's agent with a captured or guessed username and password. This assumes that there is no separate management network that the attacker cannot access, which prevents him or her from connecting to any agents. While separate management networks are ideal for safe and secure management, implementation of out-of-band management networks is not only very costly but adds a significant amount of complexity to a network.

SSH can be used as a secure management alternative by providing encrypted communication for any type of system or device management. Not only does SSH provide secure communication for remote command line management, which is the most popular management method on most Unix systems; it provides secure communication of graphic user interfaces (GUIs) with less secure applications such as VNC. In addition, SSH can provide two-factor authentication for all management methods by requiring a public key and password for management access. As best practice, two-factor authentication should be used for all management methods, as it reduces the number of brute-force attacks, password-guessing attacks, and dependencies on passwords for security. SSH can enforce two-factor authentication quite easily, which supports a critical best practice in management security. Lastly, SSH can eliminate the need for an out-of-band management network, removing a significant amount of cost and adding administrative simplicity in managing the systems and devices. The following list describes the advantages of using SSH for management:

- Encrypted management
- Encrypted GUI management with port forwarding (discussed further in Chapter 6)
- Significant cost savings
- Elimination of separate out-of-band management networks
- Added simplicity
- Two-factor authentication

Proxy Services

SSH can also be used to secure proxy services. Proxy servers have been identified to contain established benefits to which SSH can add value. Deploying SSH as a proxy service to access remote systems, devices, and applications in a safe and easy manner is one of the strongest, but most unused, benefits of SSH. SSH proxies can work with traditional proxy services such as SOCKS in order to secure the application from end to end. A SOCKS server can be set up in an environment and tunnel traffic via SSH. This setup allows remote applications such as SQL, Oracle, FTP, HTTP, and MySQL to be available with client applications such as SQL*PLUS and Query Analyzer over a secure channel.

SOCKS and SSH proxies can eliminate the need for an abundance of port forwarding, as discussed in Chapter 9, and can provide secure access to applications that may not be available from the network perimeter.

Unlike the use of Secure Sockets Layer (SSL) in encrypted Web traffic (denoted by the HTTPS (Hyper-text Transfer Protocol over SSL) prefix in URLS), SSH proxies can be used in a couple of ways to secure Web traffic over hostile networks, such as the Internet or wireless networks. SSH proxies can be used to connect to remote Web servers running on internal networks, by using HTTP tunneling over SSH, over the Internet. This function adds application security and Web security when internal systems are accessed from remote sites.

Client/Server Architecture for SSH

SSH uses client/server architecture in its implementation. An SSH server can be deployed and allow several SSH clients to connect to it. The architecture is not unlike any other client/server architecture, where the server portion of the program is running a daemon or service that usually listens on port 22. SSH does provide the ability for the daemon/service to listen on any port; however, it must be listening on a TCP connection. SSH has a configuration file, where the different options can be configured, such as password/public key authentication, port options, and home directories. SSH clients just need to know the IP address of the SSH server (or hostname) and the port on which it is listening, such as port 22. Based on the configuration of the SSH server, such as login requirements, the client just needs to authenticate to the server with the predefined requirements and get access to the session, whether it is SSH or the built-in SFTP functionality. Figure 1.6 shows a very simple example of the SSH architecture.

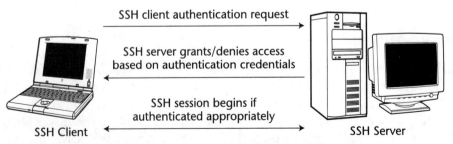

SSH client authentication request

SSH server grants/denies access based on authentication credentials

SSH session begins if authenticated appropriately

SSH Client   SSH Server

Figure 1.6   SSH Communication from an SSH client to an SSH server.

As shown in Figure 1.6, the SSH process is as follows:

- The SSH client on the left provides authentication to the SSH server on the right. In the initial connection, the client receives a host key of the server; therefore, in all subsequent connections, the client will know it is connecting to the same SSH server. This places less emphasis on the IP address of the SSH server, which can be easily spoofed, and more emphasis on the host key of the server, which cannot be spoofed very easily.

- The SSH server determines if the client is authorized to connect to the SSH service by verifying the username/password or public key that the client has presented for authentication. This process is completely encrypted.

- If the SSH server authenticates the client and the client is authorized, the SSH session begins between the two entities. All communication is completely encrypted.

The client/server architecture for SSH provides the ability for clients to have a single source for authentication and/or authorization. The single source for authentication/authorization allows access only to the SSH service, while access to various other services such as e-mail, intranets, extranets, and IRC requires further authentication. Also, with the use of SSH proxies described previously, a single source of authentication can provide access to applications without the need for more usernames and passwords.

SSH's Encryption Architecture

One of the many benefits of SSH is that it provides a fully encrypted protocol for transferring information, but what is the encryption architecture that SSH uses, and how is it deployed? This book does not explore in detail the encryption algorithms used or how they are implemented in SSH (since optimization and implementation are the focuses of this book), but I do briefly examine the architecture in order to provide some background knowledge of its deployment.

SSH's implementation architecture is just as flexible as the protocol itself. SSH is compatible with the major encryption algorithms used today, including the following:

- 3DES
- Blowfish
- Twofish (128 and 192)

- AES (128, 192, and 256)
- Arc Four
- CAST
- DES
- RC4

Any of the preceding encryption algorithms can be used for the ciphers for the SSH connection. Most of the ciphers are well supported, but the use of DES is strongly discouraged for the more secure 3DES option.

In addition to the preceding cipher algorithms, SSH offers Message Authentication Code (MAC) algorithm hashes. Two of the choices supported in most SSH implementations are MD5 and SHA1. MAC algorithm hashes are used for data integrity. Data transferred from one entity to another is hashed with a unique cryptographic signature, differentiating it from other data. The cryptographic signature, generated with MD5 or SHA1 hashes, does not change under any circumstances from one entity to the next. This ensures that the entity receiving the data has obtained it without any modification, tampering, or general abuse by unauthorized entities.

Basic Miscues with SSH

Many protocols used in enterprise networks have several security issues. SSH is no different. SSH offers a wide variety of solutions, but it is important to mention that SSH has had security issues, including severe issues that may result in remote access to unauthorized users. I do not discuss all the security issues associated with OpenSSH or other variants of SSH. I do, however, encourage awareness that SSH, like any program or service, needs to be patched on a regular basis. Inform your internal patch management process and network operations personnel to patch and monitor SSH services on a regular basis.

Some of the security issues identified with SSH involve buffer overflows, incorrect X11 forwarding, weak Challenge/Responses handling, remote information leakage, and privilege escalation. For more information, visit the following URL for OpenSSH security problems: www.openssh.com/security.html.

Types of SSH Clients/Servers

SSH clients/servers come in a variety of packages. Following is a short summary of the organizations and products mentioned throughout this book.

SSH Servers

- OpenSSH (www.openssh.com)

  - OpenSSH is a free version of the SSH protocol suite. OpenSSH servers and clients are available for both Unix and Windows.

  - OpenSSH has been ported to Windows with the popular CYGWIN utility. The project was created by Network Simplicity (www.networksimplicity.com) and has been adopted by the following site: http://lexa.mckenna.edu/sshwindows/.

- SSH2 (www.ssh.com)

  - SSH2 is a commercial version of SSH, with required license fees for commercial use (noncommercial use is free). Commercial SSH clients/servers are available for both Windows and Unix systems.

VanDyke Software (www.vandyke.com)

- VanDyke Software makes a commercial version of SSH, with required license fees for usage. Commercial SSH servers (VShell) and clients (SecureCRT) are available for the Windows operating system.

SSH Clients

- Commerical SSH
- OpenSSH
- PuTTY
- Secure-CRT
- MindTerm—SSH over Java with Web browsers
- WinSCP

Basic Setup of SSH

This section focuses on setting up an SSH server in both a Unix and Windows environment. The setup creates a base SSH server install, based on the operating system of your choice, which enables the discussion of various SSH features that appear throughout this book. The following lists the types of implementations demonstrated:

- OpenSSH on Unix (Red Hat Linux 8.0 and OpenBSD 3.1)
- OpenSSH on Windows (Windows 2000 Server)

- Commercial SSH on Unix (Red Hat Linux 8.0 and OpenBSD 3.1)
- Commercial SSH on Windows (Windows 2000 Server)
- VShell SSH server on Windows (Windows 2000 Server)

Many operating systems, such as OpenBSD, are loaded with OpenSSH by default. For the purposes of this section, I assume that your system has not been pre-loaded with any type of an SSH server. If you have a machine that already has the SSH service/daemon listening, feel free to skip this section.

OpenSSH

The following paragraphs describe the prevalent servers using OpenSSH.

Red Hat Linux 8.0

The following is a step-by-step procedure to install SSH on Red Hat 8.0.

RPM-Based Implementation

After the full installation of a Red Hat 8.0 server, use your favorite FTP client, such as the command line client or built-in Web browser FTP functionality, to download the latest RPM (Red Hat Package Manager) from ftp://ftp5.usa .openbsd.org/pub/OpenBSD/OpenSSH/portable/rpm/RH80. I will be using version 3.5 (openssh-3.5p1-1.i386.rpm). Download the RPM to the directory of your choice; I recommend /usr/local/src. Once the file has been downloaded, follow these directions:

1. From a shell, change directories to the location where the OpenSSH RPM was downloaded:

   ```
   # cd /usr/local/src
   ```

2. Install the OpenSSH RPM:

   ```
   # rpm -i openssh-3.5p1-1.i386.rpm
   ```

To start the daemon, change to the installation directory and start the service:

```
# cd /usr/sbin
# ./sshd -p 22
```

Note, the –p option is not needed if you are using the default port (22).

You should now have the SSH server running on port 22 on your Red Hat 8.0 machine. To confirm this, type **netstat –an** and you should see the screen shown in Figure 1.7.

```
Active Internet connections (servers and established)
Proto Recv-Q Send-Q Local Address          Foreign Address      State
tcp      0      0 0.0.0.0:1024           0.0.0.0:*            LISTEN
tcp      0      0 0.0.0.0:22             0.0.0.0:*            LISTEN
tcp      0      0 127.0.0.1:25           0.0.0.0:*            LISTEN
tcp      0      0 127.0.0.1:5180         0.0.0.0:*            LISTEN
udp      0      0 0.0.0.0:1024           0.0.0.0:*
udp      0      0 0.0.0.0:68             0.0.0.0:*
udp      0      0 0.0.0.0:111            0.0.0.0:*                            |
```

Figure 1.7   Out of "netstat –an" command.

Notice that all the interfaces, denoted by 0.0.0.0, are listening on port 22, which is SSH.

Package-Based Implementation

After the full installation of a Red Hat 8.0 server, use your favorite FTP client, such as the command line clients or built-in Web browser FTP functionality, to download the latest package from ftp://ftp3.usa.openbsd.org/pub/OpenBSD/ OpenSSH/portable/openssh03.5p1.tar.gz. I will be using version 3.5 (openssh-3.5p1.tar.gz). Download the package to the directory of your choice; I recommend /usr/local/src. Once the file has been downloaded, implement the following directions:

1. From a shell, change directories to the location where the OpenSSH package was downloaded:

   ```
   # cd /usr/local/src
   ```

2. Unzip the tarball using gunzip:

   ```
   # gunzip -c openssh-3.5p1.tar.gz | tar xvf -
   ```

3. Change directories to SSH:

   ```
   # cd openssh-3.5p1
   ```

4. Configure the object file and the dependencies:

   ```
   # ./configure
   ```

5. Make the binary:

   ```
   # make
   # make install
   ```

You're done!

To start the daemon, change to the installation directory and start the service:

```
# cd /usr/local/src/ssh
# ./sshd -p 22
```

Note, the –p option is not needed if you are using the default port (22).

You should now have the SSH server running on port 22 on your Red Hat 8.0 machine. To confirm this, type **netstat –an** and you should see the same results as in Figure 1.7. Notice that all the interfaces, denoted by 0.0.0.0, are listening on port 22, which is SSH.

OpenBSD 3.1

After the full installation of an OpenBSD 3.1 server, use your favorite FTP client, such as the command line clients or the built-in Web browser FTP functionality, to download the latest tarball from ftp://ftp.openbsd.org/pub/OpenBSD/OpenSSH/. I will be using version 3.5 (openssh-3.5.tgz). Download the tarball to the directory of your choice; I recommend /usr/local/src. Once the file has been downloaded, follow the subsequent directions.

1. From a shell, change directories to the location where the OpenSSH package was downloaded:

   ```
   # cd /usr/local/src
   ```

2. Unzip the tarball using gunzip:

   ```
   # gunzip -c openssh-3.5.tgz | tar xvf -
   ```

3. Change directories to SSH:

   ```
   # cd ssh
   ```

4. Make the object file and the dependencies:

   ```
   # make obj
   # make cleandir
   # make depend
   ```

5. Make the binary:

   ```
   # make# .make install
   ```

To start the daemon, change to the installation directory and start the service:

```
# cd /usr/local/src/ssh
# ./sshd -p 22
```

Note, the –p option is not needed if you are using the default port (22).

You should now have the SSH server running on port 22 on your OpenBSD 3.1 machine. To confirm this, type **netstat –an** and you should see the same results as in Figure 1.7.

Notice that all the interfaces, denoted by 0.0.0.0, are listening on port 22, which is SSH.

Windows 2000 Server

After the full installation of a Windows 2000 server, use your favorite FTP client, such as ftp.exe or Internet Explorer, to download the latest version of OpenSSH for Windows platforms from http://lexa.mckenna.edu/sshwindows/. I will be using version 3.5 (openssh35p1-3.zip). Download the zip file to the directory of your choice; I recommend c:\temp. Once the file has been downloaded, follow the subsequent directions.

1. Double-click the zip file and extract the two files to the c:\temp directory. The two files should include the executable (setupssh35.exe) and the signature file.

2. After extracting setupssh35.exe to the c:\temp folder, double-click setupssh3.5.

3. A welcome screen should appear (see Figure 1.8). Select Next to go to the next screen.

4. Fully read the License Agreement (see Figure 1.9). If you agree, select I agree. If you don't agree, hit Cancel, and send this book to deprived engineers in Silicon Valley.

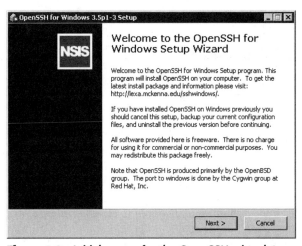

Figure 1.8 Initial screen for the OpenSSH wizard 4.

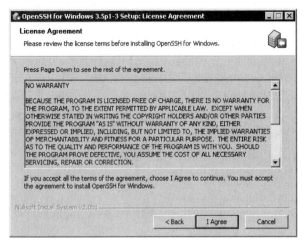

Figure 1.9   License Agreement of OpenSSH.

5. At this point, you have the option to install the client and server por-
    tions of SSH, as well as some shared tools and menu shortcuts (see Fig-
    ure 1.10). Select Next.

6. Choose the installation location; I recommend keeping the default loca-
    tion (see Figure 1.11). Select Next.

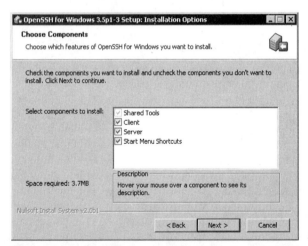

Figure 1.10   Choose Components screen for OpenSSH.

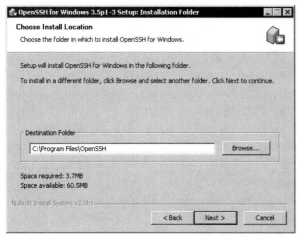

Figure 1.11   Install Location screen for OpenSSH.

7. Choose the shortcut location; I recommend keeping the default (see Figure 1.12). Click Install to begin installing the program:

8. You should see the installation in progress (see Figure 1.13).

9. During the installation process, you should see a text box, telling you that you MUST edit the password file (passwd) in order for SSH to work properly (see Figure 1.14). This is a very important step to follow after the installation has been completed. Hit OK.

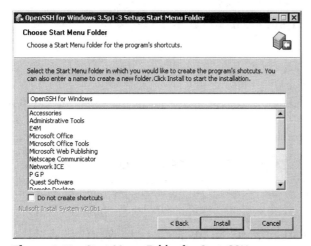

Figure 1.12   Start Menu Folder for OpenSSH.

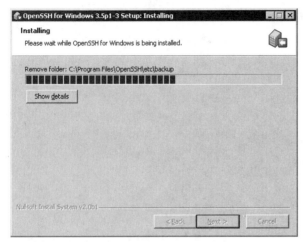

Figure 1.13   Installing screen for OpenSSH.

10. Once installation is complete, select Finish and leave the Show Quick-start guide checked.

11. The Quickstart guide should now appear in Notepad.

12. Read the guide specifications under configuration.

13. From the command prompt, change the directory to the OpenSSH bin directory.

```
c:\cd "Program Files"\OpenSSH\bin
```

14. To grant local users access to the SSH daemon, type:

```
c:\Program Files\OpenSSH\bin\mkpasswd -1 -u username >> ..\etc\passwd
```

You're done!

Change to the installation directory and start the service: \Program Files\OpenSSH\bin\net start opensshd.

To confirm the service has started, type **netstat –an** and you should see the screen shown in Figure 1.15:

Figure 1.14   Dialog box to edit the passwd file for appropriate installation for OpenSSH.

Figure 1.15   Result of the netstat –an command.

Notice that all the interfaces, denoted by 0.0.0.0, are listening on port 22, which is SSH.

Commercial SSH

The following paragraphs describe the prevalent servers using the commercial version of SSH.

OpenBSD 3.1 and Red Hat Linux 8.0

After the full installation of an OpenBSD 3.1 or Red Hat 8.0 server, use your favorite FTP client, such as the command line client or the built FTP functionality in Web browsers, to download the latest tarball from ftp://ftp.ssh.com/pub/ssh/. I use the noncommercial version of SSH, specifically 3.2.3 (ssh-3.2.3.tar.gz). Download the tarball to the directory of your choice; I recommend /usr/local/src. Once the file has been downloaded, follow the subsequent directions.

1. From a shell, change directories to the location where the Commercial SSH package was downloaded:

   ```
   # cd /usr/local/src
   ```

2. Unzip the tarball using gunzip:

   ```
   # gunzip –c ssh-3.2.3.tar.gz | tar xvf -
   ```

3. Change directories to SSH:

   ```
   # cd ssh-3.2.3
   ```

4. Compile the source:

   ```
   # ./configure
   # make
   ```

5. Run the install script:

```
# make install
```

To start the daemon, change to the installation directory and start the service:

```
# cd /usr/local/src
# ./sshd2 -p 22
```

Note, the –p option is not needed if you are using the default port (22).

To confirm the service has started, type **netstat –an** and you should see the same results as Figure 1.15. Notice that all the interfaces, denoted by 0.0.0.0, are listening on port 22, which is SSH.

Windows 2000

After the full installation of a Windows 2000 server, use your favorite FTP client, such as ftp.exe or Internet Explorer, to download the latest version of Commercial SSH for Windows platforms (evaluation version unless you have purchased the license) from www.ssh.com/support/downloads/secureshellserver/evaluation.mpl. I use version 3.2.3 (SSHSecureShellSever-3.2.3.exe). After you have filled out the appropriate evaluation form, download the executable to the directory of your choice; I recommend c:\temp. Once the file has been downloaded, follow the subsequent directions.

1. Double-click on the exe file.

2. A welcome screen should appear (see Figure 1.16). Select Next to go to the next screen.

Figure 1.16 Welcome screen for Commercial SSH.

Figure 1.17   License Agreement for Commercial SSH.

3. Fully read the License Agreement (see Figure 1.17). If you agree, select Yes. If you don't agree, hit Cancel and send this book to deprived engineers in Brookings, South Dakota.

4. Choose the installation location. I recommend keeping the default. (See Figure 1.18.) Click Next.

5. Choose the program folder, we recommend keeping the default (see Figure 1.19). Click Next.

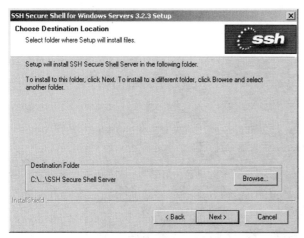

Figure 1.18   Destination Location folder for the installation of Commercial SSH.

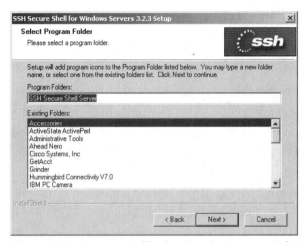

Figure 1.19 Program Folder location for Commercial SSH.

6. Let the system create a host keypair; click Next.

7. Once installation is complete, select Finish and leave the View the ReadMe File checked.

8. Read the ReadMe file; then close the file.

To start the service, select Start ⇨ Programs ⇨ SSH Secure Shell Server ⇨ Tools ⇨ Start Server. The screen shown in Figure 1.20 should appear.

To confirm the service has started, type **netstat –an** and you should see the screen as in Figure 1.15. Notice that all the interfaces, denoted by 0.0.0.0, are listening on port 22, which is SSH.

Figure 1.20 Screen indicating that the SSH service has started.

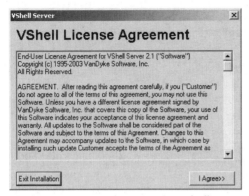

Figure 1.21   License screen for Vshell.

VShell SSH Server

After the full installation of a Windows 2000 server, use your favorite FTP client, such as ftp.exe or Internet Explorer, to download the latest version of VanDyke's Software's VShell SSH for Windows platforms (30-day evaluation version unless you have purchased the license) from www.vandyke.com/download/vshell/. I use version 2.14 (vshell214.exe). Download the executable to the directory of your choice; I recommend c:\temp. Once the file has been downloaded, follow the subsequent directions.

1. Double-click the exe file.

2. The VShell License Agreement should appear (see Figure 1.21). Read the agreement. If you agree, select I Agree to go to the next screen. If you do not agree, send this book to deprived engineers in Nashville, Tennessee.

3. The Welcome screen appears next (see Figure 1.22). Select Next to continue.

Figure 1.22   Welcome screen for VShell.

Figure 1.23   Destination location folder for the installation of VShell.

4. Choose the installation location; I recommend keeping the default (see Figure 1.23). Click Next.

5. The next screen asks about the location of the program's icons. Choose your preferred location and select Next (see Figure 1.24).

6. The next screen discusses the authentication options with VShell (described more in Chapter 4). In order to use public-key authentication, an LSA module must be created. Ensure that the checkbox to install the public key LSA module is selected and choose Next (see Figure 1.25).

7. Once all the options are selected, choose Finish.

8. Once the installation is complete and successful, choose OK.

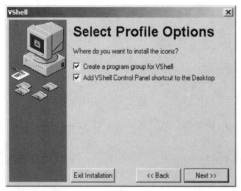

Figure 1.24   Icon location option screen.

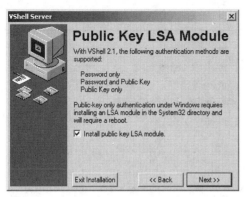

Figure 1.25 Authentication and LSA module screen.

9. In order to complete the installation, the system must be restarted. Select OK to restart the system or Cancel to restart the system at another time (be sure to restart the system before attempting to use VShell).

Once the system has been rebooted, the VShell SSH server should be started automatically. It will be installed as a service called VanDyke Software: VShell. To confirm that the service has started, type **netstat –an** and you should see the same results as in Figure 1.20.

Optimal Uses of SSH

SSH can be optimized in a variety of ways, both for security purposes and functionality purposes. One of the great things about SSH is that it can be optimized for so many different things, usually with a single installation. Following is a list of issues that SSH can help solve. This list presents different options that can be addressed by SSH:

- Secure Remote Access solution (VPN) via the Internet
- Remote access to internal applications, such as Road Warrior applications (Time and Expense)
- Secure file sharing (replacing NFS, CIFS, and SMB)
- Secure command line execution
- Secure GUI management (X11 connections and port forwarding)
- Secure Wireless connections

As you can see in the preceding list, SSH can address a variety of network issues that concern security and functionality. For example, the process of port forwarding an application protocol, such as Windows Terminal Server, may not necessarily be a security requirement, but might be a functional require-ment that limits the number of holes punched though a firewall. This allows a single firewall rule to allow access from outside connections to the internal SSH server and to port forward other applications, such as Windows Terminal Server's 3389 port, to internal hosts.

On the other hand, there could be a security requirement that all manage-ment traffic should not only be encrypted but should enforce two-factor authentication. By setting up an SSH proxy that requires two-factor authenti-cation, all clients are required to use a username/password and public key for authentication, while all information is encrypted. These uses fulfill the secu-rity requirements of the network without the extra costs and complexities of a separate solution.

The benefits of using and optimizing SSH will continue to grow. As this book unfolds, I will explore the different methods for using SSH on both Unix and Windows environments for security and functionality. I will also demon-strate many examples of using SSH with the greatest amount of flexibility to meet the needs of complex and convoluted networks.

Summary

In this chapter, some of the basics of SSH are discussed. Discussions about the differences between SSH1 and SSH2 and the different uses of SSH itself estab-lish an understanding of the protocol. The chapter also addresses the architec-ture of SSH, both client/server and encryption architecture, with a brief description of the types of SSH servers and clients. The chapter concludes with a detailed, step-by-step guide to installing SSH. This provides a basic under-standing of the protocol as well as basic setup of the application. In the next two chapters, I discuss the basic implementation and setup of several different SSH servers and clients, allowing you to proceed with optimal usages for SSH in Chapter 4 and the rest of the book.

From this point forward, you should have two SSH servers deployed in some type of network environment: one Unix based and one Windows based.

SSH Servers

There are three main SSH servers that provide different types of functionality and usage: OpenSSH, SSH Communications' SSH server, and VanDyke Software's VShell SSH server. In chapter one, we install all three of these servers; however, we do not discuss the configuration, the uses, and the different features of these servers. While the three main SSH servers offer similar SSH services, they provide different levels of functionality, several of which may be better for your environment than others. The type of SSH server you use can significantly affect the type of SSH experience you have. For example, several SSH servers offer both command line access and secure file transfer; however, if SSH is being deployed for port forwarding only (discussed in Chapters 6 and 7) or for file transfer, giving the user command line access may not be acceptable.

This chapter discusses the three main SSH servers available for Unix and Windows. Also, the focus of the chapter is on selected configuration items and the menus of the three SSH servers, in terms of customization and optimal usage. The following SSH servers are examined in this chapter:

- OpenSSH server
  - Unix and Windows
- SSH Communications' SSH server
  - Unix
  - *Windows
- VanDyke's Software VShell SSH server
  - Windows

OpenSSH

OpenSSH servers are available on both Windows and Unix environments. The Windows version is actually a port of OpenSSH's Unix version using the popular Cygwin utility (see www.cygwin.com for more details). While the Windows port of OpenSSH uses Cygwin, note that the port is not a full installation of Cygwin and does not require additional Cygwin utilities, which is ideal since Cygwin requires a separate installation procedure. Since both the Unix and Windows versions of OpenSSH use the same configuration file for the SSH server, the sshd_config file, I discuss the file itself in detail. It can apply to both Windows and Unix platforms. To view the configuration file, enter the following commands.

On Unix:

```
#cd /etc/ssh
#more sshd_config
```

On Windows:

```
C:\cd "Program Files"\OpenSSH\bin
C:\Programe Files\OpenSSH\bin\type sshd_config
```

NOTE All lines in the sshd_config file that are changed must be uncommented (the # must be deleted from the beginning of the line).

The first section I present is the simple network configuration:

```
#Port 22
#Protocol 2,1
#ListenAddress 0.0.0.0
#ListenAddress ::
```

Table 2.1 describes the first four options in the sshd_config file.

Table 2.1 Options in the sshd_config File

OPTION	DESCRIPTION

Port	Sets the port number for SSH to listen on. The default port is 22; however, listening on several ports, including other nonstandard ports, such as 80, 443, or 8080, may be optimal, since business travelers may not be able to make outbound connections on port 22, but since port 80 or 443 are usually available. To listen on multiple ports, add the following lines:
	`Port 22`
	`Port 80`
	`Port 443`
	`Port 8080`

Protocol	Allows the usage of only SSH version 1, SSH version 2, or both. Since SSH version 1 is more insecure, it may be a good option to only use version 2; however, several devices do not support SSH version 2 yet. To use only SSH version two, add the following line: `Protocol 2`

ListenAddress	Sets the IP address to have the SSH daemon listen on. The default, which is `0.0.0.0`, enables the SSH services on all interfaces. If there are interfaces where SSH should not be listening, such as the external interface of a firewall, remove `0.0.0.0` and add the appropriate IP addresses. To listen on only select interfaces, addl the following lines:
	`ListenAddress 172.16.1.1`
	`ListenAddress 192.168.0.1`

The next section discusses the host-key section. The host-key section discusses parameters around the SSH server's host key, which is the fingerprint used to identify the SSH server.

```
# HostKey for protocol version 1
# HostKey /etc/ssh/ssh_host_key
# HostKeys for protocol version 2
# HostKey /etc/ssh/ssh_host_rsa_key
# HostKey /etc/ssh/ssh_host_dsa_key
```

This section of the sshd_config file is fairly straightforward. It simply states the location of the host-key file for both the SSH version 1 format and the SSH version 2 format. Also, for SSH version 2, the section states the location of both the RSA and DSA keys.

The next section addresses the server key:

```
# Lifetime and size of ephemeral version 1 server key
#KeyRegenerationInterval 3600
#ServerKeyBits 768
```

This section sets specifics on the server key. The KeyRegenerationInterval is the time, in seconds, to regenerate the server key; the ServerKeyBits is the number of bits to be used.

The next section addresses logging:

```
# Logging
#obsoletes QuietMode and FascistLogging
#SyslogFacility AUTH
#LogLevel INFO
```

This section sets the logging option for the SSH service. The differentiation between QuiteMode and FascistLogging is that QuiteMode logs only fatal errors, whereas FascistLogging enables verbose logging. SyslogFacility specifies the syslog code to use when logging messages from SSH, such as Daemon and Auth. Loglevel specifies the level used when logging messages from SSH, such as only informational messages (INFO).

The next section addresses authentication options with SSH:

```
#Authentication
#LoginGraceTime 120
#PermitRootLogin yes
#StrictModes yes

#RSAAuthentication yes
#PubkeyAuthentication yes
#AuthorizedKeysFile                              .ssh/authorized_keys
```

Table 2.2 describes the authentication options available for the SSH server.

Table 2.2   Authentication Options

OPTION	DESCRIPTION
LoginGraceTime	The amount of time the user has to complete the authentication process. Specifically, from the time the user initiates the connection to the time the user enters his or her username/password or public/private key password.

Table 2.2 *(continued)*

OPTION	DESCRIPTION
PermitRootLogin	Option to allow (yes) or disallow (no) the root user to log in to the SSH session. Best practice is to restrict root access and have only users 'su' or 'sudo' to root. Also, if the root account must be able to log in directly, the value of "nopwd" can allow root to log in directly, but only with public-key authentication.
StrictModes	Enables (yes) or disables (no) the checking of a users' permission in their home directory and rhosts files before accepting authentication. This should be set to yes to protect against world-writeable files in home directories.
RSAAuthentication	Option to allow RSA authentication.
PubkeyAuthentication	Option to allow public-key authentication; possible values are yes and no.
AuthorizedKeysFile	The directory where the user's public key will be stored. The default is .ssh/authorized_keys, which is the users' home directory in the .ssh folder (for example, /home/<username>/.ssh/authorized_keys on Program Files\OpenSSH\.ssh on Windows).

Under the authentication section in the ssh_config file is an authentication option for using rhosts with RSH. While rhosts usage is not recommended due to its poor security standards, the following lines address rhost configuration options:

```
# rhosts authentication should not be used
#RhostsAuthentication no
# Don't read the user's ~/.rhosts and ~/.shosts files
#IgnoreRhosts yes
# For this to work you will also need host keys in
/etc/ssh/ssh_known_hosts
#RhostsRSAAuthentication no
# similar for protocol version 2
#HostbasedAuthentication no
# Change to yes if you don't trust ~/.ssh/known_hosts for
# RhostsRSAAuthentication and HostbasedAuthentication
#IgnoreUserKnownHosts no
```

Table 2.3 describes the rhost authentication options available for the SSH server.

Table 2.3   Rhost Configuration Options

OPTION	DESCRIPTION
RhostAuthenication	To allow rhosts authentication
Ignore Rhosts	To ignore (yes) or read (no) rhosts files in the users home directory, stored in .rhosts or .shosts files
RhostsRSAAuthenication	To attempt rhosts authentication from RSA host keys
HostbasedAuthenication	Enable (yes) or disable (no) host-based authentication under SSH version 2
IgnoreUserKnownHosts	Ignore (no) or read (yes) the known hosts file in the users' home directory

The last authentication section for the sshd_config file addresses more password options, including Kerberos usage:

```
# To disable tunneled clear text passwords, change to no here!
#PasswordAuthentication yes
#PermitEmptyPasswords no

# Change to no to disable s/key passwords
#ChallengeResponseAuthentication yes

# Kerberos options
#KerberosAuthentication no
#KerberosOrLocalPasswd yes
#KerberosTicketCleanup yes

#AFSTokenPassing no

# Kerberos TGT Passing only works with the AFS kaserver
#KerberosTgtPassing no
```

Table 2.4 describes the password and Kerberos authentication options available for the SSH server.

Table 2.4   Password and Kerberos Options

OPTION	DESCRIPTION
PasswordAuthentication	To enable (yes) or disable (no) password authentication.
PermitEmptyPasswords	To allow (yes) or disallow (no) the use of blank passwords.

Table 2.4   *(continued)*

OPTION	DESCRIPTION
ChallengeResponse Authentication	Enable (yes) or disable (no) challenge/response authentication. Challenge/Response authentication occurs when the server sends the client a challenge; the client's response will determine if authentication is allowed.
Kerberos Authentication	To enable (yes) or disable (no) Kerberos authentication, which involves session tickets.
KerberosOrLocalPasswd	To permit (yes) Kerberos or local-system passwords for authentication.
KerberosTicketCleanup	To enable (yes) or disable (no) the ability to automatically delete the Kerberos ticket upon logout.
AFSTokenPassing	To enable (yes) or disable (no) the ability to use AFS tokens for authentication.
KerberosTgtPassing	To enable (yes) or disable (no) the ability to use Kerberos Ticket Granting Tickets for authentication.

The next section of the sshd_config file addresses X11 options that can be used with forwarding:

```
#X11Forwarding no
#X11DisplayOffset 10
#X11UseLocalhost yes
```

X11 forwarding can be enabled or disabled in this section of the sshd_config file. If X11 forwarding is enabled, the offset can be set, where 10 is the default, and the option to use the localhost can be enabled, which is the most typical installation of X11 forwarding. Using the localhost to forward X11 connections allows all X11 traffic to prorogate from the local machine.

The last section of the sshd_config file addresses a variety of options that can be set with the service, such as printing, banner information, and subsystems:

```
#PrintMotd yes
#PrintLastLog yes
#KeepAlive yes
#UseLogin no
#UsePrivilegeSeparation yes
#PermitUserEnvironment no
#Compression yes
```

```
#MaxStartups 10
# no default banner path
#Banner /some/path
#VerifyReverseMapping no

# override default of no subsystems
Subsystem    sftp    /usr/libexec/sftp-server
```

Table 2.5 describes the various miscellaneous options that are available for the SSH server.

Table 2.5   Miscellaneous Options for the SSH Server

OPTION	DESCRIPTION
PrintMotd	Enables (yes) or disables (no) any text located in the motd (Message of the day) file (/etc/motd) to be displayed at login. This is very useful since messages can be displayed to all users who are logging in to the system, such as system downtime, security issues, and so on.
PrintLastLog	Enables (yes) or disables (no) information to be displayed to the screen about the last time a user logged in to the service.
UseLogin	Enables (yes) or disables (no) the authentication process to be handled internally using /usr/bin/login instead of the SSH utility.
UserPrivilegeSeparation	Enables/Disables the use of separate privileges for users using the SSH service.
PermitUserEnvironment	Allow (yes) or disallow (no) users to have their environment variables loaded after authentication.
Compression	Enable (yes) or disable (no) compression of the SSH transmission process.
Banner	Path to the file that holds the banner messages that will be displayed after login.
Subsystem sftp	Path to the secure file transfer subsystem.

You may have noticed that many of the options in the sshd_config file are specific to Unix implementations of OpenSSH. While a full sshd_config file can be used on Windows platforms, many of the items will not apply, since they do not exist in the Windows world, such as Syslog and rhost authentication. Once you have opened the sshd_config on the Windows machine, you should see only an abbreviated portion of the bigger sshd_config file on Unix, as the following code shows:

```
HostKey                          /ssh/ssh_host_key
HostDSAKey                       /ssh/ssh_host_dsa_key
PidFile                          /ssh/sshd.pid
Protocol                         2
Port                             22

PermitRootLogin                  yes
PasswordAuthentication           yes
IgnoreRhosts                     yes
IgnoreUserKnownHosts             yes
RhostsAuthentication             no
RhostsRSAAuthentication          no
RSAAuthentication                no

Subsystem        sftp     /ssh/sftp-server
```

Despite the abbreviated portion of the sshd_config file, all the entries have the same definition described in the previous file portion.

SSH Communications' SSH server

SSH Communications' SSH servers are also available on both Windows and Unix environments. The sshd2_config file is used by SSH Communications' SSH server for all configuration management for the service. The Windows version has a different configuration utility, which uses a graphical user interface (GUI) to display and report changes to the sshd2_config configuration file. On the other hand, the Unix version provides only the sshd2_config file for configuration management without any extra configuration tools. Since the Unix and Windows versions provide different configuration utilities, I address the sshd2_config file first, since both platforms either rely (Unix) or refer (Windows) to this file for configuration; then I address the Windows GUI for configuration management.

SSH Communications' SSH Server: Unix

To view the configuration file, enter the following commands:

```
#cd /etc/ssh2
#more sshd2_config
```

SSH Communications' sshd2_config file is similar to the sshd_config file of OpenSSH; however, there are many differences that distinguish the two. The following paragraphs discuss the various sections of the sshd2_config file.

General

The general section of the sshd2_config file should look similar to the following:

```
## General
#       VerboseMode             no
#       QuietMode               yes
#       ForcePTTYAllocation     no
#       SyslogFacility          AUTH
#       SyslogFacility          LOCAL7
```

Table 2.6 describes the general options available for the SSH server.

Table 2.6   Options in the General Section of the ssch2_config File (Unix)

OPTION	DESCRIPTION
VerberosMode	Enables (yes) or disables (no) the SSH session's debugging and connection related information to be displayed to standard output
QuietMode	Enables (yes) or disables (no) the SSH session's warning and error messages to be displayed to standard output
ForcePTTYAllocation	Enables (yes) or disables (no) the ability to force allocation of PTTY sessions
SyslogFacility	Identifies the Syslog code to use when logging a message from SSH, such as Daemon, Auth, and Local

Network

The network section of the sshd2_config file should look like the following:

```
        Port                    22
#       ListenAddress           any
#       RequireReverseMapping   no
#       MaxBroadcastsPerSecond  0
#       MaxBroadcastsPerSecond  1
#       NoDelay                 yes
#       KeepAlive               yes
#       MaxConnections          50
#       MaxConnections          0
```

Table 2.7 describes the network options available for the SSH server.

Table 2.7 Options in the Network Section (Unix)

OPTION	DESCRIPTION

Port	Sets the port number for SSH to listen on. Default port is 22; however, listening on several ports, including other nonstandard ports, such as 80, 443, or 8080, may be optimal since business travelers may not be able to make outbound connections on port 22, but since port 80 or 443 is usually available. To listen on multiple ports, add the following lines:
	
	`Port 22`
	`Port 80`
	`Port 443`
	`Port 8080`

ListenAddress	Sets the IP address to have the SSH daemon listen on. The default, which is `0.0.0.0`, enables the SSH services on all interfaces. If there are interfaces where SSH should not be listening, such as the external interface of a firewall, remove `0.0.0.0` and add the appropriate IP addresses. To listen on only select interfaces, add the following lines:
	
	`ListenAddress 172.16.1.1`
	`ListenAddress 192.168.0.1`

RequireReverseMapping	Enables (yes) or disables (no) the requirement of DNS lookups to succeed, in order to work with AllowHost and DenyHost entries. If enabled and the DNS lookup fails, the request is denied. If disabled and the DNS lookup fails, the IP address in AllowHosts and DenyHosts is checked.
MaxBroadcastPerSecond	Identifies the number of UDP broadcasts the server should handle per second. The default value, which is zero, has no broadcast handled.
NoDelay	Enables (yes) or disables (no) the socket option for TCP_NODELAY.
KeepAlive	Enables (yes) or disables (no) whether the SSH server should send KeepAlive packets to the SSH clients. This value helps prevent hanging sessions by determining if the client on the other side is still running and hasn't crashed or blue-screened.
MaxConnections	Identifies the number of concurrent connections the SSH server will handle. If the value is set to zero, the number of concurrent connections is unlimited.

Crypto

The Crypto section of the sshd2_config file should look similar to the following:

```
#      Ciphers                    AnyCipher
# Following includes "none" 'cipher':
#      Ciphers                    AnyStd
#
#      Ciphers                    AnyStdCipher
#      Ciphers                    3des
# Following includes "none" 'mac':
#      MACs                       AnyMAC
#
#      MACs                       AnyStd
#      MACs                       AnyStdMAC
#      RekeyIntervalSeconds       3600
```

Table 2.8 describes the Crypto options available for the SSH server.

Table 2.8   Options in the Crypto Section (Unix)

OPTION	DESCRIPTION
Ciphers	Lists the types of cipher-text to be used when encrypting the SSH session. Triple-DES (3DES), Blowfish, Arcfour, Twofish, CAST – 128, and DES are supported. More global options can be set, such as Any, Anystd, anycipher, and anystdcipher. Any and anystd allows standard ciphers; anycipher allows any ciphertext; anystdcipher allows any cipher listed in the IETS SSH draft. The entry of none offers no cipher.
MACs	Message Authentication Code (MAC) is a hash algorithm used to verify the integrity of the data before and after transmission. The algorithms supported are SHA1, MD5, SHA1-96, and MD5-96. Multiple MACs can also be set.
RekeyIntervalSeconds	Specifies the amount of time before the key exchange process is executed again. The default is 3600 seconds, which is one hour. The key exchange process can be disabled by setting the value to zero.

Users

The Users section of the sshd2_config file should look like the following:

```
#    PrintMotd                yes
#    CheckMail                yes
#    UserConfigDirectory      "%D/.ssh2"
#    UserConfigDirectory      "/etc/ssh2/auth/%U"
#    UserKnownHosts           yes
#    LoginGraceTime           600
#    PermitEmptyPasswords     no
#    StrictModes              yes
#    IdleTimeOut              1h
```

Table 2.9 describes the various miscellaneous options available for the SSH server.

Table 2.9   Miscellaneous Options in the User Section (Unix)

OPTION	DESCRIPTION
PrintMotd	Enables (yes) or disables (no) any text located in the motd (Message of the Day) file (/etc/motd) to be displayed at log in. This is very useful since messages can be displayed to all users who are logging in to the system, such as system downtime, legal statements, and security issues.
CheckMail	Enables (yes) or disables (no) the ability of the SSH server to check for new mail after the user has been authenticated.
UserConfigDirectory	Identifies the locations of user-specific configuration data, such as keys and identification files. The default is the .ssh2 folder in the users' home directory, such as /home/<username>/.ssh2 or Documents and Settings\<username>\.ssh2. More than one location can be identified for configuration data.
UserKnownHosts	Identifies the locations of user-specific known host file. The default is the .ssh2 folder in the users' home directory, such as /home/<username>/.ssh2 or Documents and Settings\<username>\.ssh2. More than one location can be identified.

(continued)

Table 2.9 *(continued)*

OPTION	DESCRIPTION
LoginGraceTime	The amount of time, in seconds, the user has to compete the login process after initiating an authentication request. Values range from zero, no limit, to 600 seconds.
PermitEmptyPasswords	Allows (yes) or rejects (no) the ability for users to have empty passwords. In most situations, this should be no.
StrictModes	Enables (yes) or disables (no) the checking of a users' permission in their home directory and rhosts files before accepting authentication. This should be set to yes to protect against world-writeable files in home directories.
IdleTimeOut	The amount of time, in minutes, the session can remain unused before it is automatically closed. A setting of zero specifies no timeout, which may be ideal in certain backup processes.

User Public Key Authentication

The User Public Key Authentication section of the sshd2_config file should look like the following:

```
#    HostKeyFile                hostkey
#    PublicHostKeyFile          hostkey.pub
#    RandomSeedFile             random_seed
#    IdentityFile               identification
#    AuthorizationFile          authorization
#    AllowAgentForwarding       yes
```

Table 2.10 describes the User Public Key options available for the SSH server.

Table 2.10 Options in the User Public Key Authentication Section (Unix)

OPTION	DESCRIPTION
HostKeyFile	Identifies the location of the private host-key file. The default is called hostkey, located on the local file system.
PublicHostKeyFile	Identifies the location of the public host-key file. The default is called hostkey.pub, located on the local file system.
RandomSeedFile	Identifies the location of the random seed file. This file is used to generate randomness for the SSH server.

IdentityFile	Identifies the location of the identity file, usually name identification. It is located in the users' home directory on the SSH client. This file is used by the SSH client to indicate which private keys are authorized for use during the process of authentication. For example, if a user has two private keys for authentication, such as id_dsa_2048_a and id_rsa_2048_a, the contents of the identification file will look like the following:
	
	`IdKey    id_dsa_2048_a`
	`IdKey    id_rsa_2048_a`
	
	Note: The private keys listed in the identification file need to be in the users' home directory also, discussed further in Chapter 4.

AuthorizationFile	Identifies the location of the authorization file, usually name authorization and located in the users' home directory on the SSH server. This file is used by the SSH server to indicate which public keys are authorized for acceptance during the process of authentication. For example, if a user has two public keys for authentication, such as id_dsa_2048_a.pub and id_rsa_2048_a.pub, the contents of the authorization file will look like the following:
	
	`Key    id_dsa_2048_a.pub`
	`Key    id_rsa_2048_a.pub`
	
	Note: The public keys listed in the authorization file need to be in the users' home directory also, discussed further in Chapter 4.

AllowAgentForwarding	Enables (yes) or disables (no) the SSH agent utility to forwarded logins remotely over SSH. This option uses the ssh-agent2 binary, a program that stores private keys for automated authentication.

Tunneling

The Tunneling section of the sshd2_config file should look similar to the following:

```
#    AllowX11Forwarding            yes
#    AllowTcpForwarding            yes
#    AllowTcpForwardingForUsers    sjl, cowboyneal@slashdot\.org
#    DenyTcpForwardingForUsers     2[[:isdigit:]]*4,peelo
#    AllowTcpForwardingForGroups   priviliged_tcp_forwarders
#    DenyTcpForwardingForGroups    coming_from_outside
```

Table 2.11 describes the tunneling options available for the SSH server.

Table 2.11   Options in the Tunneling Section (Unix)

OPTION	DESCRIPTION
AllowX11Forwarding	Enables (yes) or disables (no) the ability for X11 applications to forward over SSH.
AllowTcpForwardingForUsers	Enables specific users to forward ports, both locally and remotely. This setting accepts usernames and patterns, such as DNS patterns.
DenyTcpForwardingForUsers	Disables the ability for specific users to forward ports, both locally and remotely. This setting accepts usernames and patterns, such as DNS patterns.
AllowTcpForwardingForGroups	Enables groups to forward ports, both locally and remotely. This setting accepts usernames and patterns, such as DNS patterns.
DenyTcpForwardingForGroups	Disables the ability for specific groups to forward ports, both locally and remotely. This setting accepts usernames and patterns, such as DNS patterns.

Authentication

The Authentication section of the sshd2_config file should look like the following:

```
#    BannerMessageFile             /etc/ssh2/ssh_banner_message
#    BannerMessageFile             /etc/issue.net
#    PasswordGuesses                                                3
#    AllowedAuthentications        hostbased,publickey,password
#    AllowedAuthentications        publickey,pam-1@ssh.com
```

```
#     AllowedAuthentications        publickey,password
#     RequiredAuthentications       publickey,password
#     HostbasedAuthForceClientHostnameDNSMatch no
#     SshPAMClientPath              ssh-pam-client
```

Table 2.12 describes the authentication options available for the SSH server.

Table 2.12   Options in the Authentication Section (Unix)

OPTION	DESCRIPTION
BannerMessageFile	Identifies the location of the file that contains the text to be displayed before the client logs in to the SSH server. This is very useful for legal disclaimers.
PasswordGuesses	Identifies the number of attempts a user is given before being disconnected if valid authentication is not submitted.
AllowedAuthentications	Identifies the types of authentication methods that are valid. Options include password, publickey, and hostbased.
RequiredAuthentications	Identifies the types of authentication methods required for authentication. If the value is empty, any values in AllowedAuthentication will be honored.
HostbasedAuthForce ClientHostnameDNSMatch	Requires an exact match of the SSH client's hostname and the client's DNS entry.
SshPAMClientPath	Identifies the location of the SSH PAM client to use in order for PAM authentication to take place. The default location is /usr/local/bin/ssh-pam-client.

Host Restrictions

The Host Restrictions section of the sshd2_config file should look like the following:

```
#AllowHosts              localhost, foobar.com, friendly.org
##AllowHosts             t..l.\..*
##     AllowHosts        ([[:digit:]]{1\,3}\.){3}[[:digit:]]{1\,3}
##     AllowHosts        \i.*
##
#      DenyHosts                evil\.org, aol\.com
#      AllowSHosts              trusted\.host\.org
#      DenySHosts               not\.quite\.trusted\.org
#      IgnoreRhosts             no
#      IgnoreRootRHosts         no
```

Table 2.13 describes the Host Restrictions options available for the SSH server.

Table 2.13   Options in the Host Restrictions Section (Unix)

OPTION	DESCRIPTION
AllowHosts	Identifies the only hostnames, IP addresses, and/or patterns allowed to log in to the SSH server
DenyHosts	Identifies the hostnames, IP addresses, and/or patterns not allowed to log in to the SSH server
AllowSHosts	Identifies the hosts that are allowed hostbased authentication, based on /etc/shosts.equiv and AllowSHosts entries
DenySHosts	Identifies the hosts that are not allowed hostbased authentication, based on /etc/shosts.equiv and AllowSHosts entries
IgnoreRhosts	Enables (yes) or disables (no) the ability to allow only global configuration files (hosts.equiv and shosts.equiv)
IgnoreRootRHosts	Enables (yes) or disables (no) the ability to allow only root's global configuration files (hosts.equiv and shosts.equiv)

Users Restrictions

The Users Restrictions section of the sshd2_config file should look like the following:

```
#    AllowUsers         sj.*,s[[:isdigit:]]*,s(jl|amza)
#    DenyUsers          skuuppa,warezdude,31373
#    DenyUsers          don@untrusted\.org
#    AllowGroups        staff,users
#    DenyGroups         guest
#    PermitRootLogin                                    nopwd
     PermitRootLogin                                    no
```

Table 2.14 describes the Users Restrictions options available for the SSH server.

Table 2.14   Options in the Users Restrictions Section (Unix)

OPTION	DESCRIPTION
AllowUsers	Identifies the only users allowed to log in to the SSH server. This entry can contain a list of users, separated by a comma, or a pattern-matching variable.
DenyUsers	Identifies the users not allowed to log in to the SSH server. This entry can contain a list of users, separated by a comma, or a pattern-matching variable.
AllowGroups	Identifies the only groups allowed to log in to the SSH server. This entry can contain a list of groups, separated by a comma, or a pattern-matching variable.
DenyGroups	Identifies the groups not allowed to log in to the SSH server. This entry can contain a list of groups, separated by a comma, or a pattern-matching variable.
PermitRootLogin	Enables (yes) or disables (no) the ability for the root user to log in to the SSH server. As best practice, this setting should be set to no, forcing admin-users to su (switch user) to root. If the root account must be able to log in directly, the value of "nopwd" can allow root to log in directly, but with only public-key authentication.

SSH1 Compatibility

The SSH1 Compatibility section of the sshd2_config file should look similar to the following:

```
#     Ssh1Compatibility              <set by configure by default>
#     Sshd1Path                      <set by configure by default>
#     Sshd1ConfigFile          /etc/sshd_config_alternate
```

Table 2.15 describes the SS1 Compatibility options available for the SSH server.

Table 2.15   Options in the SSH1 Compatibility Section (Unix)

OPTION	DESCRIPTION
Ssh1Compatibility	Enables (yes) or disables (no) compatibility with SSH version 1, which is an entirely different implementation of SSH when compared with SSH version 2. SSH version 1 is insecure, but may be required.
Sshd1Path	Identifies the location of the SSH version 1 binary (for example, /usr/local/sbin/sshd1).
Sshd1ConfigFile	Identifies the location of the SSH version 1 configuration file (for example, /etc /ssh1/sshd1_config).

Chrooted Environment

The Chrooted Environment allows specific users to be limited to their home directories, either with a shell or with file transfer. In addition to entering the correct information in the sshd2_config file, the ssh-chroot manager needs to be initiated. The Chrooted Environment section of the sshd2_config file should look like the following:

```
#    ChRootUsers              ftp,guest
#    ChRootGroups             guest
```

Table 2.16 describes the Chroot options available for the SSH server.

Table 2.16   Options in the Chrooted Environment Section (Unix)

OPTION	DESCRIPTION
ChRootUsers	Identifies the users that should be limited to their home directories, thus chroot users
ChRootGroups	Identifies the groups that should be limited to their home directories, thus chroot groups

Subsystem Definitions

The Subsystem Definitions section of the sshd2_config file should look like the following:

```
subsystem-sftp              sftp-server
```

Table 2.17 describes the SFTP options available for the SSH server.

Table 2.17   Options in the Subsystem Definitions Section (Unix)

OPTION	DESCRIPTION
subsystem-sftp	Identifies the path for the SFTP (secure file transfer protocol) subsystem to be used with SSH (usually located in /usr/local/bin)

SSH Communications' SSH server: Windows

SSH Communications' SSH server in a Windows environment still uses the sshd2_config file; however, a GUI is included with the package, which is the recommended method of management. In this section, I discuss both the contents of the sshd2_config file, location in Program Files\SSH Secure Shell Server, and GUI management tool, located at Start ⇨ Programs ⇨ SSH Secure Shell Server ⇨ Configuration.

To view the contents of the sshd2_config file, the file that is used to configure the SSH server, enter the following commands:

```
C:\cd "Program Files\SSH Secure Shell Server"
C:\notepad sshd2_config
```

To view the configuration GUI, browse to the following shortcut:

Start ⇨ Programs ⇨ SSH Secure Shell Server

The configuration screen shows the subheadings on the left that are the same subsections in the sshd2_config file above. The GUI is just a graphical tool to modify the sshd2_config file. I will examine both the GUI tool and the sshd2_config file.

The first screen that appears using the GUI tool is the SSH server settings, as shown in Figure 2.1. This screen provides information about server status, event log, and default settings. Server status allows you to start or stop the server by simply clicking the button. This button starts or stops a service associated with SSH, which is called SSH Secure Shell 2. The next button, View Event Log, opens the Windows Event Log in order to view any error or warning messages from SSH. Lastly, the Restore Default Settings button reinstates default settings on the SSH server.

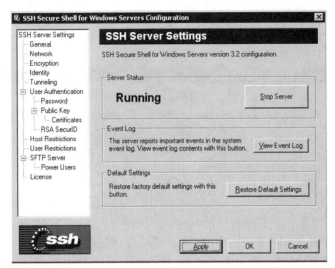

Figure 2.1   Configuration menu of SSH Communications' SSH server.

The Windows version of sshd2_config file is similar to the Unix version; however, many differences distinguish the two versions. The following sections address the Windows sshd2_config file.

General Settings

The general section of the sshd2_config file should look like the following:

```
## General settings
        MaxConnections                  0
        EventLogFilter                  error, warning
        IdleTimeout                     0
        BannerMessageFile               ""
        TerminalProvider                "cmd.exe"
        DoubleBackspace                 yes
#       ProtocolVersionString
```

The general section of the SSH configuration GUI should look like Figure 2.2.

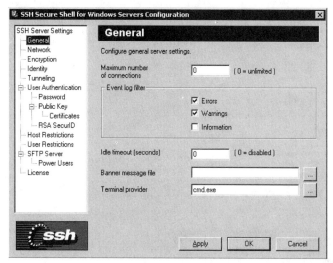

Figure 2.2 General screen from the SSH server configuration tool.

Table 2.18 describes the General options available for the SSH server.

Table 2.18 Options from the General Section of the sshd2_config File (Windows)

.OPTION	DESCRIPTION
MaxConnections	Identifies the number of concurrent connections the SSH server will handle. If the value is set to zero, the number of concurrent connections is unlimited.
EventLogFilter	Identifies the filter for Windows Event Log settings. Possible filters can be error, warning, and information.
IdleTimeout	The amount of time, in minutes, the session can remain unused before it is automatically closed. A setting of zero specifies no timeout, which may be ideal in certain backup processes.
BannerMessageFile	Identifies the location of the file containing text to be displayed before the client logs in to the server. This is very useful for legal disclaimers.
TerminalProvider	Identifies the executable that will provide terminal access to the remote user, which is usually the command prompt program (cmd.exe).

Network Settings

The network section of the sshd2_config file should look like the following:

```
Port                          443
ListenAddress                 0.0.0.0
RequireReverseMapping         no
ResolveClientHostName         yes
MaxBroadcastsPerSecond        0
NoDelay                       yes
KeepAlive                     yes
```

The network section of the SSH configuration GUI should look like Figure 2.3.

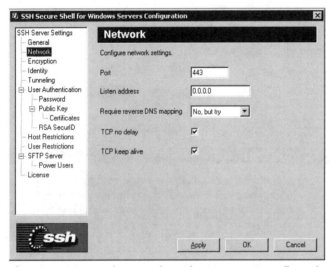

Figure 2.3 Network screen from the SSH server configuration tool.

Table 2.19 describes the Network options available for the SSH server.

Table 2.19 Options in the Network Section (Windows)

OPTION	DESCRIPTION

Port	Sets the port number for SSH to listen on. Default port is 22; however, listening on several ports, including other nonstandard ports, such as 80, 443, or 8080, may be optimal since business travelers may not be able to make outbound connections on port 22, but since port 80 or 443 is usually accessible. To listen on multiple ports, add the following lines:
	`Port 22`
	`Port 80`
	`Port 443`
	`Port 8080`

ListenAddress	Sets the IP address to have the SSH daemon listen on. The default, which is `0.0.0.0`, will enable the SSH services on all interfaces. If there are interfaces where SSH should not be listening, such as the external interface of a firewall, remove `0.0.0.0` and add the appropriate IP addresses. To listen on only select interfaces, add the following lines:
	`ListenAddress 172.16.1.1,192.168.0.1`
	`ListenAddress 10.0.0.1`

RequireReverseMapping	Enables (yes) or disables (no) the requirement of DNS lookups to succeed, in order to work with AllowHost and DenyHost entries. If enabled and the DNS lookup fails, the request is denied. If disabled and the DNS lookup fails, the IP address in AllowHosts and DenyHosts is checked.
ResolveClientHostname (sshd2_config file only)	Enables (yes) or disables (no) the server resolving (via DNS) the client's IP address.
MaxBroadcastPerSecond (sshd2_config file only)	Identifies the number of UDP broadcasts the server should handle per second. The default value, which is zero, has no broadcast handled.

(continued)

Table 2.19 *(continued)*

OPTION	DESCRIPTION
NoDelay	Enables (yes) or disables (no) the socket option for TCP_NODELAY.
KeepAlive	Enables (yes) or disables (no) whether the SSH server should send KeepAlive packets to the SSH clients. This value helps prevent hanging sessions by determining if the client on the other side is still running and hasn't crashed or blue-screened.

Crypto Settings

The Crypto section of the sshd2_config file should look like the following:

```
Ciphers                    AnyStdCipher
MACs                       AnyStdMac
RekeyIntervalSeconds       0
RandomSeedFile             "server_random_seed"
```

The Encryption section of the SSH configuration GUI should look like Figure 2.4.

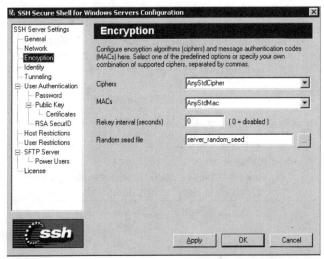

Figure 2.4 Encryption screen from the SSH server configuration tool.

Table 2.20 describes the Encryption options available for the SSH server.

Table 2.20   Options in the Encryption Section (Windows)

OPTION	DESCRIPTION
Ciphers	Lists the types of cipher-text to be used to encrypt the session. Triple-DES (3DES), Blowfish, Arcfour, Twofish, CAST – 128, and DES are supported. More global options can be set, such as Any, Anystd, anycipher, and anystdcipher. Any and anystd allow standard ciphers; anycipher allows any ciphertext; anystdcipher allows any cipher listed in the IETS SSH draftA setting of none offers no cipher.
MACs	Message Authentication Code (MAC) is a hash algorithm that verifies the integrity of the data before and after transmission. The algorithms supported are SHA1, MD5, SHA1-96, and MD5-96. Multiple MACs can also be set.
RekeyIntervalSeconds	Specifies the amount of time before the key-exchange process is executed again. The default is 3600 seconds, which is one hour. The key-exchange process can be disabled by setting the value to zero.
RandomSeedFile	Identifies the location of the random seed file. This file is used to generate randomness for the SSH server.

Users Settings

The Users section of the sshd2_config file should look like the following:

```
LoginGraceTime              600
PermitEmptyPasswords        no
UserConfigDirectory         "%D/.ssh2"
AuthorizationFile           "authorization"
PrivateWindowStation        yes
```

The User Authentication section of the SSH configuration GUI should look like Figure 2.5.

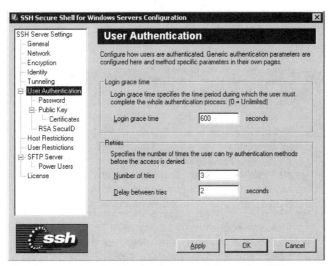

Figure 2.5   User Authentication screen from the SSH server configuration tool.

Furthermore, the User Authentication–Password section should look like Figure 2.6.

Lastly, the User Authentication–Public Key section should look like Figure 2.7.

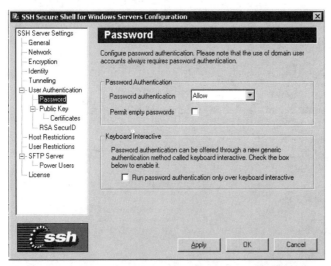

Figure 2.6   User Authentication–Password screen from the SSH server configuration tool.

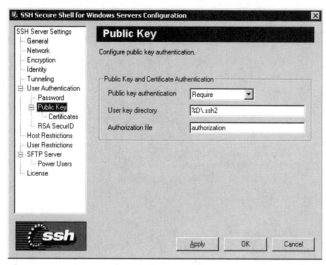

Figure 2.7 User Authentication–Public Key screen from the SSH server configuration tool.

Table 2.21 describes the User Authentication options available for the SSH server.

Table 2.21 Options in the User Authentication Section (Windows)

OPTION	DESCRIPTION
LoginGraceTime	The amount of time, in seconds, the user has to complete the log in process after initiating an authentication request. Values range from zero, no limit, to 600 seconds.
PermitEmptyPasswords	Allows (yes) or rejects (no) the ability for users to have empty passwords. In most situations, this should be no.
UserConfigDirectory (sshd2_config file)	Identifies the locations of user-specific configuration data, such as keys and identification files. The default is the .ssh2 folder in the users' home directory, such as /home/<username>/.ssh2 or Documents and Settings\<username>\.ssh2 (%D is user home dir; %U is user login name). More than one location can be identified for configuration data.

(continued)

Table 2.21 *(continued)*

OPTION	DESCRIPTION

User key directory (GUI)	Identifies the location of the authorization file, usually named authorization and located in the users' home directory on the SSH server. This file is used by the SSH server to indicate which public keys are authorized for acceptance during the process of authentication. For example, if a user has two public keys for authentication, such as id_dsa_2048_a.pub and id_rsa_2048_a.pub, the contents of the authorization file will look like the following:
	`Key  id_dsa_2048_a.pub`
	`Key  id_rsa_2048_a.pub`
	
	Note: The public keys listed in the authorization file need to be in the users' home directory also, discussed further in Chapter 4.

PrivateWindowStation (sshd2_config file only)	Enables (yes) or disables (no) any terminal created to be in a fully private window or not.

Server Public Key Configuration

The Server Public Key Configuration section of the sshd2_config file should look like the following:

```
#    HostKeyFile                hostkey
#    PublicHostKeyFile          hostkey.pub
```

The Identity section of the SSH configuration GUI should look like Figure 2.8.

Table 2.22 describes the Server Public Key options available for the SSH server.

Table 2.22 Options in the Server Public Key Configuration Section (Windows)

OPTION	DESCRIPTION
HostKeyFile	Identifies the location of the private host-key file. The default location is in the /etc/ssh2 directory, located on the local file system.
PublicHostKeyFile	Identifies the location of the public host-key file. The default is hostkey.pub, located on the local file system.

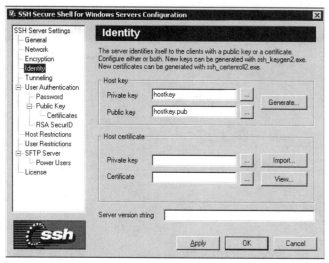

Figure 2.8   Identity screen from the SSH server configuration tool.

Server Certificate Configurations

The Server Certificate Configuration section of the sshd2_config file should look like the following:

```
#        HostKeyFile               " "
#        HostCertificateFile       " "
#        Pki                       " "
#        MapFile                   " "
#        LDAPServers
#        SocksServer
#        PkiDisableCRLs            no
```

Table 2.23 describes the Server Certificate options available for the SSH server.

Table 2.23   Options in the Server Certificate Configuration (Windows)

OPTION	DESCRIPTION
HostKeyFile	Identifies the location of the private host-key file. The default is hostkey, located on the local file system.
HostCertificateFile	Identifies the location of the certificate file.
PKI	Enables (yes) or disables (no) user authentication using certificates.

(continued)

Table 2.23   *(continued)*

OPTION	DESCRIPTION
MapFile	Identifies the keyword-mapping file for the preceding PKI keyword.
LDAPServers	Identifies the LDAP server to be used for CRLs.
SocksServer	Identifies the name of the SOCKS server, which is used for certificate CRL on remote servers.
PKIDisableCRLs	Disables CRL checking.

Tunneling Configurations

The Tunneling section of the sshd2_config file should look similar to the following:

```
        AllowTcpForwarding              no
#       AllowTcpForwardingForUsers
#       DenyTcpForwardingForUsers
```

The Tunneling section of the SSH configuration GUI should be similar to Figure 2.9.

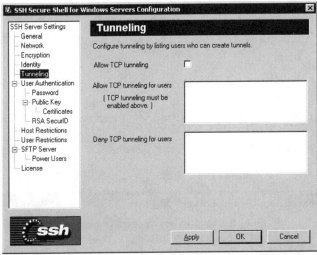

Figure 2.9 Tunneling screen from the SSH server configuration tool.

Table 2.24 describes the Tunneling options available for the SSH server.

Table 2.24 Options in the Tunneling Section (Windows)

OPTION	DESCRIPTION
AllowTcpForwarding	Enables (yes) or disables (no) the ability to forward ports, both locally and remotely for all users.
AllowTcpForwardingForUsers	Enables the ability for specific users to forward ports, both locally and remotely. This setting accepts usernames and patterns, such as DNS patterns.
DenyTcpForwardingForUsers	Disables the ability for specific users to forward ports, both locally and remotely. This setting accepts usernames and patterns, such as DNS patterns.

Authentication Methods

The Authentication section of the sshd2_config file should look like the following:

```
        PasswordGuesses                3
        AllowedAuthentications         "publickey,password,"
        RequiredAuthentications        "publickey,"
        AuthInteractiveFailureTimeout  2
        AuthKbdInt.NumOptional         0
#       AuthKbdInt.Optional            ""
#       AuthKbdInt.Required            ""
        AuthKbdInt.Retries
```

Table 2.25 describes the Authentication options available for the SSH server.

Table 2.25 Options in the Authentication Section (Windows)

OPTION	DESCRIPTION
PasswordGuesses (Shown in Figure 4.5)	Identifies the number of attempts a user is given before being disconnected if a valid authentication is not submitted.
AllowedAuthentications (Shown in Figure 4.6 and 4.7 with the Password Authenication drop down box or the Public Key drop down box)	Identifies the types of authentication methods that are valid. Options include password, publickey, and hostbased.

(continued)

Table 2.25   *(continued)*

OPTION	DESCRIPTION
RequiredAuthentications (Shown in Figure 4.6 and 4.7 with the Password Authenication drop down box or the Public Key drop down box)	Identifies the types of authentication methods that are required for authentication. If the value is empty, any values in AllowedAuthentication will be honored.
AuthInteractiveFailureTimeout (sshd2_config file only)	Identifies the number of failures a keyboard-interactive session may have.
AuthKbdInt.NumOptional (sshd2_config file only)	Identifies the number of submethods required before valid authentication.
AuthKbdInt.Optional (sshd2_config file only)	Identifies the optional submethod that Keyboard-Interactive will use. The options can be SecureID, plugin, and password.
AuthKbdInt.Required (sshd2_config file only)	Identifies the required submethods that must be present in order for valid authentication.
AuthKbdInt.Retries (sshd2_config file only)	Identifies the number of retries a user can attempt the keyboard-interaction process in order to authenticate to the SSH server.

Host Restrictions

The Host Restrictions section of the sshd2_config file should look like the following:

```
#    AllowHosts
#    DenySHosts
```

The Host Restrictions section of the SSH configuration GUI should look like Figure 2.10.

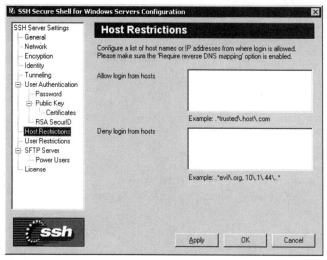

Figure 2.10   Host Restrictions screen from the SSH server configuration tool.

Table 2.26 describes the Host Restrictions options available for the SSH server.

Table 2.26   Options in the Host Restrictions Section (Windows)

OPTION	DESCRIPTION
AllowHosts	Identifies the only hostnames, IP addresses, and/or patterns allowed to log in to the SSH server
DenyHosts	Identifies the hostnames, IP addresses, and/or patterns not allowed to log in to the SSH server

User Restrictions

The User Restrictions section of the sshd2_config file should look like the following:

```
#    AllowUsers
#    DenyUsers
#    PermitRootLogin
     PermitUserTerminal
```

The User Restrictions section of the SSH configuration GUI should look like Figure 2.11.

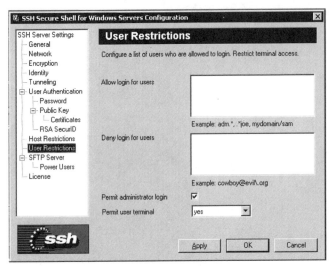

Figure 2.11 User Restrictions screen from the SSH server configuration tool.

Table 2.27 describes the User Restriction options available for the SSH server.

Table 2.27 Options in the User Restrictions Section (Windows)

OPTION	DESCRIPTION
AllowUsers	Identifies the only users allowed to log in to the SSH server. This entry can contain a list of users, separated by a comma, or a pattern-matching variable.
DenyUsers	Identifies the users not allowed to log in to the SSH server. This entry can contain a list of users, separated by a comma, or a pattern-matching variable.
PermitRootLogin	Enables (yes) or disables (no) the ability for the root user to log into the SSH server. As best practice, this setting should be set to no, forcing admin-users to su (switch user) to root. If the root account must be able to log in directly, the value of "nopwd" can allow root to log in directly, but with only public key authentication.
PermitUserTerminal	Enables (yes) or disables (no) the ability for a user to access a terminal session. If this option is set to admin, only administrators can access the terminal. This admin option works well for SFTP file servers giving the remote user access to cmd.exe.

Subsystem Definitions

The Subsystem Definitions section of the sshd2_config file should look like the following:

```
subsystem-sftp                          sftp-server2.exe
SftpLogCategory                         16
Sftp-DirList                            "HOME=%D"
Sftp-Home                               "%D"
Sftp-AdminDirList                       "HOME=%D, C:=C:, D:=D:"
#        Sftp-AdminUsers
```

The SFTP Server section of the SSH configuration GUI should look like Figure 2.12.

The SFTP Server–Power Users section should look like Figure 2.13.

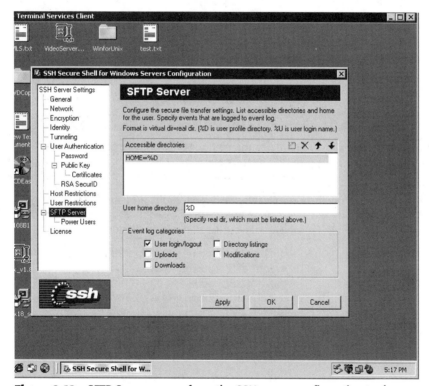

Figure 2.12 SFTP Server screen from the SSH server configuration tool.

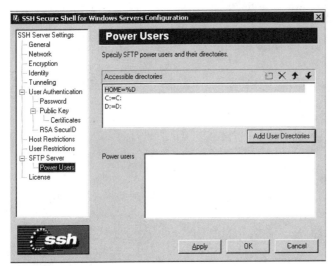

Figure 2.13   SFTP Server–Power Users screen from the SSH server configuration tool.

Table 2.28 describes the SFTP options available for the SSH server.

Table 2.28   Options in the Subsystem Definitions (Windows)

OPTION	DESCRIPTION
subsystem-sftp (sshd2_config file only)	Identifies the path for the SFTP (secure file transfer protocol) subsystem to be used with SSH; usually located in Program Files/SSH Secure Shell Server.
Sftplogcategory (sshd2_config) Event Log categories (GUI on Figure 4.12)	Specifics the SFTP operations that are logged in the Windows Event Viewer. The default value is 16, which only logs user logins and logouts.
Sftp-DirList (sshd2_config) Accessible Directories (GUI on Figure 4.12)	Identifies the directories available for a regular SFTP user. Format is virtual dir=real dir. This setting will restrict any SFTP access to only the specific directories. This option works well with secure file servers by restricting users to only a certain share or folder on a remote file server, such as D:\applications, and disabling access to core operating system folders, such as c:\winnt\system32\config, discussed further in Chapters 6 and 7.
Sftp-Home (sshd2_config) User Home Directory (GUI on Figure 4.12)	Identifies the SFTP home directory for all users.

Table 2.28   *(continued)*

OPTION	DESCRIPTION
Sftp-AdminDirList	
Accessible Directories (GUI on Figure 4.13)	Identifies the available directories for administrators.
Sftp-AdminUsers Power Users (GUI on Figure 4.13)	Identifies the usernames that are SFTP administrators.

VanDyke Software's VShell SSH Server

VanDyke Software's VShell SSH server is available only for Windows environments. The VShell server uses a GUI to display, edit, and report configuration options for the SSH server. The following paragraphs address the various settings and capabilities of the VShell SSH server.

General Settings

To view the configuration screen (see Figure 2.14), browse to the VShell short-cut, Start ⇨ Program ⇨ VShell ⇨ VShell.

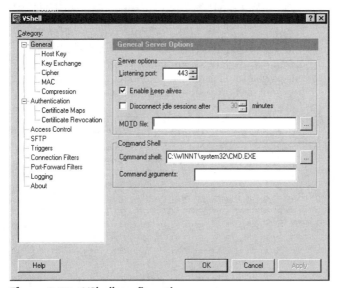

Figure 2.14   VShell configuration screen.

In the configuration screen, highlight the general section first. The general section describes some of the global options for the SSH server, which are listed in Table 2.29.

Table 2.29   Options in the General Section (VShell)

OPTION	DESCRIPTION

ListeningPort	Sets the port number for SSH to listen on. Default port is 22; however, listening on several ports, including other nonstandard ports, such as 80, 443, or 8080, may be optimal since business travelers may not be able to make outbound connections on port 22, but since port 80 or 443 is usually accessible. To listen on multiple ports, add the following lines:
	`Port 22`
	`Port 80`
	`Port 443`
	`Port 8080`

Enable Keep Alives	Enables (check) or disables (no check) whether the SSH server should send KeepAlive packets to the SSH clients. This value helps prevent hanging sessions by determining if the client on the other side is still running and hasn't crashed or blue-screened.
Disconnect idle session after __minutes	Sets the amount of time, in minutes, the session can remain unused before it is automatically closed.
MOTD file	Identifies the path to the MOTD (Message of the day) file (Program Files\VShell\) to be displayed at login. This is very useful since messages can be displayed to all users who are logging in to the system, such as system downtime, security issues, and so on.
Command Shell	Identifies the executable that will provide terminal access to the remote user, which is usually the command prompt program (cmd.exe).
Command arguments	Identifies any arguments or flags to provide with the command shell specified previously.

General–Host Key

Highlight the General–Host Key section next (see Figure 2.15). The General–Host Key section describes the host-key location as well as the fingerprint. Various options are given in Table 2.30.

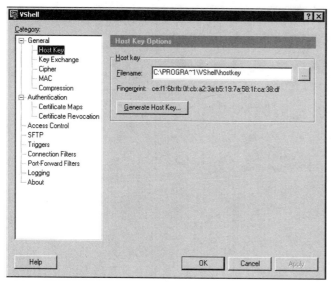

Figure 2.15 General–Host Key screen from the VShell server.

Table 2.30 Options in the General–Host Key Section (VShell)

OPTION	DESCRIPTION
Filename	Identifies the path to the host key for the VShell SSH server
Fingerprint	Displays the fingerprint for the VShell SSH server
Generate Host Key...	A wizard that creates a host key for the VShell SSH server

General–Key Exchanges

Highlight the General–Key Exchanges section next (see Figure 2.16). The General–Key Exchanges section describes the key exchange options. Various options are given in Table 2.31.

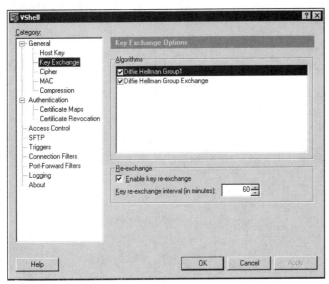

Figure 2.16   General–Key Exchanges screen from the VShell server.

Table 2.31   Options in the General–Key Exchanges Section (VShell)

OPTION	DESCRIPTION
Algorithms	Identifies the algorithms available for the key-exchange process
Re-exchanges	Enables (check) or disables (no check) the re-exchange of keys. If checked, an interval, in minutes, should be selected

General–Cipher

Highlight the General–Cipher section next (see Figure 2.17) The General–Cipher section describes the encryption options, which are listed in Table 2.32.

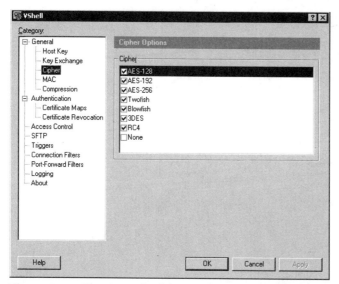

Figure 2.17   The General–Cipher screen from the VShell server.

Table 2.32   Options in the General–Cipher Section (VShell)

OPTION	DESCRIPTION
Cipher	Identifies the types of cipher-text to be used to encrypt the session. AES-128, AES-192, AES-256, Twofish, Blowfish, Triple-DES (3DES), RC4, and no encryption (none) are supported

General–MAC

Highlight the General–MAC section next (see Figure 2.18). The General–MAC section describes the hash options, which are listed in Table 2.33.

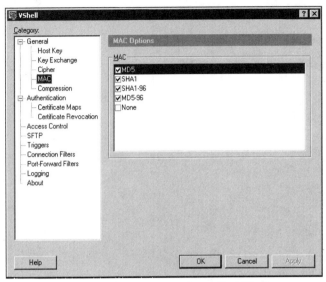

Figure 2.18   General–MAC screen from the VShell server.

Table 2.33   Options in the General–MAC Section (VShell)

OPTION	DESCRIPTION
MAC	Message Authentication Code (MAC) is a hash algorithm used to verify the integrity of the data before and after transmission. The algorithms supported are SHA1, MD5, SHA1-96, and MD5-96. No hash can also be set.

General–Compression

Highlight the General–Compression section next (see Figure 2.19). The General–Compression section describes the compression options, which are listed in Table 2.34.

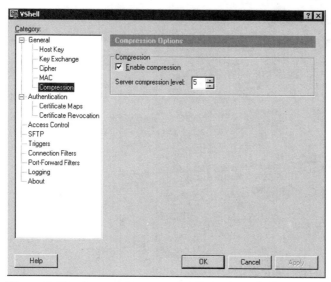

Figure 2.19   General-Compression from the VShell server.

Table 2.34   Options in the General-Compression Section (VShell)

OPTION	DESCRIPTION
Enable Compression	Enables (checkbox selected) or disables (checkbox not selected) the use of compression during the SSH session.
Server Compression Level	If Enable Compressed is checked, this sets the level of compression to be used for the SSH session.

Authentication

Highlight the Authentication section next (see Figure 2.20). The Authentication section describes the key exchange options, which are listed in Table 2.35.

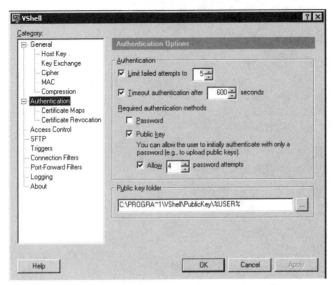

Figure 2.20   Authentication screen from the VShell server.

Table 2.35   Options in the Authentication Section (VShell)

OPTION	DESCRIPTION
Limit failed attempts to	The number of failed attempts a user can have before the session is disconnected.
Time authentication after	Sets the amount of time the user has to complete the authentication process. Specifically, from the time the user initiates the connection to the time the user enters a username/password or private-key password.
Required authentication methods – Password	Requires a password for authentication.
Required authentication methods – Public Key	Requires a public key for authentication.
Required authentication methods – Public Key Uploads	Sets the number of times a user can log in with only a password in order to upload a public key. This feature is very useful if public-key authentication is the only method for authentication, giving the user a method to upload a public key.
Public key folder	The location where the users' public keys will be stored. The default is Program Files\VShell\Publickey\<username>.

Access Control

Highlight the Access Control section next (see Figure 2.21). The Access Control section describes the rights and privileges for different users, which are listed in Table 2.36.

Table 2.36 Options in the Access Control Section (VShell)

OPTION	DESCRIPTION
Name	Identifies the names or groups allowed to access the VShell SSH server. This option is very valuable since it can limit only a specific amount of users and/or groups without exposing SSH to all users on the machine.
Permissions	This option allows or denies specific rights to be associated with a user, such as log in, shell, remote execution, SFTP, Port Forwarding, and Remote Port Forwarding. This option provides a lot of value that is absent from other SSH implementations. For example, if SSH is being deployed as a secure management tool, a secure file transfer tool, and a remote access solution, using only one VShell SSH service, users in the Administrators group can be given Shell and Port Forwarding rights to manage the server. Furthermore, users in the File Transfer group can be explicitly denied rights to everything, including Shell, but allowed SFTP rights. This protects against users having a command prompt (cmd.exe) to the remote server, but having full file access to the specified directory (for example, d:\share\applications). Lastly, the Remote Access group can be explicitly denied access to everything, such as shell and SFTP, but granted access to Port Forwarding, which would allow them to tunnel ports, such as mail ports, for remote access but restrict them from getting a command prompt or file access to the VShell SSH server.

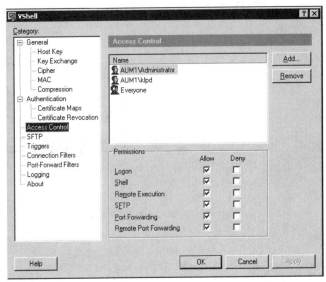

Figure 2.21   Access Control screen from the VShell server.

SFTP Section

Highlight the SFTP section next (see Figure 2.22). The SFTP section describes the secure file transfer options, which are listed in Table 2.37. These options are also excellent because they allow the control of specific folders to publish to SFTP users. This can help secure a file server by allowing only authorized directories on a file server, such as d:\Common files\, while restricting the users from sensitive operation system files and folders, such as c:\winnt\. This option allows an SSH server to provide full file-system security over an SFTP session without any worries that the user may be able to access and download other files that may be on the SSH server.

Table 2.37   Options in the SFTP Section (VShell)

OPTION	DESCRIPTION
SFTP Root	Sets the SFTP root directory to allow users to access
SFTP Root <Directory> that has been specified	Shows the permissions of the SFTP root directory

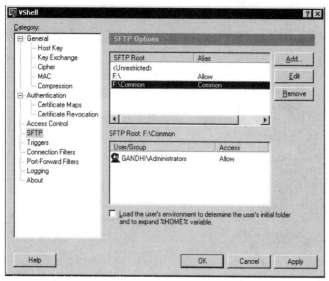

Figure 2.22 SFTP screen from the VShell server.

Triggers

Highlight the Triggers section next (see Figure 2.23). The Triggers section describes any triggers options that can be executed to SFTP uploads or failed authentications, which are listed in Table 2.38.

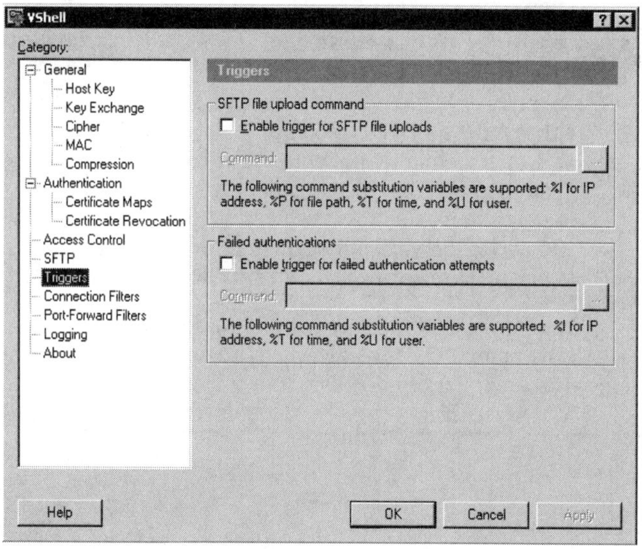

Figure 2.23 Triggers screen from the VShell server.

Table 2.38   Options in the Triggers Section (VShell)

OPTION	DESCRIPTION
SFTP file upload commands	Enables (checkbox selected) or disables (checkbox not selected) triggers to be executed during an SFTP upload process. The triggers can be simple batch files, visual basic scripts, perl scripts, or java scripts that will be executed once an Upload process is requested.
Failed Authentications	Enables (checkbox selected) or disables (checkbox not selected) triggers to be executed during a failed authentication. The triggers can be simple batch files, visual basic scripts, perl scripts, or java scripts that will be executed once an authentication request has failed.

Connection Filters

Highlight the Connection Filters section next (see Figure 2.24). The Connection Filters section describes who can and cannot connect to the SSH server. Options are shown in Table 2.39. When a VShell SSH server is deployed on a network, access to everyone, which may be all internal machines or all Internet machines, may not be desired. This option allows you to set filters and restrict access to the VShell SSH server.

Table 2.39   Options in the Connection Filters Section (VShell)

OPTION	DESCRIPTION
Filter Entries	Describes the filters that have been set. Options are either Allow or Deny, based on a particular IP address, hostname, network mask, or Domain. For example, if an SSH server is deployed for remote management, a list of specific IP address can be allowed, which will limit access to only authorized users while restricting all other accounts.
Test Filter	Tests any filters. By entering an IP address or hostname, the connectivity can be tested to the specified IP address/hostname to ensure that the SSH server can access the specified machine.

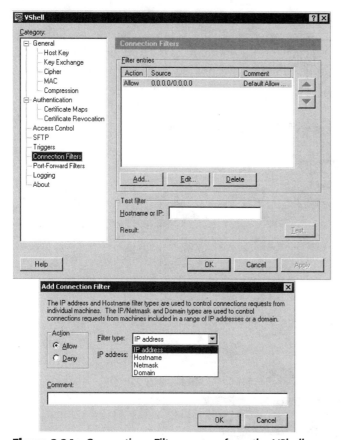

Figure 2.24 Connections Filters screen from the VShell server.

Port-Forward Filters

Highlight the Port-Forward Filters section next (see Figure 2.25). The Port-Forward Filters section describes the port-forwarding options, which are listed in Table 2.40. The Port-Forward Filters section describes which machines can be accessed on which ports via SSH tunneling. When a VShell SSH session is established between a source and a destination, port forwarding to remote servers may not be desired for security purposes. This option allows you to set filters that specify the servers and ports allowed to be accessed, eliminating the security risk of authorized SSH users tunneling to machines they should not be accessing. For example, an SSH session may allow remote management to a Windows Terminal Server on port 3389 (Terminal Services); however, access to the FTP (port 21) service on the same machine may be not be desired. If a filter is set to allow only 3389 to be tunneled to the Windows machine, access to the FTP service via a port-forward tunnel will be denied.

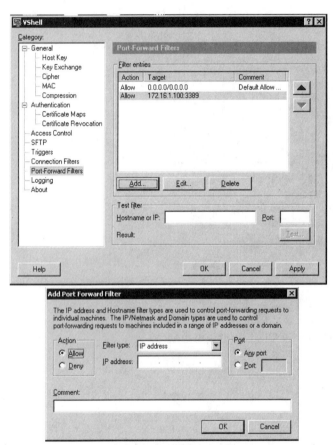

Figure 2.25 Port-Forward Filters screen from the VShell server.

Table 2.40 Options in the Port-Forward Filters Section (VShell)

OPTION	DESCRIPTION
Filter Entries	Describes the filters that have been set. Options are either Allow or Deny, based on a particular IP address, hostname, network mask, or Domain. For example, if an SSH server is deployed on the perimeter of the network to allow remote management to a Windows Terminal Server in the internal network, the Target value will be the Windows Terminal server (for example, 172.16.1.100) on the specific port (for example, 3389). This will limit port-forwarding access to the remote terminal server on port 3389 only, denying port forwarding access to everything else. This provides a significant level of security.
Test Filter	Tests any filters. By entering in an IP address or hostname, the connectivity can be tested to the specified IP address/hostname.

Logging

Highlight the Logging section next (see Figure 2.26). The Logging section describes the logging options, which are listed in Table 2.41.

Table 2.41 Options in the Logging Section (VShell)

OPTION	DESCRIPTION
Log File Messages	Enables (checkbox selected) or disables (checkbox not selected) specific types of logs to be sent to a log file. Possible options are Errors, Warnings, Informational, Connection, Authentication, SFTP, port Forwarding, and Debug. It is best practice to log as much as possible and to create scripts to view only certain parts of the Log file that are desired (for example, every port-forwarding request established).
Log file folder	Identifies the path to the specific log file to record the VShell SSH event specified by the preceding options.

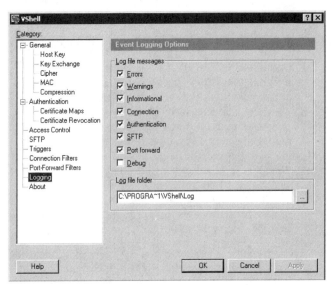

Figure 2.26 Logging section from the VShell server.

Comparison of OpenSSH, SSH Server, and VShell

The SSH servers discussed in this chapter have similar functionality, but significant differences exist among them. For example, VShell SSH server offers easy configuration methods to restrict shell access to an SSH client but also allows other SSH options such as SFTP or port forwarding. If SSH needs to be set up for secure file transfer, shell access should probably be restricted. If Vshell is used, this restriction can be set quite easily. On the other hand, OpenSSH does not offer quite the same ease of restricting shell access to users. Similarly, if SSH needs to be set up for remote management to internal servers only, all three SSH servers can be used; however, if remote management needs to be limited to a specific number of machines and ports, VShell and SSH Communications' are probably good choices, since they offer SSH access with port-forwarding restrictions.

If SSH is being deployed in an environment where several different SSH servers exist, OpenSSH is probably a good choice, since it offers the most flexibility and interoperability with any other SSH server that may be a different installation.

Your choice of an SSH server is highly dependant on the type of functionality required for SSH. Because SSH can be used in a variety of ways, you need to understand the different servers and the specific functionality that each offers.

Summary

This chapter examines three SSH servers that can be used with any SSH client: OpenSSH, SSH Communications' SSH Server, and VanDyke Softare's VSHell SSH server. Many more, equally effective SSH servers exist than the ones discussed here; however, in the interests of time and space, they have not been covered. Be aware that most of the other servers are very similar to the ones examined in the previous paragraphs. For example, F-Secure's SSH server and SSH Communications' SSH server are practically alike.

When deciding on the choice of an SSH server for your organization, it is important to know the business and technical requirements in addition to the different options available with each. While many SSH servers offer similar functionality, many offer features that might not be present in others. For example, if your SSH architecture is being used for terminal access, port forwarding, SFTP, or all of the above, different SSH servers have strengths and weaknesses that should influence your decision.

In this chapter, I have described in detail the various options available in each SSH server and use this information throughout the rest of this book to highlight the strengths and weakness of the SSH servers. This approach will not only help you understand the features of the SSH servers, but will also allow you to make an informed decision when choosing a server.

Chapter 1 of this book has covered the basics of SSH (namely, the deployment of SSH servers), and Chapter 2 has covered the detailed descriptions of SSH servers themselves. The next chapter focuses on SSH clients.

Secure Shell Clients

Many SSH clients provide different types of functionality and usage. The list of SSH clients includes freeware, downloadable easily from the information superhighway; noncommercial freeware, available for all development and learning environments; and pay commercial clients, used only for commercial use and commercial development. While there may be several SSH clients that can be used for various operating systems, all SSH clients are not created equal. The type of SSH client you use can significantly affect the type of SSH experience you have. For example, several SSH clients do not have built-in SFTP or SCP functionality. The absence of such functionality requires you to download and use two separate tools: one for SSH usage and one for SFTP/SCP usage. Although using two tools may be simple enough, the cumbersome process might discourage novice users. The SSH clients that provide built-in SFTP/SCP functionality might offer you a superior SSH experience.

This chapter explores several SSH clients available for Unix and Windows. Also, the configuration of various SSH clients and customization for optimal usage is discussed. The following clients are the focus of this chapter:

Command-Line SSH Clients

- Secure Shell Communications
- OpenSSH
- GUI SSH clients

- SecureCRT
- PuTTY
- WinSCP
- MindTerm
- MacSSH

The discussion of SSH clients in this chapter, and throughout this book, is limited to the major ones. Keep in mind that there are many other types of SSH clients, very similar to and as good as the ones covered here. For example, F-Secure's SSH client and SSH Communications' SSH client are extremely similar.

Although many of the SSH clients discussed in this chapter offer similar functionality, there are various subtle differences among them. For example, SSH Communications' SSH client offers an integrated SFTP client that can be used in a seamless fashion. On the other hand, SecureCRT does not provide a fully integrated tool for SFTP in its SecureCRT SSH client; however, Secure-CRT does contain an HTTP proxy tunnel that is very easily configurable but not so simple on SSH Commutations' SSH client. Furthermore, MindTerm's FTP-to-SFTP bridging capability provides an easy method for connecting non-SSH enabled clients to gain access to an SFTP server. Despite the fact that the connection from the FTP client to the SFTP client is still insecure, the connection from the SFTP server to SFTP client is still secure, which might be the only connection used over an insecure network such as the Internet.

Your choice of an SSH client is highly dependant on the type of functionality required for SSH. Since SSH can be used in a variety of ways, it is important to understand the various clients and the specific functionality that each offers. This chapter will allow your SSH-client decision to be as informed as possible. For example, if SSH is being deployed primarily for its file-transfer capabilities, WinSCP and SSH Communications' SSH clients are probably good choices. On the other hand, if SSH is being deployed for remote shell access via an HTTP proxy server, the SecureCRT and PuTTY clients are probably good choices. Lastly, if SSH is being deployed for remote access from undefined and uncontrolled terminal locations, MindTerm is probably a good choice, since it offers SSH access with the need of only a Web browser.

The SSH client you choose does not have to be based exclusively on technical capabilities; personal preference is important as well. While there may be many differences among SSH clients, their basic principle is the same: encrypted communication.

Command-Line SSH Clients

Secure Shell Communications (www.ssh.com) and OpenSSH (www.openssh .org) produce two of the most-used command-line clients for both Windows and Unix. Since the OpenSSH and Secure Shell Communications' clients are so similar, the following paragraphs cover both of the clients' features. Also, since the command-line clients contain similar features, if not the same features, on Windows and Unix versions, the following section can be used on Windows command-line clients or Unix command-line clients.

The SSH clients can be purchased and/or downloaded for commercial or noncommercial use from the following Web site:

www.ssh.com/support/downloads/secureshellwks/

Since we will be using SSH for a noncommercial use, the noncommercial version can be downloaded from www.secondstory.org/mirror/ssh/. Also, the OpenSSH client for Unix can be downloaded from the following site:

ftp://ftp3.usa.openbsd.org/pub/OpenBSD/OpenSSH/portable
/openssh03.5p1.tar

The Windows command-line client can be downloaded from the following site:

http://lexa.mckenna.edu/sshwindows/

Windows Installation

Installing the SSH client is a relatively easy process on a Windows operating system. Once you have downloaded the executable files from http://lexa.mckenna.edu/sshwindows/ (OpenSSH) or www.ssh.com (SSH Communications), a wizard will walk you through the installation process. Keep in mind that you need to install only the clients for the purposes of this chapter. Installation of the server is discussed in Chapter 1. Many of the client binaries are installed automatically when an SSH server has been installed on a Windows machine.

Unix Installation

Once you have downloaded the SSH client from www.ssh.com or www.openssh.com on a Unix operating system, it must first be extracted. (The letters XYZ that follow are a variable that signifies the version number of the SSH client you will be downloading):

```
#gunzip -c ssh-XYZ.tar.gz | tar xvf -
```

After extraction, change directories to the SSH folder. Once inside the SSH folder, the binary must be compiled and created:

```
#cd ssh-XYZ
#./configure
```

```
#make
#make install
```

Once the binary has been compiled, it will place the binary in /usr/local/bin. At this point, the help file should be ready for viewing. SSH Communications' SSH client binary is called ssh2 on both Windows and Unix. On Windows, the file can be located at \Program Files\SSH Secure Shell\ssh2.exe. On Unix, the file can be located at /usr/local/bin/ssh2. OpenSSH client binary is called ssh on both Unix and Windows. On Windows, the file can be located at \Program Files\OpenSSH\bin\ssh.exe. On Unix, the file can be located at /usr/local/bin/ssh. Once you have located the SSH client binary, type **ssh2 –h** for the SSH Communications' binary or **ssh –h** for OpenSSH's binary. The following help should appear:

```
Usage: ssh2 [options] [user@]host[#port] [command]

Options:
  -l          login_name Log in using this user name.
  -n          Redirect input from /dev/null.
  +a          Enable authentication agent forwarding.
  -a          Disable authentication agent forwarding.
  +x          Enable X11 connection forwarding (treat X11 clients as
              UNTRUSTED).
  +X          Enable X11 connection forwarding (treat X11 clients as
              TRUSTED).
  -x          Disable X11 connection forwarding.
  -i file     Identity file for public key authentication
  -F file     Read an alternative configuration file.
  -t          Tty; allocate a tty even if command is given.
  -v          Verbose; display verbose debugging messages.
Equal to '-d 2'
  -d level    Set debug level.
  -V          Display version string.
  -q          Quiet; don't display any warning messages.
  -f[o]       Fork into background after authentication.
              With optional 'o' argument, goes to "one-shot" mode.
  -e char     Set escape character; 'none' = disable (default: ~).
  -c cipher   Select encryption algorithm. Multiple -c options are
              allowed and a single -c flag can have only one cipher.
  -m MAC      Select MAC algorithm. Multiple -m options are
              allowed and a single -m flag can have only one MAC.
  -p port     Connect to this port. Server must be on the same port.
  -S          Don't request a session channel.
  -L          listen-port:host:port  Forward local port to remote address
  -R          listen-port:host:port  Forward remote port to local address
  -g          Gateway ports, i.e. remote hosts may connect to locally
              forwarded ports.
```

```
+g          Don't gateway ports.
+C          Enable compression.
-C          Disable compression.
-4          Use IPv4 to connect.
-6          Use IPv6 to connect.
-o          'option'  Process the option as if it was read from a
            configuration file.
-1[ti]      Choose ssh1-protocol fallback type.
-h          Display this help.
```

As shown previously, the SSH help file is exhaustive and shows the wide array of options that SSH can provide. In its simplest sense, SSH can connect an SSH server listening on its default port, which is 22. The –p switch is required in order to specify a port other than 22; however, if –p is not used, port 22 will be used as the default. Similarly, the –l switch needs to be used in order to specify a username. If you do not use the –l switch, the current user that the command is being executed from will be used:

```
ssh 10.0.0.3 -l cdwivedi -p 22
cdwivedi's password:
Authentication successful.
Last login: Thurs June 12 05:52:06 2003 from 172.16.11.17
```

As an alternative, the same command can be written without any switches, using SSH defaults:

```
ssh cdwivedi@10.0.0.3#22
```

–l and –p are two of the various switches used with the SSH client. The following section describes some of the more important switches used throughout the rest of this book.

The first switch is –i. The –i switch can be used to point to a pubic-key file used to authenticate to an SSH server. A copy of the public-key file needs to exist on the SSH server for public-key authentication, discussed further in Chapter 4. An example of the –i switch follows:

```
ssh 10.0.0.3 -l cdwivedi -p 60599 -i publickey.pub
```

The –L and –R switches are used for local port forwarding and remote port forwarding. Port forwarding is discussed in Chapter 6; however, a general understanding of its syntax is required now. Local port forwarding allows the local connection to a port to be forwarded to a remote server on any remote port through the SSH server. For example, a mail server that has the IP address 10.0.0.100 and is listening on port 143 can be accessed using SSH. The SSH server, which has the IP address 10.0.0.3, needs a valid route to the machine. The following is an example of using the –L switch for local port forwarding:

```
ssh 10.0.0.3 -1 cdwivedi -L 143:10.0.0.100:143
```

Remote port forwarding can also be conducted; it is discussed further in Chapter 6. The following is an example of remote port forwarding:

```
ssh 10.0.0.3 -1 cdwivedi -R 139:127.0.0.1:139
```

Options can be also set for the type of encryption desired as well as the type of MAC algorithm. For example, if the SSH server accepts only connections using Triple-DES (3DES), the –c switch should be used. Triple-DES is an algorithm that can be used to encrypt data. This allows 3DES to be used to encrypt data that traverses the network. If more than one type of encryption is supported, multiple –c options can be used. The following are two examples of the encryption options:

```
ssh 10.0.0.3 -1 cdwivedi -c 3DES
ssh 10.0.0.3 -1 cdwivedi -c 3DES -c Blowfish
```

The MAC algorithms used can either be MD5 or SHA1. Both MD5 and SHA1 are algorithms that can be used to verify the integrity of data. MD5 uses a 128-bit message digest from data input that is unique to the data. SHA1 uses a 160-bit message digest from data input that is also unique to the data. This allows the MD5 and SHA1 hashes to be used as a fingerprint for a particular piece of data. To use the MAC algorithms, the –m flag should be used with the specific option (hmac-md5 or hmac-sha1) in order to hash the data that will be transferred between to entities. The following are two examples of the MAC options:

```
ssh 10.0.0.3 -1 cdwivedi -m hmac-md5
ssh 10.0.0.3 -1 cdwivedi -m hmac-sha1
```

The –F switch is used to point to a different configuration file for the SSH session. Every SSH session uses a configuration file as input when attempting to establish a connection. Configuration files are discussed in the next section, "SSH Client Configuration File." If an end user needs to connect to two or more SSH servers that have different parameters, such as listening on different ports, it is easier to point to a different configuration file than to remember the input parameters required for the SSH servers. Let's say that SSH server *A* listens on port 101, enables local forwarding to the mail server, and requires

3DES for encryption. Furthermore, server *B* listens on port 701, enables local forwarding to the file server, and requires Blowfish for encryption. The two commands, without using configuration files, would be as follows:

```
ssh 10.0.0.3 -l cdwivedi -p 101 -L 143:172.16.1.100:143 -c 3DES
ssh 10.0.0.4 -l cdwivedi -p 701 -L 139:172.16.1.200:139 -c Blowfish
```

Although remembering two commands may not be that difficult, connecting to more than two SSH servers with different forwarding rules, different port specifications, and different encryption algorithms becomes a cumbersome process. Using two configuration files significantly eases the log in process and user experience, as shown in the following example:

```
ssh 10.0.0.3 -l cdwivedi -F mail.config
ssh 10.0.0.4 -l cdwivedi -F file.config
```

The next two switches are quite simple when you are using them with IP version 4 or IP version 6. Using IP version 6 assumes that an IP version 6 network is in use, which is beyond the scope of this book and SSH; however, SSH provides support for IP version 6 packets. IP version 4 is the default packet type, but both flags can be used if the networks are available. Following are two examples of the switches:

```
ssh 10.0.0.3 -l cdwivedi -4
ssh 10.0.0.3 -l cdwivedi -6
```

The next switches do not add functionality to the SSH client, but they do provide the opportunity to gather additional information regarding the connection. The –d switch sets the debug level for a connection. The higher the debug value, the greater the amount of information that will be printed on the screen regarding the connection. The following is an example of the –d switch. Notice all the information that comes before the password request:

```
ssh 10.0.0.3 -l cdwivedi -d 1
debug: Connecting to 10.0.0.3, port 22... (SOCKS not used)
debug: client supports 3 auth methods:* 'publickey,keyboard-
interactive,password'
debug: Ssh2Common/sshcommon.c:537/ssh_common_wrap:
local ip = 10.0.0.3, local port = 1077
debug: Ssh2Common/sshcommon.c:539/ssh_common_wrap:
remote ip = 10.0.0.3, remote port = 22
debug: Remote version: SSH-1.99-OpenSSH_3.4p1
debug: OpenSSH: Major: 3 Minor: 4 Revision: 0
```

```
debug: Remote host key found from database.
debug: server offers auth methods
publickey,password,keyboard-interactive'.
debug: SshConfig/sshconfig.c:2717/ssh2_parse_config_ext:
Unable to open /root/.ssh2/identification
debug: server offers auth methods
publickey,password,keyboard-interactive'.
debug: server offers auth methods
publickey,password,keyboard-interactive'.
cdwivedi's password:
```

The next informational switch, -V, displays the version of the remote SSH server. This is helpful when you are trying to understand what version the remote SSH server is running for patching and security purposes. The following is an example of the –V switch:

```
ssh 10.0.0.3 -V
ssh: SSH Secure Shell 3.2.3 (non-commercial version) on i686-pc-linux-gnu
```

The last informational switch discussed here is –q. In essence, it tells the SSH server to be quiet and not display any warning messages to the end-user. If the –q switch is used, the SSH server will display only the request for the user's password. The following is an example of the –q switch:

```
ssh 10.0.0.3 -q
root's password:
```

SSH Client Configuration File

Now that I have covered the switches that may be used with the SSH client, I'll discuss the configuration file itself. Table 3.1 describes where the configuration file can be located, depending on the operating system and type of SSH client.

The SSH client configuration file is divided into the following categories:

- General
- Network
- Crypto
- User Public Key Authentication
- Tunneling
- SSH1 Compatibility
- Authentication

Each of these categories is explored in the paragraphs that follow.

Table 3.1   Location of Configuration Files

CLIENT	WINDOWS OS	UNIX OS
OpenSSH	\Program Files\OpenSSH\etc	/etc/ssh_config
SSH Communications	\Program Files\SSH Secure Shell \ssh2_config	/etc/ssh2/ssh2_config

General

The general section of the of the configuration file lists generic flags and switches that can limit the number of commands the end-user needs to type when trying to access the SSH server. Fields such as VerboseMode, Quiet-Mode, Compression, GoBackground, and EscapeChar allow customized generic settings to be enabled from the profile file itself instead of typed into the command line. Some of the selected fields in the General section are provided in Table 3.2, as well as a brief description of each.

Network

The Network section of the configuration file lists networking settings required for the connection. An example of a network setting is the specific port that the SSH client should use when attempting to connect to the SSH server. Table 3.3 gives a brief description of some of the selected fields in the Network section.

Table 3.2   Fields in the General Section

FIELD	DESCRIPTION
VerboseMode	Displays verbose information of the SSH session
QuietMode	Displays warning messages
DontReadStdin	Disables input for Standard input
BatchMode	Enables/Disables batch-mode processing
Compression	Enables/Disables compression
GoBackground	Sends the connection to the background
EscapeChar	Sets the ESC character for the session
PasswordPrompt	Type of Password prompt
AuthenticationSuccessMsg	Displays success message after login
SetRemoteEnv	Sets environment variables for the session

Table 3.3 Fields in the Network Section

FIELD	DESCRIPTION
Port	Sets the port to connect to
NoDelay	Enables/Disables the delay process
KeepAlive	Keeps the connection active
SocksServer	The network ID of SOCKS server
UseSocks5	Support for SOCKS version 5

Crypto

The Crypto section of the configuration file lists the types of cryptography that can be set for the SSH clients. This section is useful when different SSH servers require different types of encryption algorithms. For example, a different SSH configuration file can be set for backups, enabling certain types of encryption that have the least effect on bandwidth and enabled data validation with MAC. Table 3.4 gives a brief description of some of the selected fields in the Crypto section.

Table 3.4 Fields in the Crypto Section

FIELD	DESCRIPTION
Ciphers	Specifies which Ciphers can be used
MACs	Specifies which MACs can be used
StrictHostKeyChecking	Enables hostkey checking server validation
RekeyIntervalSeconds	Interval length for re-keying the session

User Public Key Authentication

The Public Key Authentication section of the configuration file simply specifies the location and name of the user's public key to use for authentication. The fields in the Public Key Authentication section are described in Table 3.5.

Table 3.5 Fields in the Public key Authentication Section

FIELD	DESCRIPTION
IdentityFile	Name of identification file
RandomSeedFile	Name of random_seed file

Tunneling

The Tunneling section of the configuration file specifies the local and remote tunneling options that should be used on the SSH client. This section adds a great deal of value when the client has enabled multiple local and remote port forwards. The selected fields in the Tunnel section are described in Table 3.6.

Table 3.6 Fields in Tunnel Section

FIELD TUNNELING	DESCRIPTION
GatewayPorts	Allow interfaces to act as a gateway
ForwardAgent	Enable/Disable forwarding of packets
ForwardX11	Enable/Disable X11 emulation
TrustX11Applications	Options to trust/distrust X11
TUNNELS SET UP UPON LOGIN	
LocalForward	Local port forwarding setting (143:IP:143)
LocalForward	Local port forwarding setting (25:IP:25)
RemoteForward	Remote port forwarding setting (22:IP:23)

SSH1 Compatibility

The SSH1 Compatibility section of the configuration file specifies the options to use in order to be compatible with SSH1 version 1. In order for SSH2 clients to be compatible with SSH1 servers, the following fields must be set (shown in Table 3.7).

Table 3.7 SSH Compatibility

FIELD	DESCRIPTION
Ssh1Compatibility	Enable/Disable SSH1 support
Ssh1Path	The path to use for SSH1. The default is /usr/local/bin/ssh1
Ssh1MaskPasswordLength	Enable/Disable masking for the password length

Authentication

The Authentication section of the configuration file specifies the options supported for authentication. This section allows the client to know which type of authentication to use, whether to use a password and public key instead of just a password, in order to authenticate. Table 3.8 is a brief list of the selected fields of the authentication section.

Table 3.8 Authentication

FIELD	DESCRIPTION
AllowedAuthentication	Specifies the authentication types allowed, such as password, public key, or all of the above

GUI SSH Clients

Secure Shell Communications (www.ssh.com), VanDyke Software, PuTTY, AppGate, and WinSCP are several of the vendors that provide graphical user interfaces (GUIs) for SSH clients. Since there are several GUI clients on the market, the following section examines some of the optimal features of the GUI SSH clients. Also, since the GUI clients are primarily available for Windows, the following section focuses on Windows 2000 and Windows XP.

Table 3.9 shows where the SSH clients can be purchased and/or downloaded.

Table 3.9 Web Sites Where SSH Clients Are Available

CLIENTS	URL
SSH Communications	www.ssh.com
VanDyke Software	www.vandyke.com/
Putty	www.chiark.greenend.org.uk/~sgtatham/putty/
WinSCP	winscp.vse.cz/eng/
Mindterm	www.appgate.com/mindterm/
MacSSH	pro.wanadoo.fr/chombier/

Windows Installation

Installing Windows-based SSH clients is relatively straightforward. I do not describe the process of installing each of the SSH clients listed in Table 3.9, but a wizard of each will walk you through the installation process.

SSH Communications

SSH Communications' SSH client is the first I will discuss. Open the SSH client and initiate a simple SSH connection by executing the following steps:

1. Start ⇨ Programs ⇨ SSH Secure Shell ⇨ Secure Shell Client

2. File ⇨ Open ⇨ Quick Connect

As shown in Figure 3.1, the Host Name field is either the fully qualified DSN name for the SSH server, such as sshserver.aum.com, or the dot notation of the IP address of the SSH server, such as 172.16.11.17. The User Name field is the username on the remote SSH server. The username can either be the local account on a Windows machine or a domain account on a Windows domain, depending on how the SSH server is implemented. In Unix environments, the username is the same in the /etc/passwd file. The Port Number field is used to specify the port number. If the SSH server is listening on a nonstandard port (a port other than port 22), the appropriate port number should be placed in the port box, such as 202. Lastly, the Authentication Method specifies the type of authentication that should be used when attempting to connect to the remote SSH server. The possible values and their descriptions are in Table 3.10.

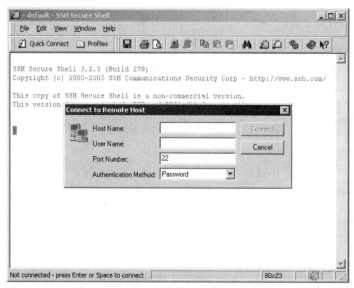

Figure 3.1 "Quick Connect" menu.

Table 3.10   Authentication Types

AUTHENTICATION TYPE	DESCRIPTION
Password	Username and password combination
Public Key	Public and Private-key authentication
SecureID	RSA SecureID tokens for authentication*
PAM	Pluggable authentication module**

* Requires RSA ACE server.
** The pluggable authentication module is a Unix authentication method that integrates various authentication methods into one.

SSH Communications offers different settings on SSH clients. Using the Menu bar, open the settings menu by selecting Edit ⇨ Settings.

Under the settings menu, there should be two sections: Profile Settings and Global Settings. Under profile and global settings, there should be several more options. In the following sections, each option is examined individually and its purpose and usage described.

Profile Settings

The profile settings are similar to the ssh2_config file discussed previously with the command-line utilities. All options under the Profile Settings section directly correlate to settings used by default when attempting to connect to an SSH server. The description and usage of the settings are provided in Table 3.11.

Table 3.11   Options Under the Profile Settings Section

SETTING	DESCRIPTION AND USAGE
Connection	The following describes the options on each of the sections to the left. The options within those sections are also explained.
	- Host Name: DNS name or IP address of the remote SSH server. - User Name: Username of the account to log in with. - Port Number: Port number that the SSH server is listening on. - Authentication Methods: Authentication types that can be used in order to log in to the SSH server. Options can be password, public key, SecureID, and PAM. - Encryption Algorithm: Sets the type of cryptography to be used for the session. -MAC Algorithm: Sets the type of hashes to be used when hashing the data being sent across the network. Options can be MD5 or SHA1. (The option chosen must be supported by the SSH server.) - Compression: Enables compression on the connection. The valid choice for compression in only zlib.

Table 3.11 (continued)

SETTING	DESCRIPTION AND USAGE
	Terminal Answerback: Set the type of emulator to receive from the SSH server. Valid choices range from VT100 to xterm. - Connect Through Firewall: This checkbox determines if the connection will be taken through a SOCKS or proxy server. - Request Tunnels Only (Disable Terminal): Enables/Disables the terminal window from appearing. If this is enabled, the user will not receive a command-line shell to execute commands, but only the session itself to port forward to.
Cipher List	Lists the types of Ciphers that can be used. Options can be 3DES, Blowfish, Twofish, AES, Arcfour, and CAST128. (The option chosen must be supported by the SSH server.)
Colors	Allows the cosmetic appearance to be modified.
Keyboard	Changes the keyboard functions.
Tunneling	Provides the ability to secure X11 connections via the SSH connection by tunneling the X11 packets inside SSH. - Outgoing: Sets Outgoing tunnels for the session (discussed more in the port-forwarding chapter). - Incoming: Sets Incoming tunnels for the session (discussed more in the port-forwarding chapter).

Global Settings

The global settings are used for any SSH connection attempt, regardless of the profile that might be used. All options under the Global Settings section directly correlate to settings used by default when attempting to connect to an SSH server. The description and usage of the settings are shown in Table 3.12.

Table 3.12 Options Under the Global Settings

SETTING	DESCRIPTION AND USAGE
Appearance	Sets some of the cosmetic items to display by default, such as profiles, hostname, color, and font.
User Keys	Manages the public and private-key pairs that can be used for authentication (instead of a password). This section allows you to create a key pair, delete an old key pair, export a key to a flat *.pub file, import a key pair to a flat *.pub file, view the flat connects of a public key, change the passphrase in order to use the public key, and upload a public key to an SSH server (the SSH server must be compatible with the type of key created). The User Keys section is discussed further in Chapter 4.

(continued)

Table 3.12 *(continued)*

SETTING	DESCRIPTION AND USAGE
Host Key	Identifies the SSH server. The host key is a virtual fingerprint of the server. The use of host keys protects against IP address attacks on IPv4 networks, such as Man-in-the-Middle and spoofing attacks.
Public Key Infrastructure (PKI)	Provides support for a certificate-based authentication system. The options can include certificates from SSH clients, certificates from integrated directory services architecture, such as LDAP, or using hardware devices. - Certificates: Allows the SSH client to import, enroll, view, delete, or change the passphrase of a certificate. - LDAP: Provides LDAP directory integration with PKI certificates. - PKCS #11: Provides a certificate-based system to access hardware devices.
File Transfer	Configures Secure FTP and Secure Copy. Options that can be configured are the display types of Icons, the display of hidden or root directories, and the ability to confirm the deletion or overwriting of a file on the SFTP server. Also, allows the configuration of the default file viewing application of an extension that is not available for a particular file.
Firewall	Configures SOCKS firewall operability. For example, socks://172.16.1.100:1117 would be used to make an SSH connection via a SOCKS server (172.16.1.100) on port 1117.
Security	Configures basic security options, such as the option to clear the host name upon exit or deleting the contents of the clipbook upon exit.
Printing	Sets the options for printing, such as fonts, margins, and header/footer information.

The profile and global settings are the primary areas where the SSH client can be configured for functionality. Like the command-line clients, the GUI client can save settings based on different SSH servers. To customize the profile settings based on a particular SSH server, go to the File Menu bar and select File ⇨ Profiles ⇨ Add/Edit Profiles.

A profile can automatically be set up after the initial valid connection to an SSH server. As shown in Figure 3.2, once the initial connect is made, the option to save the profile appears in the upper right-hand corner. The Add/Edit profile option is a simple way to customize SSH connections. After opening the File ⇨ Profiles ⇨ Edit/Add profile option, you should notice the same profile options that are available with the Edit/Setting menu. However, these options do not globally change all options; they make changes based on the specific connection.

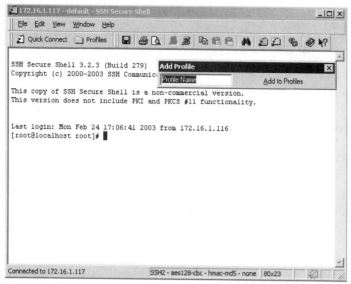

Figure 3.2 Automatic Profile save option.

One of the most useful options with SSH Communications' SSH client is the built-in SFTP client. It allows the SFTP client to be executed without the need for any secondary client or another SSH connection. The SFTP client can be executed from the menu bar with Windows ⇨ New File Transfer.

After this option has been selected, the SFTP client, with the original session to the SSH server enabled, displays the contents of the local machine on the left pane, which is the SSH Client machine, and the contents of the remote SSH server on the right pane. This allows safe and simple SFTP usage for the SSH session. Figure 3.3 demonstrates the use of the SFTP client option with an SSH session that has already been established.

The last option I will discuss for the SSH Communications' SSH client is the Log Session. This option logs the entire connection, including commands, outputs, and inputs, to a log file. The log file can be saved locally on the client machine for viewing at a later time. The log session option is also located at the file menu bar at File ⇨ Log Session.

After Log Session is chosen, the client will display a prompt for a location to save the log file to. Session-logging capabilities will be enabled for the following connection after the option is enabled.

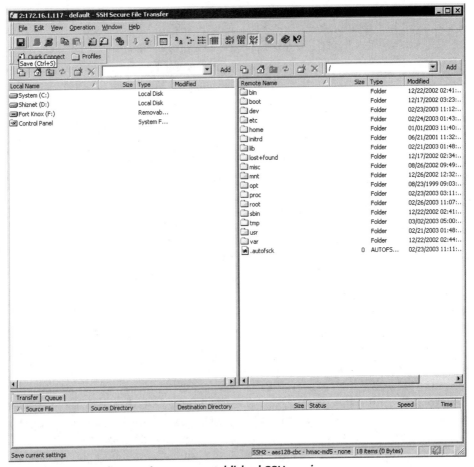

Figure 3.3   SFTP client option on an established SSH session.

VanDyke Software's SecureCRT

VanDyke Software has an SSH client called SecureCRT. Open the SSH client and initiate a simple SSH connection by selecting Start ⇨ Programs ⇨ Secure-CRT 4.0 ⇨ SecureCRT 4.0.

After you select the shortcut, SecureCRT will automatically open its Quick Connect menu (see Figure 3.4) to begin an SSH connection.

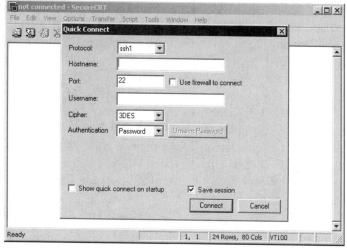

Figure 3.4 Quick Connect options for SecureCRT.

The field options shown in Table 3.13 are available in the Quick Connect display.

Table 3.13 Field Options in the Quick Connect Display

FIELD	DESCRIPTION
Protocol	Option to use SSH1, SSH2, or other non-SSH connections, such as Telnet, Rlogin, serial interfaces, or TAPI.
Hostname	The fully qualified host name for DNS resolution, such as sshserver.Aum.com. The dot notation of an IP address can also be used (for example, 10.8.15.47).
Port	The port number to use for the remote SSH server. Default SSH port is 22. The use firewall to connect checkbox enables firewall settings in the Global Options menu, such as SOCKS or Proxy settings.
Username	The username used on the remote SSH server.
Cipher	The encryption algorithm used for the SSH connection. Available options are DES, 3DES, RC4, and Blowfish.
Authentication	Authentication mechanism to be used for the SSH connection. Possible choices are RSA authentication (requires RSA ACE server on the server side of the connection), password, and TIS (requires TIS firewall server on the server side of the connection).

The last options on the Quick Connect display are two checkboxes: The Show Quick Connect on Startup checkbox displays Quick Connect upon startup, and the Save Session checkbox saves the custom settings to a profile.

SecureCRT offers different settings to be enabled on SSH clients. Using the Menu bar, open the options menu by selecting Options ⇨ Global Options.

Under the Global Options menu are seven sections, including Options, Appearance, Firewall, SSH1, SSH2, Printing, and Web Browser. Under each of the sections are several more sections that can be used to configure the client. I will select options individually and describe their purpose and usage.

All Global Options under this section directly correlate to settings that will be used by default when attempting to connect to an SSH server. The description and usage of each setting is shown in Table 3.14.

Table 3.14 Settings Under Global Options

SETTING	DESCRIPTION AND USAGE
Options	Mouse settings: - Copy - Paste - Hide Mouse Dialogs—Various Dialog information settings Other— Various appearance settings.
Appearance	Various appearance settings, including color, menu/tool bar options, margin settings, and so on.
Firewall	Enables an SSH session via a SOCKS server, version 4 or version 5, or a proxy server. Both SOCKS and proxy servers can be used to relay an SSH connection to a device on behalf of an SSH client, discussed further in Chapter 9. *Type:* - SOCKS (v4 or v5) with or without authentication. - Generic Proxy: Can be used on most proxy servers. *Parameters (SOCKS):* - Hostname or IP: DNS name or IP address of SOCKS server. - Port: Port number that the SOCKS service is listening on (default is 1080). *Parameters (Generic Proxy):* - Hostname or IP: DNS name or IP address of the proxy server - Port: Port number that the proxy service is listening on. Note: If your remote SSH server is listening on port 22 and all outbound traffic is allowed via a proxy server only, consider changing the SSH server to port 443 and using the proxy server to proxy the SSH connection (discussed in detail in Chapter 9). - Prompt: This field should be filled with the information that SecureCRT should expect from the proxy server.

Table 3.14 *(continued)*

SETTING	DESCRIPTION AND USAGE
	- Command: This field should be filled with the information that SecureCRT should provide to the proxy server once the connection with the proxy server is established. For example, to connect to an SSH server listening on port 443 via a proxy server, check the firewall checkbox in the login screen and enter the following text in the command field: CONNECT %h:%p HTTP/1.0\r\n\r\n.
SSH1	Allows the use of a pubic key, instead of a password, to authenticate an SSH server. Create Identity File: Allows the ability to create a public and private-key file.
SSH2	Allows the use of a public key, instead of a password, to authenticate an SSH server, discussed further in Chapter 4. - Create Identity File: Allows the ability to create a public and private-key file. - Use Certificate: Allows the use of X.509 certificate-based authentication, instead of a password or public key. Requires the use of a Certificate Authority. -Agent: Add keys to agent: Allow the use of the SecureCRT agent, which allows the ability to connect to multiple SSH servers with a single public key. Enable OpenSSH agent forwarding: Allow the ability to connect to an SSH server via an intermediate server. - Host Keys: Host keys are public keys used to identify the SSH server. The host key is virtually a fingerprint of the server. The use of host keys protects against IP-address attacks on IPv4 networks, such as Man-in-the-Middle and spoofing attacks.
Printing	Set the options for printing, such as fonts, margins, and header/footer information.
Web Browser	Sets the default Web browser to use when opening a URL via Secure CRT. In order to use this open, right-click on the URL string in Secure CRT, such as www.theonion.com, and select "Open URL".

SecureCRT offers different settings to be enabled once a session has been established. Once a connection has been enabled with the Quick Connect dialog, open the session options menu using the Menu bar; select Options ⇨ Session Options.

Under the settings menu are seven sections: Connection, Emulation, Appearance, Options, File Transfer, Log File, and Printing. Under each of the sections are several more sections that can be used to configure the client. I will select options individually and describe the purpose and usage of each.

All Session Options directly correlate to settings that will be used only when connecting to the appropriate SSH server. The description and usage of the settings are provided in Table 3.15.

Table 3.15   Session Options Settings and Descriptions

SECTION	USAGE AND DESCRIPTION
Connection	Connection-specific information can be configured under this section. *Logon Scripts* - Automate Logon: Creates a script to automate the login process to an SSH server. - Logon Scripts: Allows the Secure CRT client to run automatic scripts to be used when logging on to a remote SSH server. *SSH2* - Use Compression: Enables compression on the connection. - Cipher: Encryption algorithm to be used for the connection. - MAC: Sets the type of hashes to be used when hashing the data being sent across the network. - SSH Server: Sets the type of SSH server being used on the remote server. Options are: Auto Detect, which is the best option; DataFellows, SSH Communications, and Standard. *Port Forwarding* - Locally sets outgoing tunnels for the session (discussed more in Chapters 6 and 7). - Remote: Set Incoming tunnels for the session (discussed more in Chapters 6 and 7). *X11* Allows the ability to secure X11 connections via the SSH connection by tunneling the X11 packets inside SSH
Emulation	Sets options and properties for emulated terminals with Secure CRT.
Appearance	Sets cosmetic appearances for the session.
Options	Sets keyboard options for the session.
File Transfer	Allows the specific location to be set for the Upload and Download of file with the Xmodem and Zmodem utilities. - Xmodem: File transfer utility that supports error detection during transfer. Note: Xmodem functionality is required on the remote server. - Zmodem: File transfer utility to download and upload files. Note: Zmodem functionality is required on the remote server.

Table 3.15   *(continued)*

SECTION	USAGE AND DESCRIPTION
Log File	Allows the location of the log file to set to a specific location. Note: Logging must be enabled with "File > Log Session" or "File > Raw Log Session."
Printing	Allows printing information to be configured.

File-transfer capabilities are partially available via the SecureCRT client. Another client, SecureFX, is the fully supported SFTP/SCP client for VanDyke Software. Some utilities, such as Zmodem and Xmodem, allow basic file-transfer options, located under the Transfer menu bar.

To further automate Secure CRT, ActiveX scripting is available with VBScript and Jscript by selecting Script ➪ Run.

Any VB script, Microsoft Java script, and even certain Perl scripts can be loaded from the client's machine to the SecureCRT SSH client, to be executed within the SSH session.

Secure CRT also offers the ability to create and use public keys for authentication instead of passwords. To use a public key for authentication, a key must be generated. Use the utilities under the Tools menu, which can create keys for SecureCRT clients.

1. Select Tools ➪ Create Public Key. This creates a public key for the user.

2. Select Tools ➪ Public-key Assistant. This manages the public key for the current user on the remote SSH server.

To use a created public key that has been uploaded on the remote SSH server, the PublicKey option needs to be set under the Authentication drop-down box in the Connection or Quick Connect dialog.

The last options I will discuss for SecureCRT are Log Session and Trace. The log options simply log the entire SSH session, including commands, outputs, and inputs, to a log file. There are two options with Log Session: formatted, which only logs selected items; or Raw, which logs everything in an unformatted fashion. The log file can be saved locally on the client machine for viewing at a later date. The Log Session option is also located at the file menu bar. Open the SSH client and complete the following steps:

1. Select File ➪ Open ➪ Quick Connect.

2. Choose File ➪ Log Session or File ➪ Raw Log Session.

After Log Session or Raw Log Session is chosen, the client will save the session under the location specified in the Session Options section. The only difference between the two settings is that the Raw Log Session records connections between the SecureCRT client and the SSH service, including escape commands.

The Trace options menu allows the display of hidden communication between the SSH server and the SecureCRT SSH client. To enable the Trace options, select the option File ⇨ Trace Options.

PuTTY

PuTTY is a free Telnet and SSH client for Win32 platforms, available from www.chiark.greenend.org.uk/~sgtatham/putty/. PuTTY has similar functionality as described in other SSH clients. After downloading PuTTY, double-click the executable and the configuration menu should appear.

As shown in Figure 3.5, four sections can be configured using PuTTY: Session, Terminal, Window, and Connection. The description and usage of the settings are provided in Table 3.16.

Figure 3.5 The PuTTY client.

Table 3.16   Options for PuTTY Settings and Descriptions

SETTING	DESCRIPTION AND USAGE
Session	Configurations for the specific SSH session. - Host Name (or IP address): Fully qualified DNS name or dot notation of IP address of the SSH server. - Port: Port that the remote SSH server is listening on, typically port 22. - Protocol: Since PuTTY can be used for various items, the SSH radio box should be used for SSH connections. - Saved Sessions: Provides the ability to save a session or load a session that has been saved beforehand. - Logging: Provides the ability to log the SSH session.
Terminal	Allows the ability to set specific options for the terminal session of the SSH connection.
Windows	Allows the ability to make cosmetic changes to the SSH connection.
Connection	Allows the ability to set session specific information, such as terminal type and username. *Proxy:* Settings to configure to enable an SSH connection via a proxy server (either a Web proxy (HTTP) or a SOCKS server). *SSH:* SSH specific settings.- Remote Command: Commands to automatically to send to the SSH server after the session has been established. - Protocol Options: Options for SSH 1 or 2, compression, and pseudo-terminals. - Encryption Options: Options for encryption algorithms to use for the SSH connection, including AES, Blowfish, 3DES, and DES. - Auth: Authentication settings for the session, including keyboard (password) or key options. - Tunnels: X11 and Port forwarding options for the SSH sessions. Supports both Local and Remote forwarding (discussed further in the port-forwarding chapter). - Bugs: Allows the ability to configure options to subvert problems in the SSH connection, specifically in the SSH server.

WinSCP

WinSCP is a free secure copy (SCP) client for Win32 platforms. WinSCP provides a terminal session similar to other clients we have discussed, but its primary feature is a Win32 secure copy client. After downloading WinSCP, open the client by selecting Start ➪ Programs ➪ WinSCP2 ➪ WinSCP2.

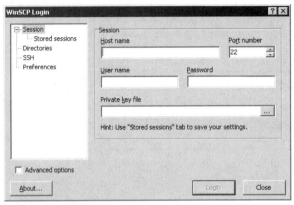

Figure 3.6   WinSCP display.

As shown in Figure 3.6, WinSCP has four main sections for configuration: Session, Directories, SSH, and Preferences. The description and usage of the settings are provided in Table 3.17.

Table 3.17   Options for WinSCP Settings

OPTION	DESCRIPTION AND USAGE
Session	Configurations for the specific SSH session.
	- Host Name: Fully qualified DNS name or dot notation of IP address of the remote SSH server.
	- Port Number: Port number the SSH server is listening on, usually port 22.
	- User name: Username on the remote SSH server to log in with.
	- Password: Password on the remote SSH server, which correlates to the username used in the Username field.
	- Private-key file: If key authentication is being used instead of a password, the location of the private key file to use for authentication.
	- Stored Session: Options to load stored sessions that have been saved or to create new sessions.
	- Logging (Advanced Option): Enabled logging SSH session to local files.

Table 3.17 *(continued)*

OPTION	DESCRIPTION AND USAGE
Shell (Advanced Option)	Allows various items to be customized with the Shell, including the Shell itself, the return code submitted, and Unix or Windows types of displays.
Directories	Specifies the path for the local and remote directories. - Remote Directory: Path of the remote directory (of the remote SSH server) to display in the right-hand panel of WinSCP (for example, /home/ssh or d:\ssh\share). - Local Directory: Path to local directory to be displayed in the left-hand panel of WinSCP.
Connection (Advanced Option)	Settings to configure to enable an SSH connection via a proxy server (either a Web proxy (HTTP) or a SOCKS server).
SSH	Specifies the SSH options that can be used, such as protocol version, encryption type, authentication type, and bugs. - Protocol Options: Options for SSH 1 or 2, and compression. - Encryption Options: Options for encryption algorithms to use for the SSH connection, including AES, Blowfish, 3DES, and DES. - Authentication (Advanced Option): Authentication settings for the session, including keyboard (password), or key options. - Bugs (Advanced Options) Allows the ability to configure options to subvert problems in the SSH connection, specifically in the SSH server.
Preferences	Allows the display to be customized.

To configure the advanced options for WinSCP, click the checkbox in the lower right-hand corner of the WinSCP display.

MindTerm

AppGate provides an SSH client called MindTerm. MindTerm is an SSH client that uses a Java applet. Using MindTerm, it is possible to connect to an SSH server with any Java-enabled Web browser such as Internet Explorer, Netscape, Mozilla, and Opera. To install MindTerm, Java Runtime Environment (JRE) needs to be installed. JRE can be downloaded from the following locations:

Linux:	www.blackdown.org/java-linux.htmlwww.ibm.com/developer/java
Win32 and Solaris:	www.javasoft.com/products/
Macintosh:	www.apple.com/java/
Other platforms:	http://java.sun.com/cgi-bin/java-ports.cgi

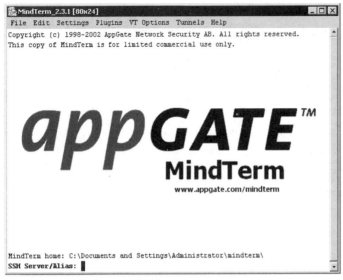

Figure 3.7 Mindterm SSH client.

After downloading and installing the JVM, follow the directions in MindTerm's readme.txt file to install the client. In many environments, the following command can be used to install the client:

```
java -jar mindterm.jar
```

As shown in Figure 3.7, the AppGate MindTerm client can also be used outside of a Web browser. Once the MindTerm client is displayed, the prompt allows a connection to a remote SSH server to be established. Table 3.18 lists some of MindTerm's prompts.

Table 3.18 MindTerm Prompts and Description of Usage

PROMPT	DESCRIPTION
SSH Server/Alias	Alias or dot notation of the IP address
Save as alias	Name to save the connection using an alias
Do you want to add this host to your set of Known hosts (check fingerprint)	Yes or No option to save the host file of the remote SSH server
Login	Username to log in to the remote SSH server
Password	Password to use for the remote SSH server, correlating to the username used

MindTerm allows several settings other than user prompts. Table 3.19 summarizes some of the selected functions of the SSH client.

To fully use a MindTerm client with a Web browser, the AppGate server needs to be deployed on the server side of the connection. The AppGate server provides the MindTerm SSH client via a Web browser; however, the session is still secure with SSH (versus HTTPS).

Table 3.19 Settings of SSH Client

SETTINGS	DESCRIPTION
File > Create Keypair	Allows the ability to create a public/private key pair for authentication, instead of using a password
File > Edit/Convert Keypair	Allows the ability to edit or convert the key to a different format
File > Capture to File	Enables logging of the SSH session
Setting > Preferences	Allows the ability to set session-specific options such as: - Protocol: SSH1 or SSH2, or auto detect - Cipher: Encryption algorithm to be used - Mac: Hash algorithm to be used - Compression: Level of compression to be used
Plugins > SFTP file transfer	Allows the ability to transfer files with the remote SSH server over the SFTP protocol
Plugins > SCP file transfer	Allows the ability to transfer files with the remote SSH server over the SCP protocol
Plugins > FTP to SFTP bridge	Allows the ability to bridge an SFTP connection to an FTP connection. For example, if a client is connected to an SSH server with MindTerm and the "FTP to SFTP bridge" is enabled, any other machine that makes an FTP connection to the SSH client with be able to view the contents of the folder on the remote SFTP server (FTP client > SSH client (with MindTerm bridge enabled) > SFTP server).
Tunnels > Basic	Allows the ability to set local port-forwarding tunnels
Tunnels > Advances	Allows the ability to set remote port-forwarding options

MacSSH

MacSSH is an SSH client for Macintosh environments. MacSSH supports SSH2 only, with no support for SSH1. MacSFTP is similar to MacSSH but is used for the file-transfer portion of the connection. There are some other good clients for the Macintosh environment, including JellyfiSSH (www.arenasoftware .com/grepsoft/) and Rbrowser (www.rbrowser.com).

Summary

This chapter explores several SSH clients that can be used in enterprise architectures and different options. Each SSH client has been examined in detail in this chapter, with coverage of the options, settings, and configuration steps in a typical environment.

Chapters 1, 2, and 3 of this book have covered the basics: SSH servers and SSH clients. The focus of this book now turns from descriptions and implementation steps of servers and clients to specific features and options of SSH servers and clients. Chapter 4 discusses the authentication methods provided by SSH. Although I have covered the client-configuration options with authentication in this chapter, I have not discussed how to implement the various options and the best methods for optimal usage.

The remaining portions of this book assume that you are familiar with most of the features of the SSH clients discussed in Chapter 3, as well as the major uses of SSH servers from Chapter 2.

Authentication

The first three chapters of this book focus on the various aspects of SSH servers and SSH clients. I now shift the focus from the actual packages of SSH to the detailed options and optimal uses of SSH. The first topic is authentication.

Authentication is the process of determining if an entity is actually who or what it claims to be. The entity can be a person, a server, an application, a service, or even a process. In most networks, authentication is commonly used with usernames and passwords. In this type of authentication, the password is the only object that guarantees that the entity is actually what it claims to be. While users can choose and change their own passwords for successful authentication, the fact that passwords are often stolen, shared, sticky-noted (a manual technique of writing passwords on a Post-It note and sticking it to a monitor), or simply forgotten makes the use of passwords for authentication a less-than-ideal solution.

Since passwords may not be the best solution for sensitive information or for hostile environments, SSH offers the use of a more stringent authentication process. The use of public keys or digital certifications can be the required method of authentication across any SSH environment that uses sensitive information or transcends hostile networks, such as the Internet or internal networks. Furthermore, since authorization is highly dependant on authentication, the authentication process needs to be as strong as possible, since most authorization processes do not perform a second layer of error checking for validity.

This chapter's focus is common authentication methods used in SSH, primarily passwords, host-based authentication, and public keys. The chapter summarizes some of the other authentication options available via SSH, such as server authentication, where the client authenticates the server, and general-option authentication settings. The order of the discussions is as follows:

- General options
- Passwords
- Host-based authentication
- Server authentication
- Public keys

General Options

SSH offers several general authentication options depending on the type of SSH server deployed. The options range from valid password attempts to the use of blank passwords. The following paragraphs describe the SSH servers and the authentication options they provide.

SSH Communications' SSH server (Windows)

SSH Communications' SSH server offers a few options for authentication. Open the SSH Server configuration screen (Start ➪ Programs ➪ SSH Secure Shell Server ➪ Configuration) and highlight the User Authentication section of the screen. See Figure 4.1 for the authentication screen.

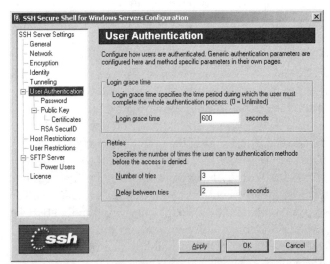

Figure 4.1   The User Authentication section of the screen for SSH Communications' SSH server.

Tables 4.1 through 4.3 describe the general authentication options for SSH Communications' SSH server.

Table 4.1 describes the general user-authentication options. Parameters such as login grace time, number of retries, and delay between retries can be configured.

Table 4.2 describes the user-authentication password options under the password section. Parameters such as password authentication, empty password permissions, and keyboard interactive can be configured.

Table 4.3 describes the user authentication public key options under the public key section. Parameters such as public key authentication, key directory, and authorization file can be configured.

Table 4.1 User-Authentication Options

OPTION	DESCRIPTION
Login grace time	Sets the amount of time the user has to complete the authentication process. Specifically, from the time the user initiates the connection to the time the user enters a username/password or private-key password
Retries – Number of Retries	Stipulates the number of times a user can attempt to log in
Retries – Delay between tries	Specifies the duration between retries

Table 4.2 User-Authentication Password Options

OPTION	DESCRIPTION
Password authentication	Allows, requires, or denies password authentication
Permit empty passwords	Enables blank passwords to be used for accounts
Keyboard interactive	Permits keyboard-interactive authentication with password authentication

Table 4.3 User-Authentication Public-Key Options

OPTION	DESCRIPTION
Public-key authentication	Allows, requires, or denies public-key authentication.

(continued)

Table 4.3   *(continued)*

OPTION	DESCRIPTION
User-key directory	Specifies the directory where the user's public key will be stored. The default is %D\.ssh2, which is the users' home directory in the .ssh2 folder (for example, /home/<username>/.ssh2 on Unix and Documents and Settings\<username>\.ssh2 on Windows).
Authorization file	Stores a valid list of public keys that will be authorized for public-key authentication. The default is the authorization file, which is stored in the users' home directory (for example, /home/<username>/.ssh2 on Unix and Documents and Settings\<username>\.ssh2 on Windows).

SSH Communications' SSH Server (Unix)

The SSH server for Unix offers authentication options similar to the Windows platform. One difference is that the Windows Server configuration screen is simply a GUI that points to the SSH configuration file, which is sshd2_config; the Unix version of the SSH Communications' server does not use a GUI but directly uses the configuration file itself. To view the authentication options, enter the following commands.

```
#cd /etc/ssh2
#more sshd2_config
```

Options in the authentication section are listed in Table 4.4, along with a description of each option.

Table 4.4   Authentication

OPTION	DESCRIPTION
BannerMessageFile	Denotes the location of the file that contains the banner message, such as "The only way to win is not to play." Default path is /etc/ssh2/ssh_banner_message.
PasswordGuesses	Specifies the number of attempts a user has in order to enter the correct password.

Table 4.4   *(continued)*

OPTION	DESCRIPTION
AllowedAuthentication	Indicates the types of authentication methods that are allowed by the SSH server. Options include hostbased, publickey, password, and PAM.
RequiredAuthentication	Names the types of authentication methods required by the SSH server. Options include hostbased, publickey, password, and PAM.
HostbasedAuthForce ClientHostnameDNSMatch	Forces a DNS match for authentication. Possible choices are yes and no.
SshPAMClientPath client is used	States the location of the PAM client, if a PAM

VShell SSH Server

VanDyke Software's VShell SSH server offers a few options for authentication. Open the VShell configuration screen (Start ➪ Programs ➪ VShell ➪ VShell) and highlight the Authentication section of the screen. (See Figure 4.2.)

Table 4.5 describes the general authentication options for VShell.

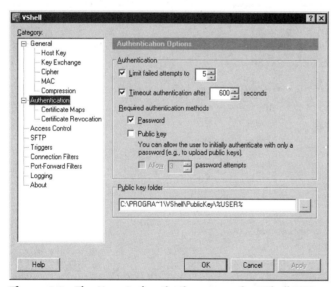

Figure 4.2   The User Authentication screen for VShell SSH server.

Table 4.5   Authentication Options for VShell

OPTION	DESCRIPTION
Limit failed attempts to	Restricts the number of failed attempts a user can have before the session is disconnected.
Time authentication after	Sets the amount of time the user has to complete the authentication process. Specifically, from the time the user initiates the connection to the time the user enters a username/password or private-key password.
Required authentication methods—Password	Requires a password for authentication.
Required authentication methods—Public Key	Requires a public key for authentication.
Required authentication methods—Public Key Uploads	Sets the number of times a user can log in with only a password in order to upload a public key. The feature is very useful if public-key authentication is the only method for authentication, giving the user a method to upload a public key.
Public-key folder	Specifies the location where the users' public keys will be stored. The default is Program Files\VShell\ Publickey\<username>.

OpenSSH (Unix and Windows)

OpenSSH server offers similar authentication options to those of VShell and SSH Communications' SSH server. To view the authentication options, enter the following commands:

```
#cd /etc/ssh
#more sshd_config
```

or

```
c:\cd "Program Files"\OpenSSH\ssh
c:\notepad sshd_config
```

The options for the authentication section for OpenSSH are described in Table 4.6.

Table 4.6 Authentication Options for OpenSSH

OPTION	DESCRIPTION
LoginGraceTime	Specifies the amount of time the user has to complete the authentication process. Specifically, from the time the user initiates the connection to the time the user enters a username/password or private key password.
PermitRootLogin	Allows (yes) or disallows (no) the root user to log in to the SSH session. Best practice is to restrict root access and have authorized users 'su' to root.
StrictModes	Enables (yes) or disables (no) the checking of a user's permission in his or her home directory and rhosts files before accepting authentication. This should be set to yes to protect against world-writeable files in home directories.
RSA Authentication	Allows RSA authentication.
Publickey Authentication	Allows public-key authentication; possible values are yes and no.
AuthorizedKeysFile	Names the path to the authorized key-validation file on the SSH server. The default is .ssh/authorized_keys, which is the users' home directory in the .ssh folder (for example, /home/<username>/.ssh/authorized_keys on Program Files\OpenSSH\.ssh on Windows).
Rhost Authentication	Permits rhosts authentication for RSH
RhostsRSA Authentication	Allows rhosts authentication from RSA host keys
Hostbased Authentication	Authorizes host-based authentication
Password Authentication	Enables (yes) or disables (no) password authentication
PermitEmptyPasswords	Allows (yes) or disallows (no) the use of blank passwords

Passwords

Password authentication is the basic method of authentication for SSH. SSH servers support authentication for both Windows and Unix platforms. SSH servers on Unix platforms have two methods for password authentication:

- /etc/passwd or /etc/shadow
- PAM (Pluggable Authentication Module)

Similarly, password authentication on Windows supports the use of the SAM (Security Accounts Manager) database file, located at %System-Root%\winnt\system32\config, or the NTDS.DIT database file, located at %SystemRoot%\NTDS\ntds.dit.

Despite the database files that SSH supports, the location and type of operating system is irrelevant to the actual setup and usage of passwords. It should be noted that password authentication is enabled by default on most, if not all, SSH servers. However, it is important to know how to disable/enable password authentication in order to possibly disable it in favor of stronger authentication, such as public-key authentication.

To enable password authentication, the process is quite simple. For a SSH server installation on a Unix environment, there exists a configuration file called sshd2_config (Commercial SSH) and sshd_config (OpenSSH). Both configuration files are quite similar. Sshd_config is usually located in /etc/ssh, and sshd2_config is located /etc/sshd2. Enter the following command to show the contents of the OpenSSH configuration file:

```
#cd /etc/ssh
#more sshd_config
```

An abbreviated portion of the output is listed as follows:

```
# Authentication:
#LoginGraceTime 600
#PermitRootLogin yes
#StrictModes yes

# To disable tunneled clear text passwords, change to no here!
#PasswordAuthentication yes
#PermitEmptyPasswords no
```

Under the Authentication section, denoted by #Authentication, many settings are given that can be used for the SSH server. The option you are most concerned with is the PasswordAuthentication setting. This setting needs to be set to Yes in order for password authentication to be valid, which is the default. Furthermore, if password authentication should be disabled in favor of other authentication methods, this setting should be set to No and uncommented, which means deleting the # from the beginning of the line. An example follows:

```
# To disable tunneled clear text passwords, change to no here!
PasswordAuthentication no
#PermitEmptyPasswords no
```

Enter the following command to show the contents of the SSH configuration file for Commercial SSH:

```
#cd /etc/ssh2
#more sshd2_config
```

An abbreviated portion of the output follows:

```
## Authentication
## publickey and password allowed by default

#        AllowedAuthentications         publickey,password
#        AllowedAuthentications         hostbased,publickey,password
#        AllowedAuthentications         hostbased,publickey,keyboard-
#        RequiredAuthentications        publickey,password
#        LoginGraceTime                 600
#        AuthInteractiveFailureTimeout  2
```

Under the Authentication section, denoted by ##Authentication, are many settings that can be set for the SSH server. The option you are most concerned with is the AllowedAuthentications setting. This setting by default accepts both password and public keys. In order for password authentication to be valid, password must be written on this line, even though that is the default setting. Furthermore, if password authentication is not required or desired, simply remove password from all the AllowedAuthentications lines, which disables the use of passwords for authentication. As with OpenSSH, be sure to uncomment the line, which means deleting the # at the beginning. Refer to the following example to disable password for authentication:

```
## Authentication
## publickey and password allowed by default

         AllowedAuthentications         publickey
#        AllowedAuthentications         hostbased,publickey,password
#        AllowedAuthentications         hostbased,publickey,keyboard-
#        RequiredAuthentications        publickey,password
#        LoginGraceTime                 600
#        AuthInteractiveFailureTimeout  2
```

The process of enabling password authentication on Windows-based operating systems is equally simple; however, the process is different for OpenSSH than Commercial SSH or VanDyke's VShell SSH server. For OpenSSH installations on Windows environments, there exists a configuration file called sshd_config located at Program Files\OpenSSH\ssh\. Enter the following commands to show the contents of the OpenSSH configuration file:

```
C:\cd "Program Files"\OpenSSH\ssh\
C:\type sshd_config
```

The following is an abbreviated portion of the output:

```
PermitRootLogin                    yes
PasswordAuthentication             yes
```

Similar to OpenSSH on Unix, yes must be present on the Password Authentication line in order for passwords to be used; however, password authentication is enabled by default. In order to disable the use of password, no must be present. The following example disables password authentication:

```
PermitRootLogin                    yes
PasswordAuthentication             no
```

Enabling password authentication with VanDyke Software's VShell is also quite easy. Using the configuration tool (Start ➪ Programs ➪ VShell ➪ VShell), there is an Authentication section for the Authentication options. Under the Authentication section, you will see many options that can be set. One of the options is Required authentication methods. Under this option are two checkboxes: one for Password and one for Public Key. Simply click the checkbox for Password and hit the Apply button in the lower right-hand corner. Password authentication has now been enabled for all SSH users on the server. If password authentication is not required or desired, simply uncheck the Password checkbox and select the Public Key checkbox, which means public-key configuration must take place (discussed in the following section). Figure 4.3 shows VShell's Authentication menu.

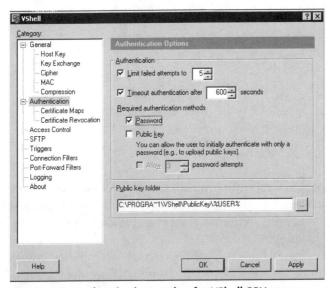

Figure 4.3   Authentication section for VShell SSH server.

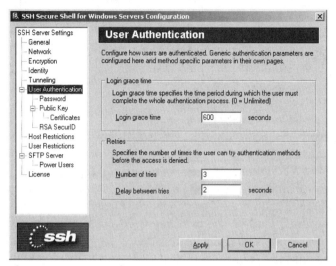

Figure 4.4 User Authentication section for SSH Communications SSH Server.

Similarly, enabling password authentication for SSH Communications' SSH server on Windows platforms is quite easy. Using the configuration menu (Start ➪ Programs ➪ SSH Secure Shell Server ➪ Configuration), there is a User Authentication section for the Authentication options. Under the User Authentication section, you will see many options that can be set. One of the options is Password authentication. Under this option are three choices in the drop-down menu. In order to permit password authentication, simply set the drop-down menu to Allow and select Apply on the lower-half of the menu. Password authentication has now been enabled for all SSH users on the server. If password authentication is not required or desired, simply select Deny from the drop-down menu and hit Apply. Be sure to configure public-key configuration in order for authentication to occur (discussed in the following section). Figure 4.4 shows the SSH User Authentication menu.

Host-Based Authentication

Host-based authentication is another method of authentication in a SSH environment. Each entity in a SSH architecture, either an SSH server or SSH client, can contain a host key for identification. The host key is used to uniquely distinguish the client or server from any other entity. Furthermore, the host key is unique only to the operating system and cannot be easily duplicated from one machine to the next. Host-key-based authentication is used to replace IP address authentication used in RSH (remote shell) authentication. Since an

IP address can be easily spoofed, using an IP address as a method of authentication is extremely insecure. Furthermore, host keys cannot be easily spoofed and can be used to uniquely authenticate a SSH server or a SSH client. Host-based authentication is best suited for scripted environments, where username/password combinations cannot be used or are too cumbersome for the required business use (for example, nightly encrypted backups). Table 4.7 shows the locations of the host keys in SSH servers.

Once the host keys have been located and identified, the public host keys, denoted by the .pub extension, should be copied to the remote server. For example, if a machine called AUM wants to connect to another machine called OM with host-based authentication, the public key host key should be copied to the OM SSH server. This will allow the OM SSH server to accept authentication from the AUM machine based on the host key itself, without any need for a password. The following steps should be conducted in order to set up host-based authentication with the AUM server and OM server.

1. Host AUM should generate a host key. (Depending on the type of operating system and environment, the syntax may be different.) The following is a list of the syntax depending on the environment:

   ```
   ssh-keygen -P Aum (OpenSSH)
   ssh-keygen2 -P Aum (SSH Communications)
   ```

2. This will create the private host key and the public host key. The public host-key file is Aum.pub and the private host-key file is Aum.

3. Copy Aum.pub to the knownhost folder in /etc/ssh2 for SSH Communications' SSH server and /etc/ssh/ssh_known_hosts for OpenSSH SSH's server. For SSH Communications, copy Aum.pub to /etc/ssh2/knownhosts; however, rename Aum.pub to the fully qualified DNS name in the following form: hostname.domain.ssh-dss.pub. (A fully qualified domain name is a full DNS name of a machine on a given network.) For example, if machine AUM belongs to the eNapkin domain, its name should be changed to Aum.eNapkin.ssh-dss.pub. For OpenSSH, just add the key to the authorized key file, as the following shows:

   ```
   #cd .ssh
   #cat Aum.pub >> authorized_keys
   ```

4. On the OM server, create a file called named .shosts. Place Aum .eNapkin.com <tab> and the username, such as root. The following is an example:

   ```
   Aum.eNapkin.com    root
   ```

Table 4.7 Types of SSH Software and the Locations of the Host Keys

SSH SOFTWARE	HOST KEY LOCATION
SSH Communications' server (Unix)	/etc/ssh2
SSH Communications' server (Windows)	Program Files\SSH Secure Shell Server
VShell SSH server	Program Files\VShell\hostkey
OpenSSH server	/etc/ssh

5. Configure the OM SSH server to accept host-based authentication by editing the configuration file. Edit sshd2_config to enable host keys for authentication for SSH Communications' SSH server:

```
## Authentication
## publickey and password allowed by default

AllowedAuthentications        publickey, hostbased
```

6. To enable host-based authentication for OpenSSH, edit the sshd_config file and change the line to yes:

```
HostbasedAuthentication yes
```

7. Test the configuration by resetting the SSH server and typing the following syntax:

```
ssh root@OM
```

Server Authentication

In addition to traditional host-based authentication for user access, a SSH client can confirm the identification of a SSH server with host-key information. When a SSH client first attempts to authenticate to a SSH server, the SSH server sends its public host key to the client in order to identify itself. The client can then accept and save the host key locally in order to authenticate or verify the connection the next time the SSH client attempts to log in. The host key accepted by the client is added to the host-key database that the SSH client stores locally on the client machine. Each time the SSH client attempts to log in to the SSH server, the client will compare the SSH server's host key with the host key in the SSH client's host-key database to make sure it matches. If the keys do not match, the SSH client can choose not to log in to the SSH server, due to possible tampering with the SSH server or possibly a man-in-the-middle attack.

Table 4.8 The Type of SSH Software and the Location of the Host Keys

SSH SOFTWARE	HOST KEY LOCATION
SSH Communications' client (Unix)	/root/.ssh2/hostkeys
SSH Communications' client (Windows)	Documents and Settings\Administrator\ Application Data\SSH\HostKeys
SecureCRT	C:\DocumentsandSettings\Administrator\ Application Data\Van Dyke Technologies\ SecureCRT\HostKeyDatabase
OpenSSH client	/etc/ssh/hostkeys

The server-authentication process protects against pure IP-address based verifications, where a SSH client would trust a SSH server based solely on its IP address. Since IPv4 networks are susceptible to IP address spoofing, reliance on IP addresses for identification is not secure. Public host keys for SSH servers offer an excellent method for a SSH client to verify and authenticate the SSH server that they will be communicating with. Table 4.8 shows the location of the host-key database for SSH clients.

SecureCRT and SSH Communications' SSH clients both show the host-key database on their respective client GUI, as shown in Figures 4.5 and 4.6.

Figure 4.5 shows the host-key database for SecureCRT. This is the repository for the SSH client for all host keys obtained after a connection is made to a SSH server. This host-key database will be referenced each time the SSH client connects to the same SSH server to make sure the host keys match.

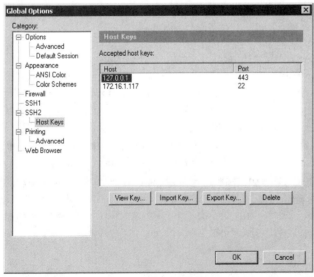

Figure 4.5 SecureCRT host-key database.

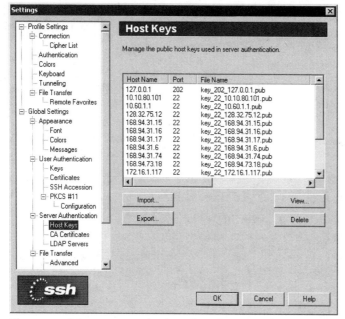

Figure 4.6 SSH Communications' host-key database.

Figure 4.6 shows the host-key database for SSH Communications' SSH client. Similar to SecureCRT, this is the repository for the SSH client for all host keys obtained after a connection is made to a SSH server. This host-key database will be referenced each time the SSH client connects to the same SSH server to make sure the host keys match.

Public Keys

Public-key authentication is one of the best authentication methods provided by SSH. Unlike password authentication, public-key authentication requires each user to contain a public-key file in order to authenticate. The fact that many corporate networks rely on user passwords, no matter how strong or weak, to protect sensitive and propriety information leaves many networks vulnerable to simple attacks. The following sidebar provides several reasons why using passwords on sensitive systems may not be the best decision in order to attain an acceptable level of security:

WHY PASSWORDS MAY NOT PROVIDE THE BEST SECURITY

- ◆ Passwords are often weak.
- ◆ Passwords can be shared easily.
- ◆ Brute-force attacks, the act of trying every password combination based on a dictionary list of words, can guess passwords in an automated fashion.
- ◆ If a password is compromised, it is very difficult to detect an incident, since all communication would look like that of an authorized user.
- ◆ Hostile SSH clients could contain key-loggers to capture a password.
- ◆ Passwords alone do not force two-factor authentication.
- ◆ Passwords are susceptible to the Sticky-Note attack (the act of writing down a password on a Post-It note and sticking it to a computer monitor).
- ◆ Passwords can be shared from one application, such as SSH, to another application, such as FTP or NTLM authentication. A hostile attacker could sniff other weak protocols, such as FTP and NTLM, for passwords. If the user has the same password for all three accounts, which is the case in many situations, the malicious attacker would have a valid SSH password.

Now that you have seen some of the security issues with passwords, you will learn about using public keys for authentication and why the use of key-based authentication can virtually eliminate many of the issues described previously. The following sidebar lists the strengths that public-key authentication offers in a typical network environment, both internally to the network and externally.

Key-based authentication in a SSH environment uses public and private keys. The following is a summary of the steps required to generate a key pair for SSH:

1. An authorized user must generate a public and private key pair.

2. The user has the option of password protecting the private key, which is recommended in almost all environments.

3. The user's public key needs to be securely uploaded to the SSH server, usually stored in the user's home directory. For example, the user Kusum would have a public key stored in /home/Kusum/.ssh/ or Documents and Settings\Kusum\.ssh of the SSH server.

4. Authorization, Identification, and authorized_keys files need to be populated.

5. Public-key authentication needs to be configured on the SSH server, which is enabled by default on many SSH installations.

That is it!

STRENGTHS OF PUBLIC-KEY AUTHENTICATION

◆ Key-based authentication supports industry best practice of two-factor authentication.

◆ Public/Private keys cannot be shared as easily as passwords (Public and private keys can still be shared from one machine to the next!)

◆ If a private key is stolen or compromised, the private key can be password protected, which enforces another level of security, protecting it from being used successfully by a malicious user.

◆ Sole reliance on user passwords is virtually eliminated.

◆ Brute-force attacks, and other password attacks, cannot be executed against public keys.

◆ Sniffing, key loggers, and the Sticky-Note attack are no longer significant threats with public-key authentication.

◆ In order for an unauthorized user to successfully authenticate to a SSH server, a malicious user would have to compromise an authorized user's machine, obtain a copy of his or her pubic and private key, and guess the passphrase of the private key. This scenario may require more effort for an attacker than moving to an easier target or easier network.

For key-based authentication to be implemented, each valid user must contain a public and private key pair. The process of creating a public and private key pair is the responsibility of the SSH client, not the SSH server. The public and private keys are stored on the local machine—the user's machine—and a copy of the user's public key is stored on the SSH server. To authenticate, the user must contain both the public and private keys. The user must authenticate, using a password, to his or her local private key, which decrypts the private-key file and enables it. Once authentication is granted, the public key is used to authenticate to the SSH server. The SSH server receives the public key and determines if the public key matches the same public key that the server holds for that particular user. If the match is correct, the user is then authenticated. The data flow for public-key authentication is illustrated in Figure 4.7.

As noted in Step 1, creating a public and private key pair is the responsibility of the SSH client, not the SSH server. Since several different SSH clients exist, I will address the process of creating a public and private key with each of the following SSH clients:

- OpenSSH (Unix and Windows)
- SSH Communications (Unix and Windows Command Line)
- SSH Communications (Windows GUI)
- VanDyke SecureCRT

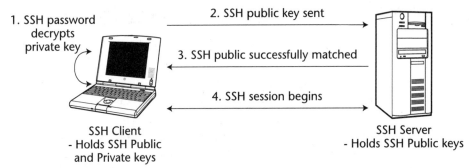

Figure 4.7   Key-based authentication in SSH.

Furthermore, I will demonstrate how to convert specific SSH client keys to fit a particular SSH server. For example, OpenSSH keys are not interpretable to SSH Communications' SSH servers by default. While it would be very nice if all public and private keys could be used from one SSH server to the other, the reality is that you need to modify your public and private keys in order to use them across multiple environments. The SSH servers you will make your client keys interoperable with are the following:

■ SSH Communications

■ OpenSSH

■ VShell

NOTE In the following sections, the use of ssh, ssh-keygen, ssh.exe, and ssh-keygen.exe refers to OpenSSH SSH clients. Furthermore, the use of ssh2, ssh-keygen2, ssh2.exe, and ssh-keygen2.exe refers to SSH Communications' SSH clients. Lastly, the use of vsh.exe and vcp.exe refers to VanDyke Software SSH clients.

Creating Keys with OpenSSH

To create keys with the OpenSSH client, complete the following steps on the client machine.

1. Change directories to the location of the ssh-keygen binary:

```
cd /usr/bin
C:\cd "Program Files"\OpenSSH\bin
```

2. Create a DSA key pair:

```
#ssh-keygen -d
c:\Program Files\OpenSSH\ssh-keygen.exe -d
Generating public/private dsa key pair.
```

3. Enter the name of the key pair (I will call ours Shreya); then enter a passphrase, and confirm the passphrase:

```
Enter file in which to save the key (/root//.ssh/id_dsa): Shreya
Enter passphrase (empty for no passphrase):
Enter same passphrase again:
```

4. After you have confirmed the passphrase, both the public and private keys should be generated. In this case, the names will be Shreya.pub for the public-key file and Shreya for the private-key file. The key fingerprint will be displayed on the shell or command prompt:

```
Your identification has been saved in Shreya.
Your public key has been saved in Shreya.pub.
The key fingerprint is:
ed:1e:67:22:79:d8:81:c9:b4:ee:0d:f5:55:0d:cf:5c
```

5. OpenSSH client keys have been generated!

After the creation process has been completed, copy the OpenSSH client key to the SSH server, specifically to the .ssh folder in the users' home directory (for example, /home/<username>/.ssh/PublicKey.pub. The following section demonstrates how to use an OpenSSH key on an OpenSSH server, a SSH Communications' SSH server, and a VanDyke VShell SSH server.

How to Use an OpenSSH Key on an OpenSSH Server

After the OpenSSH public key has been securely uploaded to the SSH server, typically in the users' home directory (/home/Shreya/.ssh/Shreya.pub or Program Files\OpenSSH\.ssh\Shreay.pub), you also need to append the key to the authorized key-list file, which is labeled authorized_keys in the users' home directory (/home/<username>/.ssh/authorized_keys). Example syntax is as follows on the server machine:

```
[Shreya@OpenSSH]$cat Shreya.pub >> /home/<username>/.ssh/authorized_keys
```

Furthermore, the permissions on the public-key and private-key pairs need to be protected in order to be used. Set the following permission on the key files generated on the client machine:

```
[Shreya@localhost]$chmod 600 Shreya
[Shreya@localhost]$chmod 600 Shreya.pub
```

Once you have made the key pairs, uploaded the public-key file to the appropriate home directory, added the key to the authorized_keys file, and set the correct permissions, you should be able to log in with the public key. Sample syntax follows on the client machine:

```
[Shreya@localhost]$ssh <SSH server IP address> -i Shreya
```

If you attach a passphrase to the private key, the following text should appear:

```
Enter passphrase for key 'Shreya':
```

After entering your passphrase, you should be logged in to the SSH connection:

```
[Shreya@OpenSSH Shreya]$
```

How to Use an OpenSSH Key on SSH Communications' SSH Server

To use an OpenSSH key on SSH Communications' SSH server, the key must be converted to the SSH2 format, using the following commands.

1. Convert your OpenSSH client key to the SSH Communications' SSH compatible format. To convert the keys, you must set a blank passphrase for the private key (ssh-keygen -p -f Shreya). After the key conversation is complete, make sure you go back and set a passphrase for both the old OpenSSH key and the newly converted SSH2 key. Use the following commands to convert the key on the client machine:

   ```
   [Shreya@localhost]$ssh-keygen -e -f Shreya.pub > SSH2-Shreya.pub
   [Shreya@localhost]$ssh-keygen -e -f Shreya > SSH2-Shreya
   ```

2. Once you have copied the public key to the SSH Communications' SSH server in the users' home directory, specifically in the .ssh2 folder in the users' home directory (/home/<username>/.ssh2/publickey.pub on Unix and Documents and Settings\<username>\.ssh2\publickey.pub on Windows), you need to add a public-key entry to the authorization file, which is labeled Authorization, also in the users' home directory on the SSH server. The contents of the authorization file on the SSH server should be Key, followed by the actual public-key name.

   ```
   Key      SSH2-Shreya.pub
   ```

3. After the authorization file has been created on the SSH server, an iden-tification file needs to be created on the SSH client, typically in the ssh2 folder in the users' home directory (/home/<username>/.ssh2 for Unix and Documents and Settings\<username>\.ssh2\ for Windows). This file is used by the SSH client to indicate which private keys to use for authentication. Furthermore, unlike OpenSSH, this file is used with the –i option to point to the correct private keys for authentication. For

example, while OpenSSH uses "–i <privatekey>" syntax, SSH Communications' uses "–i identification" for the syntax. The syntax to create the identification file is as follows on the client:

```
echo "IdKey SSH2-Shreya" >> identification
```

4. After the identification file has been created on the SSH server, the permissions on the public-key and private-key pairs need to be protected in order to be used. Set the following permission on the SSH client for the appropriate key files that were generated.

```
[Shreya@localhost]$chmod 600 SSH2-Shreya
[Shreya@localhost]$chmod 600 SSH2-Shreya.pub
```

5. Once you have made the key pairs, uploaded the public-key files to the appropriate home directory, added the entry to the authorization file, and added the entry to the identification file, you should now be able to log in with the public key. Be sure to use the identification file with the –i option, not the private-key file; otherwise you will receive a "No further authentication methods available" error. The following is sample syntax:

```
[Shreya@localhost]$ssh2 SSH-Server –i identification
```

How to Use an OpenSSH Key on a VShell SSH Server

Using an OpenSSH client key for a VShell SSH server is more straightforward than the previous section. Since VShell SSH servers accept the OpenSSH key format, it is not necessary to convert OpenSSH keys to any other format, which saves valuable time and a lot of potential headache! Since you have an OpenSSH client key, I will demonstrate how to use the OpenSSH key for VShell SSH servers.

1. Copy the OpenSSH public-key file to the remote VShell SSH server, specifically in public-key folder located at C:\ Program Files\VShell\PublicKey\%USER%.

2. Make sure public-key authentication is enabled on the remote VShell SSH server.

3. From the client machine, connect to the VShell SSH server with the following syntax:

```
ssh <VShell Server> -p 22 -i OpenSSHPrivatekey –l <username on VShell
server>
```

Using the preceding example, with Shreya as the OpenSSH private key, an example authentication process is as follows:

```
ssh VshellServer -p 22 -i Shreya -l shreya
Enter passphrase for key 'Shreya':
Authenticated with partial success
Shreya@VshellServer's password:
C:\
```

Notice that after the key is authenticated, VShell asks for a password on the VShell server. This happens only if both the password and public-key checkboxes are required on the VShell server. If public key was the only required authentication method, a password prompt would not occur; however, this is a great method of enforcing two-factor authentication, which should be required for management purposes.

Creating Keys with SSH Communications' SSH Client (Unix and Windows Command Line)

To create keys with SSH Communications' SSH client on either Windows or Unix, complete the following steps.

1. Change directories to the location of the ssh-keygen binary:

```
cd /usr/local/bin
C:\cd "Program Files"\SSH Secure Shell\bin
```

2. Create a DSA key pair:

```
ssh-keygen2
Generating 2048-bit dsa key pair
  2 Oоo.оOо.оOо.
```

3. After the key has been generated, enter a passphrase, and confirm the passphrase:

```
Key generated.
2048-bit dsa, kusum@localhost.com, Fri Aug 15 2003 11:17:00
Passphrase :
Again      :
Private key saved to /home/kusum/.ssh2/id_dsa_2048_a
Public key saved to /home/kusum/.ssh2/id_dsa_2048_a.pub
```

4. After you have confirmed your passphrase, both the public and private keys should be generated. In this case, the names will be id_dsa_2048_a.pub for the public-key file and id_dsa_2048_a for the private-key file. The key should be automatically saved to the .ssh2 folder in the users' hold directory in Unix (/home/<username>/.ssh2/) and the users' home folder in Windows (Documents and

Settings/<username>/Application Data/SSH/UserKeys). The following shows the Windows location:

```
Private key saved to C:/Documents and
Settings/Administrator/Application Data/SSH/UserKeys/id_dsa_2048_a
Public key saved to C:/Documents and
Settings/Administrator/Application
Data/SSH/UserKeys/id_dsa_2048_a.pub
```

5. The SSH Communications' SSH client keys have been generated!

After the creation process has been completed, copy the SSH public-client key to the SSH server. The following section demonstrates how to use SSH client keys with a SSH Communications' SSH Server, an OpenSSH server, and a VanDyke VShell SSH server.

How to Use SSH Client Keys with SSH Communications' SSH Server

After you have securely uploaded your public key (for example,. id_dsa_2048_a.pub) to the SSH server, typically in the users' home directory (/home/<username>/.ssh2 for Unix and Documents and Settings\<username>\.ssh2\ for Windows), you also need to add a public-key entry to the authorization file, which is labeled Authorization, also in the users' home directory. The syntax is as follows:

```
Key    id_dsa_2048_a.pub
```

After the authorization file has been created on the SSH server, an identification file needs to be created on the SSH client, typically in the ssh2 folder in the users' home directory (/home/<username>/.ssh2 for Unix and Documents and Settings\<username>\.ssh2\ for Windows). This file is used by the SSH client, with the –i flag, to indicate the private keys to use in order to authenticate. Be sure to use this file with the –i option on the SSH client. The syntax to create this file is as follows:

```
echo "IdKey  id_dsa_2048_a" >> identification
```

Once you have made the key pairs, uploaded the public-key files to the appropriate home directory, added the entry to the authorization file, and added the entry to the identification file, you should be able to log in with the public key. The following is a demonstration of the syntax:

```
ssh2 <SSH server IP address> -i identification
```

How to Use SSH Client Keys with an OpenSSH Server

To use the SSH Communications' SSH Client public-key and private-key pair with an OpenSSH server, complete the following steps.

1. Make sure your key pairs do not contain a passphrase. While it is important to remove any passphrases during the conversation process, make sure you add a passphrase to both the old key and the newly converted keys after the conversation process is completed. To change the passphrase of your key, use the –e switch.

   ```
   ssh-keygen2 -e id_dsa_2048_a
   ```

2. Once the passphrases have been removed, we must convert our SSH Communications' SSH keys to the OpenSSH compatible format, using the following commands:

   ```
   [Shreya@localhost]$ssh-keygen2 -1 id_dsa_2048_a.pub >
    id_dsa_2048_a_Open.pub
   [Shreya@localhost]$ssh-keygen2 -1 id_dsa_2048_a > id_dsa_2048_a_Open
   ```

3. Once you have copied the public key to the SSH server, using SFTP or some alternative secure method (there is no automated tool to do this), enter the following command on the OpenSSH server to add the newly converted public key to the authorized key file, located in the users' home directory, on the OpenSSH server.

   ```
   [Shreya@OpenSSHserver]$cat id_dsa_2048_a_Open.pub >>
   /home/Shreya/.ssh/authorized_keys
   ```

4. On the SSH client, the permissions on the public-key and private-key pairs need to be protected to be used. Set the following permission on the key files that were generated:

   ```
   [Shreya@localhost]$chmod 600 id_dsa_2048_a_Open.pub
   [Shreya@localhost]$chmod 600 id_dsa_2048_a_Open
   ```

5. You should now be able to authenticate, since you have converted your SSH Communications' SSH client key to OpenSSH format and have added the key to the authorized key-list file:

   ```
   /usr/bin/ssh SSH-Server -i id_dsa_2048_a_Open
   ```

How to Use SSH Client Keys with a VShell SSH Server

Using a SSH Communications' client key for a VShell SSH server is quite simple. Since VShell SSH servers accept the SSH Communications' SSH2 key format, it is not necessary to convert SSH Communications' keys to any other format, which saves valuable time and a lot of potential headache! VShell accepts the OpenSSH key format; therefore, the converted OpenSSH key from the previous section could also be used on a VShell SSH server. I will now demonstrate how to use both an SSH Communications' SSH key and a converted OpenSSH client key for VShell SSH servers.

1. Copy your SSH Communications' key and OpenSSH public key-file to the remote VShell SSH server, specifically in public-key folder located at C:\ Program Files\VShell\PublicKey\%USER%.

2. Make sure public-key authentication is enabled on the remote VShell SSH server.

3. From the client machine, connect to the VShell SSH server with the following syntax.

```
ssh2 <VShell Server> -p 22 -i identification -l <username on VShell
server>
ssh <VShell Server> -p 22 -i OpenSSHPrivatekey -l <username on VShell
server>
```

Using the previous example, with id_dsa_2048_a and the SSH Communications' key and id_dsa_2048_a_Open as the converted OpenSSH client key, complete the following steps to authenticate to the VShell SSH server.

SSH Communications' Client Key

```
ssh2 VshellServer -p 22 -i identification -l <username>
Enter passphrase for key '<username>:
Authenticated with partial success
Shreya@VshellServer's password:
C:\
```

OpenSSH Convert Client Key

```
ssh VshellServer -p 22 -i id_dsa_2048_a_Open -l <username>
Enter passphrase for key '<username>:
Authenticated with partial success
Shreya@VshellServer's password:
C:\
```

Notice that after the key is authenticated, VShell asks for a password on the VShell server. This happens only if both the password and public-key checkboxes are required on the VShell server. If public key was the only required authentication method, a password prompt would not occur; however, this is a great method of enforcing two-factor authentication, which should be required for management purposes.

Creating Keys with SSH Communications (Windows GUI)

To create keys the SSH Communications' SSH client, the following steps should be completed.

1. Open the SSH client: Start ⇨ Programs ⇨ SSH Secure Shell ⇨ Secure Shell client.

2. From the Menu bar, select Edit ⇨ Settings.

3. In the Settings display, there should be a User Authentication section. Under the User Authentication section, there is a subcategory called Keys. Select the Keys subcategory.

4. At this point, you should see a screen similar to Figure 4.8.

5. To generate a new public and private-key pair, select the option that says Generate New...

6. The wizard should be displayed, describing the process of creating a key pair. After you have read the description, select Next.

7. The Key Properties screen should appear next. This screen gives you the option of selecting a DSA or RSA key type and the key length you would like to use. In general, the better the key length, the stronger the security; however, the greater the performance hit you will have to accept. After selecting the type of key and the key length, select Next.

8. The Generation screen should appear next. This screen initiates the process of actually creating the key. The key-generation process can take several minutes. Once the process is completed, select Next.

9. The Enter Passphrase screen should appear next. This screen allows you to enter a name for the public and private-key pair, a comment for description purposes only, and a passphrase to protect the private key. Enter your preferred file name, such as your username, a comment, and a passphrase that is difficult to guess but easy to remember. After entering this information, select Next. (Note that if the passphrases do not match, the Next option will not be enabled. Make sure your passphrases match before attempting to select Next.)

10. The Finish screen should appear next. At this stage, the public and private keys have been generated and stored to your local machine. At this point, you have the option of uploading your public key to the SSH server if a valid connection currently exists. If a valid connection exists (meaning you connected to the SSH server before starting the key-generation procedure), select Upload Public Key; however, you will be uploading the key to multiple SSH servers later in this section, so select Finish and skip to Step 13 if you wish to skip this step.

Figure 4.8   Keys subcategory for SSH Communications' SSH client.

11. After selecting Upload Public Key, a new display should appear. The display should contain the name of the public key, the destination folder for the key to be placed, which is the folder on the SSH server to place the key, most likely /home/user/.ssh2, and the authorization file to add the key to, such as authorization. After verifying that all the items are correct, select Upload.

12. After selecting Upload, you will see a successful completion of the upload, where you can select finish; however, if you want to require the use of public keys only, you will have to go back and edit the sshd2_config file to require only the use of public keys and to delete password or host-based authentication. Also, if you receive an error in the upload process, probably the SSH server you are attempting to connect to is not a SSH Communications' SSH server, so the key-converting process will have to be followed, listed as follows.

13. At this point, you should be redirected to the initial Key subcategory screen. To confirm that the keys have been generated appropriately, browse to Documents and Settings\<username>\Application Data\SSH\UserKeys. There should be both the public key (*.pub) and private key located in this folder. Also, the Key subcategory screen should appear with the newly generated key in the Keys field, as shown in Figure 4.9.

14. SSH Communications' SSH keys have been generated!

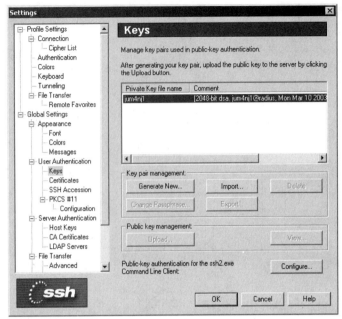

Figure 4.9   The private-key file name in SSH Communications' SSH client.

After the creation process has been completed, the process of uploading the public key is next. The following section demonstrates how to upload a SSH Communications' SSH client public-key and private-key pair to a SSH Communications' SSH server, an OpenSSH server, and a VanDyke VShell SSH server.

How to Upload an SSH Client Key Pair to SSH Communications' SSH Server

The process of uploading a SSH client key to an SSH server is quite simple if both the systems are the same, meaning they are both from the same application (OpenSSH versus Commercial). To upload the SSH Communications' SSH client public key to a SSH Communications' SSH server (Windows or Unix), complete the following steps.

1. Open the SSH Client: Start ⇨ Programs ⇨ SSH Secure Shell ⇨ Secure Shell Client.

2. Connect to the SSH Communications' SSH server using a username and password. This can be completed with the File ⇨ Quick Connect option.

3. Once authenticated and connected to the SSH server, select, Edit ⇨ Settings from the menu bar.

4. In Settings display, there should be a User Authentication section. Under the User Authentication section, there is a subcategory called Keys. Select the Keys subcategory.

5. In the Keys subcategory, there should be a Public key management section where an Upload... button should exist. Simply select the Upload... button to upload the public key to the SSH server.

6. After selecting Upload..., a new display should appear. The display should contain the name of the public key, the destination folder for the key to be placed in, which is the folder on the SSH server to place the key, most likely /home/user/.ssh2, and the authorization file to add the key to, such as authorization. The authorization file is read by the SSH server to identify which users can use public keys for authentication. After verifying that all the items are correct, select Upload.

7. If the Upload box disappears suddenly, you have successfully uploaded the public key to the SSH server. To confirm, check the home directory on the SSH server (Documents and Settings\<username>\Application Data\SSH on Windows and /home/<username>/.ssh on Unix) to verify the existence of the *.pub file, which is the public-key file for the user.

8. Using Quick connect, you should be able to authenticate with the public-key option for Authentication Method.

How to Upload an SSH Client Key Pair to an OpenSSH Server

To use the SSH Communications' SSH Client public and private-key pair to a OpenSSH server, complete the following steps.

1. Make sure your key pairs do not contain a passphrase. While it is important to remove any passphrases during the conversation process, make sure you add a passphrase to both the old key and the newly converted keys after the conversation process is completed.

    a. Select Start ⇨ Programs ⇨ SSH Secure Shell ⇨ SSH Secure Shell.

    b. Select Edit ⇨ Settings ⇨ User Authentication ⇨ Keys.

    c. Highlight the correct private-key file name, and select Change Passphrase...

    d. Enter the old passphrase, and leave the textbox blank for the new passphrases, as shown in Figure 4.10.

    e. Select Yes when the warning appears about using an empty passphrase; however, make sure you go back and add a passphrase after the conversion is completed.

    f. Hit OK to confirm the change.

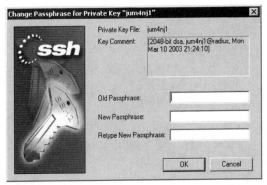

Figure 4.10 The screen to change a passphrase with SSH Communications' GUI client.

2. Once the passphrases have been removed, you must convert your SSH Communications' SSH keys to the OpenSSH compatible format, using the following commands:

> On the SSH client, use the OpenSSH ssh-keygen utility to convert the keys:

```
ssh-keygen -i -f SSH2.pub > SSH2Open.pub
ssh-keygen -i -f SSH > SSH2Open
```

3. Once you have copied the public key to the SSH server, using SFTP or some alternative secure method (there is no automated tool to do this), enter the following commands to send the newly converted public key to the authorized key files on the SSH sever.

> On the OpenSSH server:

```
cat SSH2Open.pub >> authorized_keys
```

4. At this point, you want to incorporate your newly converted OpenSSH key to your GUI client.

   a. Select Start ⇨ Programs ⇨ SSH Secure Shell ⇨ SSH Secure Shell.

   b. Choose Edit ⇨ Settings ⇨ User Authentication ⇨ Keys.

   c. Select Import ⇨ SSH2Open.pub, as shown in Figure 4.11.

   d. You will receive an error describing how the SSH client can read your public-key file; however, this is okay and will not affect the usage of the key.

5. Using Quick connect, you should be able to authenticate with the public-key option for Authentication Method, as shown in Figure 4.12.

6. After selecting Connect, you should receive a similar error, describing how it cannot read your converted OpenSSH key. Select OK and you should now be logged in with the convert OpenSSH key to an OpenSSH server using the SSH Communications' SSH client.

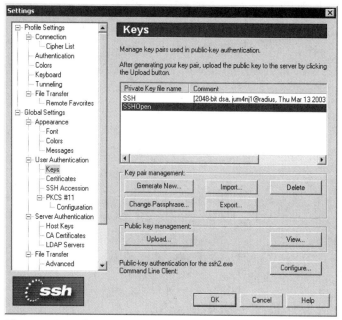

Figure 4.11   The SSH2 converted key in OpenSSH format in the SSH Communications' SSH GUI client.

How to Upload an SSH Client Key Pair to a VShell SSH Server

Using a SSH Communications' client key for a VShell SSH server is quite simple. Since VShell SSH servers accept the SSH Communications' SSH2 key format, it is not necessary to convert SSH Communications' keys to any other format, which saves valuable time and a lot of potential headache!

1. Copy your SSH Communications' public key to the remote VShell SSH server, specifically in public-key folder located at C:\ Program Files\VShell\PublicKey\%USER%.

2. Make sure public-key authentication is enabled on the remote VShell SSH server.

3. Since the public key (SSH2.pub) is already listed as a valid public key, there is no reason to import a new key; however, you can validate the

Figure 4.12   The Quick Connection option with the Public Key Authentication option.

existence of the key by selecting Edit ⇨ Settings ⇨ Keys on the SSH client. Once you have verified the existence of the SSH Communications' SSH key, hit OK.

4. On the VShell SSH Server disable password authentication and enable only public-key authentication.

   a. Start ⇨ Programs ⇨ VShell ⇨ VShell

   b. Authentication >

   ■ Uncheck Password

   ■ Check Public key

5. On the SSH Communications' SSH client, use Quick connect to authenticate with the public-key option for Authentication Method.

6. After selecting Connect, be logged-in with the SSH2 key to a VShell SSH server using the SSH Communications' SSH client.

Creating Keys with VanDyke SecureCRT

To create keys for the SecureCRT SSH client, the following steps should be completed.

1. Open the SSH client: Start ⇨ Programs ⇨ SecureCRT 4.0 ⇨ SecureCRT 4.0

2. From the Menu bar, select Tools ⇨ Create Public Key...

3. The Key Generation Wizard should appear. After reading through the introduction wizard page, select Next.

4. The Key type screen should appear next. This screen gives you the option of selecting a DSA or RSA key type. After selecting your preferred key type, select Next.

5. The Passphrase screen should appear next. This screen allows you to set a passphrase that will protect the private key. The passphrase will need to be entered in order to decrypt the private key. The screen allows you to set a comment, possibly with identification information of the public and private key pair.

6. The Key length screen should appear next. This screen allows you to set the key length, anywhere between 512 and 2048. Generally, the higher the key length, the stronger the security; however, it will have a greater performance penalty.

7. The Generation screen should appear next. This screen initiates the process of actually creating the key. Move the mouse around in order to create the key. Once the process is completed, select Next.

8. The location screen should appear next. Unless you have a particular area to store the keys, it is recommended to key in the default location (C:\Documents and Settings\Administrator\Application Data\ VanDyke\Identity); however, make sure to place NTFS permissions in the folder to restrict access to Guests, Everyone, and other unauthorized groups. After selecting the location, click Finish.

9. You should a see a pop-up box, asking if you would like to use the key as your global public key. Select No, since you may have multiple keys with one default global key.

10. VanDyke SecureCRT public and private-key pairs have been generated!

After the creation process has been completed, the process of uploading the public key is next. The following section demonstrates how to upload a SecureCRT client public and private-key pairs to a VanDyke VShell SSH server, a SSH Communications' SSH server, and an OpenSSH server.

VShell SSH Server

Using a SecureCRT public and private-key pair on VanDyke Software's SSH server is quite simple. The following steps should be complete.

1. Open SecureCRT (Start ⇨ Programs ⇨ Secure CRT ⇨ Secure CRT).

2. Make a valid connection to the VShell SSH server using the Quick Connection option.

3. Once a valid connection has been established, go back to the quick connect menu (File ⇨ Quick Connect). Under the authentication section, there should be two drop-down boxes. The Primary method should be Password. For the Secondary methods, choose PublicKey and select the Properties button to the right.

4. The Public Key Properties menu should appear. Make sure the Use global public key setting radio button is selected and the Use identify file radio button is also selected. After you have confirmed this, select the ... button and browse to the location of your public key; then select the public-key file.

5. After you have selected to your public-key file, select the Upload button to upload the public key to the VShell SSH server.

6. When SecureCRT has established a connection, it will ask you to authenticate using your username and password on the VShell SSH server. Enter the valid username and password and select OK.

7. Once the username and password are authenticated, the public key will be uploaded to the VShell SSH server. You should see a menu similar to Figure 4.13.

Figure 4.13   The confirmation of the SecureCRT public-key upload process.

8. You should now be able to use your public key to authenticate. To confirm, enable only public-key authentication on the VShell SSH server.

    a. Select Start ⇨ Programs ⇨ VShell ⇨ VShell.

    b. Highlight the Authentication section.

    c. Uncheck Password and check Public key for the required authentication methods. Be sure to uncheck the Allow 3 password attempts checkbox, since the public key is already on the VShell SSH server.

9. On SecureCRT, select PublicKey for the Primary authentication method and <None> for the Secondary authentication method. Be sure to browse to the correct public key with the Properties button.

10. Select Connect and you will authenticate with your public key and then receive a VShell SSH session.

OpenSSH

To use the SecureCRT Client public and private-key pair for an OpenSSH server, complete the following steps.

1. Make sure your key pairs do not contain a passphrase. While it is important to remove any passphrases during the conversation process, make sure you add a passphrase to both the old key and the newly converted keys after the conversion process is completed.

    a. Go to Start ⇨ Programs ⇨ SecureCRT ⇨ SecureCRT.

    b. Choose File ⇨ Quick Connect ⇨ Protocol (ssh2) ⇨ Authentication (Public Key).

    c. Select Properties ⇨ Change Passphrase.

    d. Enter the current passphrase, and leave the new passphrase blank.

    e. Select OK.

2. Once the passphrases have been removed, you must convert your SecureCRT keys to the OpenSSH compatible format. On the client machine, use OpenSSH's ssh-keygen utility to convert the keys. The keys are located at Documents and Settings\<username>\Application Data\VanDyke. Use the following commands:

```
ssh-keygen -i -f CRTpublickey.pub > CRTpublickeyOpen.pub
ssh-keygen -i -f CRTprivatekey > CRTprivatekeyOpen
```

3. Once you have copied the public key to the SSH server, using SFTP or some alternative secure method, enter the following commands to send the newly converted public key to the authorized key files on the SSH server.

On the OpenSSH server:

```
cat CRTpublickeyOpen.pub >> authorized_keys
```

4. You should now be able to authenticate, since you have converted your SecureCRT client key to OpenSSH format and have added the key to the authorized key-list file:

```
/usr/bin/ssh OpenSSH-Server -i CRTprivatekeyOpen
```

SSH Communications' SSH Server

The process of converting a SecureCRT client key to a SSH Communications' SSH server is more straightforward than the previous section. Since SSH Communications' uses SSH2 keys, converting your SecureCRT key is not required for SSH Communications' SSH servers. Since you have an SSH2 key with your SecureCRT key, I will now demonstrate how to use the SecureCRT key for SSH Communications' SSH servers.

1. Copy your SSH2 SecureCRT public-key file SSH Communications' SSH Server, specifically in the .ssh2 folder in the Documents and Settings\<username>\ directory.

2. Open or make a file-name 'authorization' located in the following directory: Documents and Settings\<username>\.ssh2. Add the new SecureCRT public key to the authorized key lists.

```
Key        CRTpublickey.pub
```

Where CRTpublickey.pub is the SSH2 SecureCRT public key.

3. On the SSH SecureCRT client, open the Quick Connect screen (File ➪ Quick Connect), and enter the following information.

   a. Protocol: ssh2

   b. Hostname: <remote SSH Communications' SSH server>

   c. Port: port number, typically 22

   d. Username: Username of the remote SSH server

   e. Authentication

- Primary: PublicKey

     - Properties: Use your identity file: c:\Documents and Settings\<username>\Application Data\VanDyke\CRTpublickey.pub

- Secondary: Password

4. Select Connect.

5. You should now be logged in to a SSH Communications' SSH server using a SSH2 key generated from SecureCRT.

While the use of public keys for authentication purposes is by far the better solution of password authentication, the process of making SSH client keys interoperate with various SSH servers may not be an easy process in an enterprise environment. For optimal usage, it is better to use tools and utilities that are interoperable with various platforms and technologies, and SSH is no different. The use of VShell SSH servers has a significant advantage, since it accepts both OpenSSH keys and SSH2 keys without any need for any conversion from any client mentioned in this chapter. Similarly, using OpenSSH keys as your primary key may be a good solution, since both OpenSSH and VShell servers accept the OpenSSH format, leaving only one conversion required to work with SSH2 servers. Nevertheless, the choice of the SSH client-key format and SSH servers will depend on many items, not just the public-key conversation process. As best practice, it is a good idea to have both formats of your public key made: one for OpenSSH and another for SSH2 formats.

SSH Agents

The SSH agent is a simple utility that allows end-users to handle passphrases attached to public-key files in a simpler way. If multiple passphrases are being used with multiple public keys, it may be cumbersome for the end-user to type and retype all the passphrases several times. The SSH agent utility remembers your passphrases for you after the first time you have authenticated with the passphrase. It is a utility that remembers your private keys and provides the authentication portion to other SSH connections. Therefore, after you initially authenticate with your passphrase, the SSH agent will prevent subsequent SSH sessions from asking you for your passphrase. The process to enable SSH agents involves the following four steps:

1. Execute the SSH agent with the shell of your choice (bash, csh, tcsh, or ksh).

2. Receive a new SSH shell (automatically).

3. Add the private keys with SSH-add command.

4. Log in to SSH sessions with the passphrase (only the first time).

In order to enable the SSH agent for OpenSSH and SSH Communications, execute the following steps:
OpenSSH:

```
ssh-agent bash
ssh-add <privatekeyfile> (e.g. ssh-add Shreya)
ssh -i OpenSSHPrivateKey <IP Address>
```

SSH Communications:

```
ssh-agent2 bash
ssh-add2 <privatekeyfile> (e.g. ssh-add2 id_dsa_2048_a)
ssh2 -i identification <IP Address>
```

Summary

This chapter discusses the various authentication options available in SSH. It should be noted that many of the authentication options, such as password attempts, are separate from the operating-system authentication options. For example, the operating system could have a password-attempts threshold at 5, while the SSH service has a password-attempts threshold at 3. While SSH servers on both Windows and Unix platforms use the local username/password database for authentication, such as /etc/shadow or the SAM database, the SSH servers can have additional or similar authentication options. Furthermore, while SSH servers are using the same password database, the actual authentication options apply to different services. For example, to log on to a Windows service requires the use of SMB, which may have authentication options tied to it. These authentication options are separate from the authentication options that apply to the SSH service on the operating system, even though both SMB and SSH are using the SAM database file.

While certain authentication options are discussed in detail in this chapter, such as password, public-key, and host-based authentication, there are several other authentications options, such as SecureID and Certificates, which are not discussed. Both SecureID and Certificate-based authentication are strong authentication methods but require the use of several other servers and/or devices, such as a RSA Ace server and a Certificate Authority, which are not included with any SSH package. RSA Ace servers and/or a certificate authority require an additional amount of setup time and implemented architecture; therefore, SecureID and Certificate-based authentication fall outside the scope of this chapter.

The key things to focus on when it comes to SSH authentication are the functional and security requirements for the application. The following is a list of questions and answers to ask when trying to determine which method of authentication is acceptable and/or optimal.

- Does the corporate culture enforce strong passwords?
    - Yes. Password authentication is an acceptable option.
    - No. Consider public-key authentication.
- Will access be from trusted segments?
    - Yes. Host-based authentication is an acceptable option.
    - No. Rely on passwords and public keys for authentication.
- Will the SSH service/daemon be facing the public Internet?
    - Yes. Consider public-key authentication.
    - No. Password authentication is an acceptable option.
- Will remote users be connecting from predefined locations?
    - Yes. Consider adding host-based authentication.
    - No. Public-key authentication is an acceptable option.
- Are the SSH servers in a layered security architecture?
    - Yes. Passwords and public keys are acceptable options.
    - No. Consider using server authentication.
- Are multiple SSH servers utilized in the environment?
    - Yes. Consider using public keys.
    - No. Passwords are an acceptable option.

Now that you understand all the authentication options with SSH and how to use them across different SSH servers, you will now shift your focus to managing servers/devices that are SSH enabled. Knowing and using different authentication methods in SSH is critical to fully understanding the security implications that exist in terms of server/device management, as well as the functional uses that SSH can enable in the process.

SSH Management

Thus far, I have described SSH in terms of application servers or SSH client applications. While using applications such as VanDyke Software's VShell, SSH Communications' SSH, and OpenSSH, or core SSH server utilities, SSH services can also be available without any of these applications. SSH services are also available on network devices such as routers, switches, firewalls, load balancers, and storage filers. These services on network devices provide the same type of secure access that SSH applications provide. Furthermore, the SSH services on these devices provide secure management capabilities while replacing insecure clear-text protocols such as Telnet, FTP, and/or SNMP.

In addition to SSH services being available on network hardware, SSH services can be integrated with other security utilities. Utilities such as Chroot, user restrictions, TCP wrappers, and IP access filters can be used with SSH to complement and enhance the overall security of network management.

Secure management is often overlooked when it comes to security. Many organizations and corporations deploy a strong perimeter defense with multiple firewalls and router-access control lists; however, they also use poor management protocols that weaken the entire network environment. For example, for remote business travelers, the use of encryption to gain access to e-mail or internal file servers is usually a requirement, either through SSH port forwarding (described in Chapters 6 and 7) or IPSec. In spite of this, many network administrators use Telnet to access perimeter devices such as routers, firewalls, and switches in order to conduct remote management. The odd thing about this situation is that many organizations do not allow insecure protocols such as IMAP and FTP for business travelers but do allow equally weak protocols such as Telnet for more sensitive actions such as router management.

One of the keys to deploying a secure environment is the use of encryption whenever possible. In the case where encryption is unavailable, the use of mitigating security controls to compensate for the lack of encryption should be used. For example, many network devices may not support standard encryption protocols such as SSH for remote management. While these devices cannot support encryption, other mitigating controls should be set, such as access-control lists, which can limit access from a predefined set of IP addresses and enforce two-factor authentication.

This chapter addresses the following features of SSH:

- Network devices
  - Cisco routers
  - Cisco switches
  - Cisco VPN concentrator
  - Cisco PIX firewall
  - Network Appliance storage filers
- Secure management
  - Management stations
  - Two-factor authentication
- SOCKS Management
  - SSH—User restrictions
  - SSH—Network access controls

Network Devices

Our discussion of secure network devices will address the installation, setup, and usage of SSH on the specified network devices in terms of secure management and secure networking. Our discussion will range from how to install SSH on network devices to actually enabling and using SSH on a regular basis on these same devices.

Cisco Routers

Cisco Internetworking Operating System (IOS) started to support the use of SSH from version 12.0.5.S for servers and 12.1.3.T for SSH clients. Since then, IOS 12.x and up has supported SSH version 1 only. While the use of SSH version 1 still has its insecurities, the replacement of Telnet on Cisco devices has added tremendous security to the network device.

To use SSH on Cisco routers, complete the following steps:

1. Download the correct IOS to the router. Make sure you are downloading an IOS version that contains SSH support. Cisco SSH servers require IPSec (DES or 3DES) encryption software image from IOS 12.1(1)T. For SSH clients, IOS 12.1(3)T is required.

2. Make sure a hostname and host domain have been configured for the router. The following commands are not SSH commands but commands on the router that are required in order to use SSH.

   ```
   Syntax:    Router(config)# hostname <hostname>
   Example:   Router(config)# hostname Belwa

   Syntax:    Router(config)# ip domain-name <domainname>
   Example:   Router(config)# ip domain-name eNapkin
   ```

3. Generate an RSA key pair for the router, which will automatically enable SSH:

   ```
   Router(config)# crypto key generate rsa
   ```

   This command will enable both local and remote SSH authentication to and from the router. When using the SSH client, be aware that it runs in EXEC mode with no specific configuration on the router. Now that SSH is enabled on the router, configure SSH appropriately.

4. Set the authentication timeout for SSH. The maximum timeout cannot exceed 120 seconds, which is also the default; however, once the session is established, the VTY timeout setting applies, not the SSH timeout setting. The following syntax sets the router's timeout session for SSH:

   ```
   Syntax:    Router(config)# ip ssh timeout(seconds)
   Example:   Router(config)# ip ssh timeout 120
   ```

5. Set the authentication retries for SSH. The maximum number of retries is five; however, the default is three. The following syntax sets the router's authentication retries for SSH:

   ```
   Syntax:    Router(config)# ip ssh authentication-retries(integer)
   Example:   Router(config)# ip ssh authentication-retries 3
   ```

6. To show and confirm the configuration results of the SSH server, enter the following commands:

```
Router# show ip ssh
SSH Enabled - version 1.5
Authentication timeout: 120 seconds; Authentication retries: 3
```

7. To view the SSH session, enter the following command:

```
Router# show ssh
```

This command shows any connections that are established, the version, the encryption, the state, and the username.

8. Once SSH is enabled and configured, it may be appropriate to prevent any non-SSH connections to access the router, such as Telnet. It is important to disable insecure protocols such as Telnet if a stronger and more secure protocol is in place and provides the same type of access. To require the use of SSH on terminal-line connections, enter the following command:

```
Router(config)# line vty 0 4
Router(config-line)# transport input ssh
```

9. Once SSH has been enabled on the Cisco router, enter the following commands to connect to the SSH service on the router:

```
Syntax:      ssh -l userid -c <des | 3des> -p <port number>
IP.Address/hostname
Example:     ssh -l <username> -c 3des <router.ip.address>
```

In addition to providing SSH access to a router, Cisco IOS provides terminal-line access with SSH, which allows SSH access to non-SSH routers that have a console or serial-port connection to an SSH-enabled router. A simple terminal-line access configuration is illustrated in Figure 5.1.

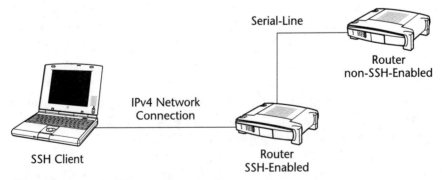

Figure 5.1 Terminal-line access.

To set up terminal-line SSH access, each line must be configured with its own rotary, and SSH must be configured to use SSH when accessing the other devices. The following steps walk you through this process.

1. Each line must be configured on the SSH-enabled router. Note that the line number refers to the port number on the remote SSH server. For example, line number 1 equates to port 2001, line number 2 equates to port 2002, and line number 3 equates to port 2003. The following syntax shows the router commands to enter a line number for SSH.

   ```
   Syntax:      Router(config)# line <line-number ending-line-number>
   Example:     Router(config)# line 1 200
   ```

2. Disable the EXEC process of each line using the following syntax:

   ```
   Router(config)# no exec
   ```

3. Define the login authentication option, which must be username/password, with the following syntax:

   ```
   Syntax:      Router(config)# login authentication <listname>
   Example:     Router(config)# login authentication default
   ```

4. Define a group of lines that will be used when SSH is enabled using the following syntax:

   ```
   Syntax:      Router(config)# rotary <group>
   Example:     Router(config)# rotary 1
   ```

5. Define the use of SSH on the line using the transport input command, as listed:

   ```
   Router(config)# transport input ssh
   ```

6. Configure SSH for the TTY lines, the port number to connect to, and the rotary group using the following syntax:

   ```
   Syntax:      Router(config)# ip ssh port <portnumber> rotary <group>
   Example:     Router(config)# ip ssh port 2001 rotary 1
   ```

7. SSH terminal-line access should now be configured! Any SSH client connection to the SSH-enabled router on port 2001 should be given access to the non-SSH enabled router via the serial-line or console to the SSH-enabled router.

Once SSH has been enabled on the Cisco router, enter the following commands to connect to the remote router via the serial-line:

```
ssh -c 3des -p 2001 <router.ip.address>
```

Cisco Switches

Cisco Catalyst Operating System (CatOS) started to support the use of SSH from version 6.1. Since then, CatOS 6.1 and up has supported SSH version 1 only. While the use of SSH version 1 still has its insecurities, the replacement of Telnet on Cisco devices has added a tremendous amount of security to the network device. SSH is supported on the following Cisco switches: Catalyst 3550, 4000, 5000, 6000, 8540, and 8510.

To use SSH on Cisco routers, complete the following steps.

1. Download the correct CatOS to the switch. Make sure you are downloading a CatOS version that holds SSH support. Cisco SSH servers require the IPSec (DES or 3DES) encryption software image from CatOS 6.1.

2. Generate the RSA Key with the following command:

   ```
   Cat6509> (enable) set crypto key rsa 1024
   ```

3. Restrict SSH to authorized host/subnets with the following commands:

   ```
   Cat6509> set ip permit 172.16.1.0 255.255.255.0
   ```

4. After the key hash has been made, enable SSH with the following command:

   ```
   Cat6509> (enable) set ip permit enable ssh
   ```

5. Once SSH has been enabled on the Catalyst switch, enter the following command to connect to the SSH services on the switch:

   ```
   ssh -c 3des -v <switch ip address>
   ```

Cisco VPN Concentrator

Cisco's VPN device, the VPN concentrator, comes with SSH operability out-of-the-box. There is no need to load software on the VPN concentrator similar to the routers and the switches. To view the SSH options on the concentrator, browse to your VPN device with any Web browser, preferably over SSL. If SSL is not enabled, consider consoling into the VPN device, but do not use clear-text protocols such as HTTP over insecure networks such as the Internet. Once you have authenticated to the Configuration screen, browse to System ⇨ Management Protocols ⇨ SSH. You should see a configuration screen similar to Figure 5.2.

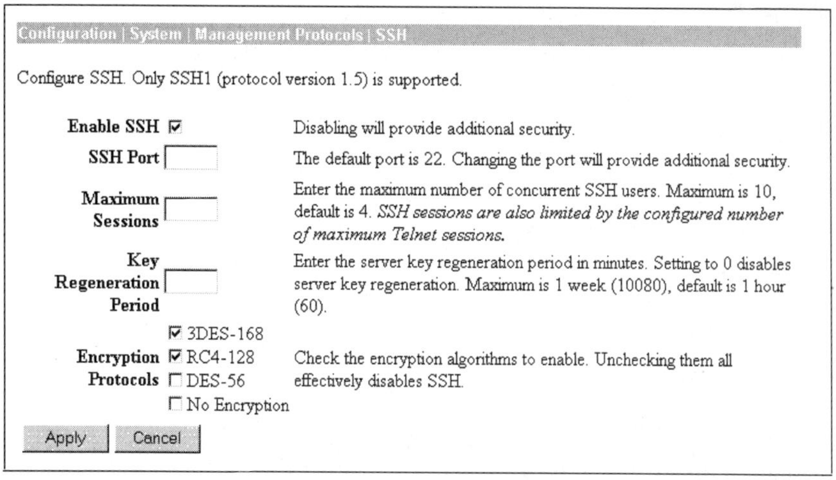

Figure 5.2   The SSH configuration screen of the Cisco VPN concentrator.

Table 5.1 lists and describes the various SSH configuration options available on the configuration screen.

Table 5.1   VPN Concentrator SSH Configuration Options

OPTION	DESCRIPTION
Enable SSH	To enable, simply click on Enable SSH checkbox. This box should be enabled by default.
SSH Port	Determines the port the SSH service should listen on. The default port is 22; however, any port can be set.
Maximum Sessions	Determines the number of simultaneous connections that are allowed. The number can range from 1 to 10, with the default setting to 4.
Key Regeneration Period	Sets the time interval to regenerate the key, specified in minutes. The range can be between 0, which disables key regeneration, and 10080, which is up to one week. The default setting is 60 minutes.
Encryption Protocols	Specifies which algorithms should be used to negotiate the SSH session between the clients and the VPN concentrator. Possible options are 3DES-168-bit key, RC4-128-bit key, DES-56-bit key, and No entry. Unselecting all options disables SSH, and choosing No Entry provides no encryption whatsoever. As best practices, select 3DES-168-bit key and RC4-128-bit key.

After the SSH options have been set, select the Apply button to apply the settings. SSH should now be enabled on the VPN concentrator on port 22 with the following settings:

- SSH Port—22
- Maximum Sessions—4
- Key Regeneration Period—45
- Encryption Protocols—3DES-168 and RC4-128

Cisco PIX Firewalls

Cisco PIX firewalls started to support the use of SSH from version 5.2. Since then, PIX versions 5.2 and above have supported SSH version 1 only. While the use of SSH version 1 still has its insecurities, the replacement of Telnet on Cisco firewalls has added a tremendous amount of security to the network device.

To use SSH on Cisco firewalls, complete the following steps:

1. Download the correct PIX version to the firewall. Make sure you are downloading a PIX version that holds SSH support. Cisco SSH servers require IPSec (DES or 3DES) encryption software image from version 5.2.

2. Make sure a hostname and host domain have been configured for the router. These are not SSH commands but are required in order to use SSH. The following information needs to be entered:

   ```
   Syntax:      PiX# hostname <hostname>
   Example:     PiX# hostname PiX-Firewall

   Syntax:      PiX# domain-name <domainname>
   Example:     PiX# domain-name Aum.com
   ```

3. Generate an RSA key pair for the firewall and save it with the following commands:

   ```
   PiX# ca generate rsa key 1024
   PiX# CA save all
   ```

4. Select the interface on the firewall to use SSH. Most likely, this will be the internal interface. The internal interface is called inside with an RFC 1918 address, as shown with the following syntax:

   ```
   PiX# ssh 172.16.1.1 255.255.255.255 inside
   ```

5. Set the authentication timeout for SSH. The maximum timeout cannot exceed 120 seconds, which is also the default; however, once the session

is established, the VTY timeout setting applies, not the SSH timeout setting. The following syntax sets the firewall's timeout session for SSH:

```
PiX# ssh timeout 60
```

6. Lastly, set the password for the firewall using the following syntax:

```
PiX# passwd superhardpasswordforl33th4x0rs
```

Once SSH has been enabled on the PIX firewall, enter the following command to connect to the SSH services on the firewall, assuming pix is the username:

```
ssh -c 3des -l pix -v <ip.address.of.pix>
```

Network Appliance Filers

Network Appliance (NetApp) storage filers provide a data repository to store data, either for backup purposes or for file-server purposes. The filer can contain data for each employee and allow access to a specified set of folders and directories, controlled by CIFS/NFS or NTFS/Unix access permissions.

Traditionally, NetApp filers use RSH, Telnet, HTTP, or even Rlogin (discussed further in Chapter 8) to access the filer for management or configuration purposes. While this access may be conducted in an internal network, several unauthorized users may have access to this segment, such as contractors, consultants, and remote VPN users, who could capture the RSH session and log in to the filer themselves. One of the key problems with this situation is that after an unauthorized user has gained access to a NetApp filer, he or she may have access to all data on the NetApp filer, not just a subset of the data.

The use of poor protocols such as RSH, Rlogin, HTTP, and Telnet can virtually negate the use of strong NTFS or NFS permission on the filer, since a possible attacker could attack the management protocol of the filer, such as RSH, to give himself access to data instead of taking the more difficult route of attacking the NTFS or NFS permission for each users.

This management issue is a common mistake in many networks where administrators deploy strong security on a backup device such as a filer to protect propriety and confidential information, but then use the weakest protocols to manage the device. From the attacker's perspective, if the choices of attack vectors are to either sniff a Telnet/RSH session over the network and gain access to an admin-level username/password or to attack the filer and break the access permissions, the sniffing attack vector is not only a lot easier but has a higher probability for success. In this situation, the attacker would always choose to attack the management method to gain access to data.

To support a higher level of security, it is important to maintain the level of security on a network or on a device with the management methods also. For example, if a NetApp filer holds the strongest level of CIFS and NTFS security, be sure to use SSH on the filer also, since it will uphold the level of security required for the device. To mitigate this issue and similar issues, NetApp has created a module to support encrypted management for its Data ONTAP software. The module that supports SSH is called SecureAdmin.

NetApp's SecureAdmin module supports SSH 1.x for command-line management. Using SecureAdmin, a remote administrator is authenticated with a username/password combination on the filer. After authentication, the session is initialized on the filer, and host-based authentication is accomplished through RSA public keys. The SSH 1.x daemon is executed with Java and RSA libraries. Supported encryption algorithms are DES and 3DES, with a key-bit range from 384 to 1024.

To set up SecureAdmin SSH on your NetApp filer, log in to the filer and gain access to a valid shell. After getting access to a shell, complete the following steps.

1. To configure the SSH server, enter the following command. This will configure SSH and allow the administrator to set the key strength for the RSA key, ranging from 384 bits to 1024 bits.

    ```
    secureadmin setup -f ssh
    ```

2. To enable SSH, enter the following command. This is a persistent command, so there is no need to re-enter the command after the server is rebooted.

    ```
    secureadmin enable ssh
    ```

3. To disable SSH, enter the following command. This is a persistent command, so there is no need to re-enter the command after the server is rebooted.

    ```
    secureadmin disable ssh
    ```

4. To show the status of the SSH session on SecureAdmin, enter the following command. This will show the current status of all SSH servers.

    ```
    secureadmin status
    ```

Secure Management

Secure management is essential for an organization to meet an acceptable level of security. While the devices mentioned previously support SSH, not all devices in a network environment will support the use of SSH. For that reason, you should examine some alternative management methods with SSH, using other network-security tools to mitigate vulnerabilities introduced by not using SSH. The five topics of discussion are as follows:

- Management servers
- Two-factor authentication
- SOCKS management
- SSH—User Restrictions
- SSH—Network Access Controls

Management Servers

Management servers are a fairly new idea in network management that is slowly growing to be a standard in many networks. The use of a management server is the restriction of management access to several systems/devices from one or two management servers only, which are accessible throughout the organization. The idea is to limit the broad management-level access to sensitive servers, such as database servers, from the entire organization and allow a set number of IP addresses, which would be management servers. Furthermore, the idea is to encrypt or secure the connection to these sensitive servers as much as possible.

From the preceding discussion, you know that SSH can be used for management on many network devices; however, what happens if SSH is not available on certain management devices? Is the right solution to use Telnet, thus lowering the security model of the network, or to allow only console access, which adds an incredible amount of overhead to managing the system?

A good architecture management model is to deploy two to four management servers throughout the network. These systems can be any flavor of Unix or Windows, as long as they are extremely secure. In fact, no services should be listening on these management servers, and some type of host-based firewall should be deployed. Install SSH on the management servers, and require the use of both passwords and public keys for authentication. Restrict access to sensitive systems/devices on the network by allowing only the management servers to have access. For example, if Web servers and database servers were considered sensitive and on the 192.168.1.0 network segment, and if the internal network were on the 172.16.1.0 network segment, access would have to be blocked from every server on the 172.16.1.0 network segment to the 192.168.1.0 network segment. Furthermore, access would have to be permitted to the 192.168.1.0 segment from the management servers that have been deployed in the internal network. Figure 5.3 describes this architecture.

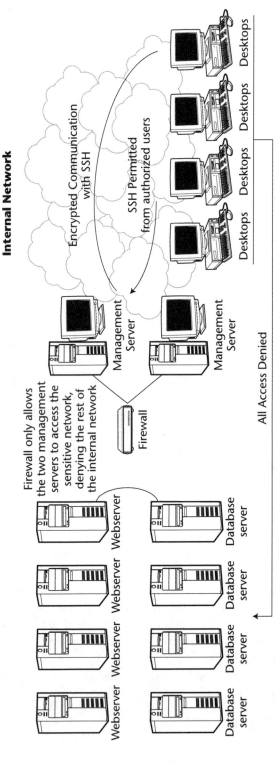

Figure 5.3   Secure administration with management servers.

Two-Factor Authentication

A very good security practice is to use two-factor authentication, which is the process of using two methods for authentication for a given entity. Two-factor authentication provides an extra level of security in the case that a single method of authentication such as a password is compromised. If a password is compromised, an additional method of authentication is still required in order to gain access to the entity. Also, since many passwords are very poor and can be compromised with a variety of attacks, the use of two-factor authentication mitigates many problems with using passwords.

SSH fully supports the use of two-factor authentication in any type of environment. While SSH can support two-factor authentication in a variety of ways, concentrate now on deploying two-factor authentication with the use of passwords and public-key files. As discussed in Chapter 4, public keys can be generated on a per-user basis and used for authentication. In addition to providing the current key for authentication, a username/password combination may be required on the remote SSH server. Therefore, once the user has authenticated to the SSH server with his/her public key, he or she is prompted for a password on the SSH server that correlates to the username that he/she is attempting to log in with. This model enforces two-factor authentication by requiring both public keys and passwords.

While the use of SSH on many network devices, described in the first half of this chapter, is a great practice for device management, several SSH installations do not support two-factor SSH authentication but just require an SSH username and SSH password to log in. While the session is still encrypted, the loss of an SSH password may leave the network device vulnerable. For example, in many network environments passwords are shared between accounts. A user may have an SSH password that is used to log in to the Cisco router, but may also use the same password to FTP files back and forth to the FTP server in the internal network. While the SSH session would be fully encrypted, the FTP session would not be. If the FTP session were sniffed by an unauthorized employee, the FTP password could be obtained and then attempted on the SSH service on the router. If the user had used the same password, the router would now be compromised, despite the use of SSH.

The use of management servers with two-factor authentication can mitigate this vulnerability. The use of management servers would already prevent direct access to the router by stopping the unauthorized employee from directly accessing the SSH-enabled router. Furthermore, if the management server were enforcing two-factor authentication and a user's FTP password is the same as his or her SSH password, which had been compromised, access to the router would still be prevented, since the unauthorized employee would not have the correct public key file to access the management server. The SSH management server would recognize the correct password for the specific account but would then reject the session, since the user would not be able to provide the correct public key that correlates to the account being accessed. Figure 5.4 shows how two-factor authentication can provide an added layer of security with SSH management servers.

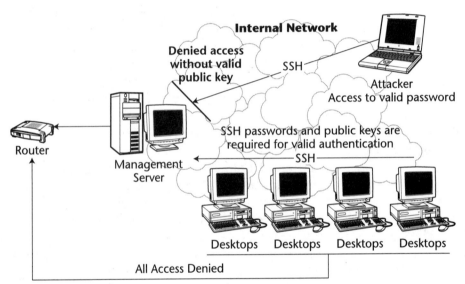

Figure 5.4   Two-factor authentication with SSH management servers.

SOCKS Management

SOCKS is an Internet Engineering Task Force (IETF) standard used as a generic proxy protocol for TCP/IP applications. SOCKS servers provide the ability to accept requests from SOCKS clients and forward them to the appropriate application server on behalf of the SOCKS client. The primary purpose of the protocol is to enable nodes on one side of the SOCKS server to gain access to hosts on the other side of the SOCKS server, allowing direct access from the SOCKS clients to the application server.

In the example configuration in Figures 5.3 and 5.4, you examined a method of using SSH and firewall rules to allow secure access to remote machines. SOCKS uses a similar configuration; however, with the use of a SOCKS server, the transitions between the clients on the right and the sensitive servers on the left is more streamlined and less cumbersome than in the configurations in the previous examples. In the architectural example with the management server and two-factor authentication, a client first needs to authenticate to the SSH server and gain a shell or command prompt on that device. After the shell/command prompt has been attained, the client needs to make another connection to the desired sensitive server in order to manage it. While this process is straightforward and relatively easy, the use of a SOCKS proxy server could cut the process in half by requiring only a connection from the client to the SOCKS server. The SOCKS server would then be authorized to forward that connection to the desired device and return the shell/command prompt to the client. Figure 5.5 shows architecture similar to that in Figures 5.3 and 5.4 but with a SOCKS implementation. Notice that the architecture is very similar, if not the same, but that access for the end-user is limited to one-step instead of two or three steps for architecture in Figures 5.3 or 5.4.

There are two current installations of SOCKS: version 4 and version 5. Most SSH clients support both versions. If a SOCKS server has been deployed in a network environment, using any SSH client such as SecureCRT is very simple. (For more detail about SSH and SOCKS, see Chapter 9.) See Figure 5.6 for SecureCRT SOCKS setup.

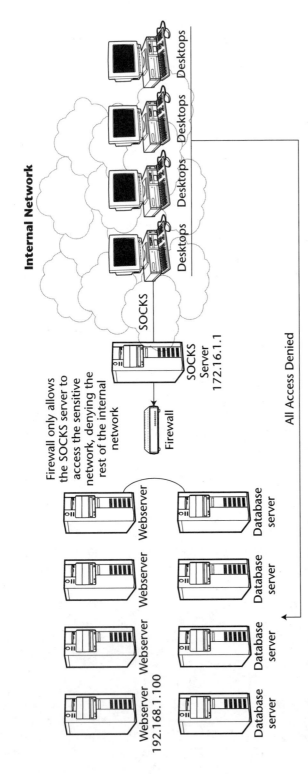

Figure 5.5 A sample SOCKS implementation.

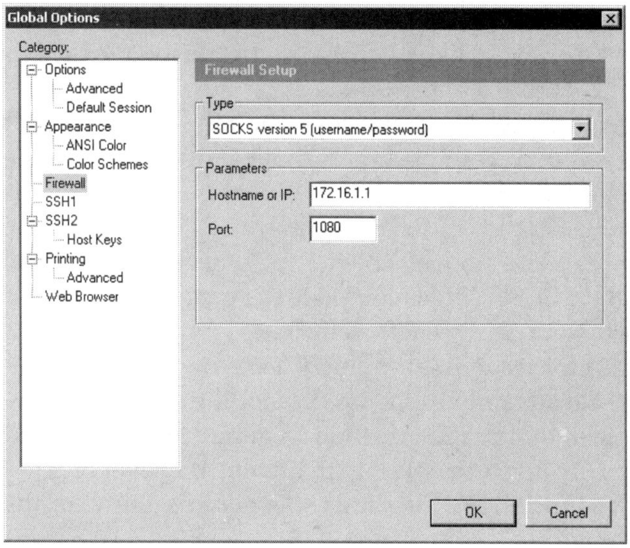

Figure 5.6 SecureCRT SOCKS configuration.

As shown in Figure 5.6, an SSH client needs to be configured in order to communicate with the SOCKS proxy (namely, 172.16.1.1, from Figure 5.5). The parameters to enter are quite simple, such as Hostname and/or IP address and the port number with which to connect to the SOCKS server. After the appropriate SOCKS server has been selected in the Type drop-down box—in this case, SOCKS version 5 (username/password)—select OK. To enable Secure-CRT to use the SOCKS server, select the "Use firewall to connect" checkbox from the Quick Connect menu. This will enable SecureCRT to use the SOCKS firewall settings that were just configured. Figure 5.7 shows the specific configuration.

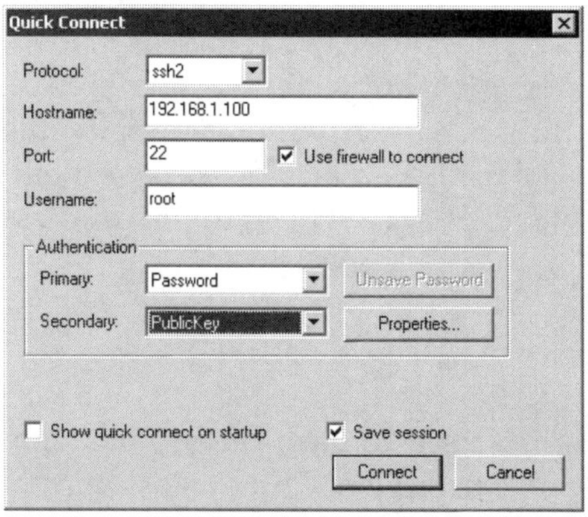

Figure 5.7 SecureCRT client using SOCKS firewall setting.

Notice that not only is the "Use firewall to connect" option selected; the hostname of the real server you would like to access, in the Hostname field, is selected as well. Referring to Figure 5.5, the desktops on the right-hand side are the machines using the SecureCRT application. The SOCKSv5 server is 172.16.1.1, which has been set up in your SecureCRT global option menu (see Figure 5.6). Lastly, when an SSH session on the Web server, which is 192.168.1.100, is desired, the SecureCRT SSH client would connect to the SOCKS server first, using the "Use firewall to connect" checkbox shown in Figure 5.7, and then have the SOCKS server complete the connection on your behalf and return the shell to your SecureCRT client.

The use of SOCKS and SSH for secure-management access reduces the number of authentication steps and streamlines the process for the end-user; however, the level of security and authentication methods required are not reduced or affected in any way. This architecture not only maintains the level of security described in Figures 5.3 and 5.4, but also adds a level of usability for the end-user.

SSH: User Restrictions

Although managing SSH on remote devices and systems is important for secure access, you might not want to allow full management access to each employee who needs to manage another device and/or system. For example, for a given system, a variety of users may need SSH access to the system, including backup operators, system administrators, and application developers. Also, if management servers are being used, even more employees may need access to the system, including network administrators, router/switch administrators, and firewall administrators. Adding all the personnel in these groups may make the SSH user base for a given device or system well over 10 percent of the user population—and possibly more, depending on the size of the organization. The fact that 10 percent of the user population needs to access an SSH management server is not an issue; however, if there is a possibility of limiting the backup administrator to backup activities, the firewall administrator to the firewall, and the router/switch administrator to the routers and switches, system security can be further escalated. The best methods to implement this type of security with SSH are SSH Chroot, user access controls, and user restrictions.

Chroot

Chroot is a Unix-only system call that restricts users to files, folders, and binaries only in a specified directory. The best way to think of Chroot is as a virtual sandbox, often called a chroot jail, where an application or user may operate.

The SSH application/process can be chrooted to prevent SSH users from breaking out of an SFTP specific directory, such as a firewall-management directory. Furthermore, the specific SSH users can be chrooted, limiting the SSH shell to a specific directory also. To chroot an SSH user using SSH Communications' Unix SSH server, complete the following steps.

1. Open the sshd2_config file in /etc/ssh2.

2. Edit the ChRootUsers line by uncommenting it (remove the # symbol) and adding all the SSH users that will need a chroot shell. The following is an example:

   ```
   ChrootUsers          SSHUser1,SSHUser2,kusum,rohan,shreya
   ```

3. If necessary, edit the ChRootGroups line by uncommenting it and adding all the groups that will need a chroot shell. The following is an example:

   ```
   ChrootGroups         FirewallAdmins,BackupAdmins,RouterAdmins
   ```

4. Uncomment the sftp-server subsystem entry, which allows SSH to initialize internal sftp-server. The following is an example:

   ```
   Subsystem-sftp       internal://sftp-server
   ```

5. Edit the /etc/passwd file, changing the SSH users shells to /bin/ssh-dummy-shell. The following is an example:

   ```
   SSHUser1:x:500:10:SSHUser1:/home/SSHuser1:/bin/ssh-dummy-shell
   SSHUser2:x:500:10:SSHUser2:/home/SSHuser2:/bin/ssh-dummy-shell
   Kusum:x:500:10:Kusum:/home/Kusum:/bin/ssh-dummy-shell
   Shreya:x:500:10:Shreya:/home/Shreya:/bin/ssh-dummy-shell
   Rohan:x:500:10:Rohan:/home/Rohan:/bin/ssh-dummy-shell
   ```

6. Restart the SSH2 daemon.

User Access Controls

User access controls are available on VanDyke Software's VShell SSH server. Unlike Chroot, user access controls are a simple access-control list applied to the specified users that attempt to access SSH services. They are not a type of jail; they limit the type of access the user or group will be able to perform. To view the User Access Control screen in VShell SSH server, complete the following steps:

1. Select Start ⇨ Programs ⇨ VShell ⇨ VShell.

2. Highlight the Access Controls section on the left-hand pane.

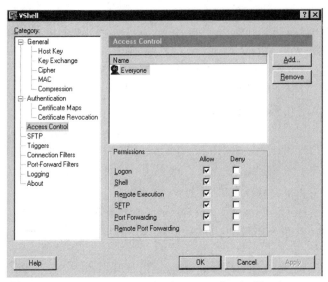

Figure 5.8   User Access Control screen of VShell's SSH server.

The VShell User Access Control screen (see Figure 5.8) shows two separate sections: the Name section and the Permissions section. The Name section is the section where the user names the operating system that needs to be set. The Permissions section sets the different types of permission that will be allowed to each user, including Logon, Shell, Remote Execution, SFTP, Port Forwarding, and Remote Port Forwarding.

Let's say you want to grant access to the SSH server for the Backup group, to back up files on the SSH server. The Backup group is called Backup Operators and will need SFTP access but will not need shell access to the SSH server (as shown in Figure 5.9). Complete the following steps to add the appropriate connection filters:

1. Select the Add button.

2. Scroll down on the Windows Select User or Group menu and choose the Backup Operations group.

3. Select the checkbox in the Allow column for the SFTP row.

4. Select the checkbox in the Allow column for the Remote Execution row.

5. Select the checkbox in the Deny column for the Shell row.

6. Now the Backup Operators group has full SFTP access to the SSH server but does not have shell access to the server.

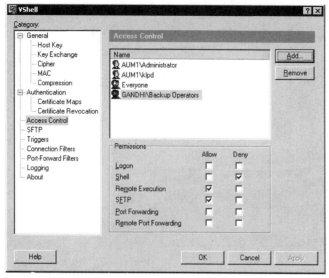

Figure 5.9   Access control permission for the Backup Operators group.

SSH User Restrictions

User restrictions are available with SSH Communications' Windows SSH server. SSH user restrictions are very similar to VShell's user access controls. Both are simple access-control lists applied to the usernames on the SSH server. To view the User Restrictions screen in SSH Communications' SSH server, complete the following steps:

1. Select Start ⇨ Programs ⇨ SSH Secure Shell Server ⇨ Configuration.

2. Highlight the User Restrictions section.

The SSH Communications' User Restrictions screen (see Figure 5.10) shows two separate sections, the Allow login for users and the Deny login for users.

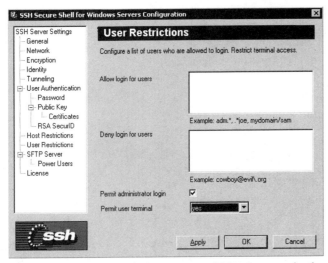

Figure 5.10   Host Restrictions screen of SSH Communications' SSH.

Let's say you want to grant access to the SSH server for the Backup Operator account, known as BackupAdmin, to back up files on the SSH server. The backup operator will need SFTP access but will not need shell access to the SSH server. Also, besides allowing access to the Backup Operator account, you want to make sure the backup operator does not use a personal account to log in to the SSH server, which is called Sudhanshu. Complete the following steps to add the appropriate connection filters:

1. Move the mouse inside of the Allow login from hosts.

2. Type **BackupAdmin**.

3. Move the mouse inside of the Deny login from hosts.

4. Type **Sudhanshu**.

5. Select the no option for the Permit User Terminal option.

6. Select Apply.

7. Now the Backup Operator account is allowed to make an SFTP connection to the SSH server, but is not permitted to use the SSH terminal session. Also, the backup operator's personal account, Sudhanshu, is fully restricted.

Note the use of patterns in Figure 5.11. For example, to permit any user with admin in front of his or her username, such as adminSANFRAN, the following syntax can be used: admin.*. Furthermore, to deny any user with test in front of his or her username, such as test1234, test.* can be used as a pattern-matching utility.

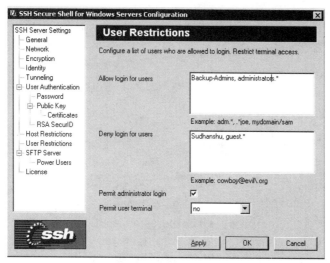

Figure 5.11   The new set of user restrictions.

SSH: Network Access Controls

Installing an SSH management server adds tremendous flexibility and security to any network environment. The use of SOCKS and Chroot helps further streamline and secure management access to sensitive servers and devices. Another method to help secure the SSH management server is the use of TCP wrappers on Unix SSH servers and connection filters on Windows SSH servers.

SSH TCP wrappers

TCP Wrappers is a Unix utility that permits or denies network access to a particular port to a specified set of IP addresses. TCP wrappers functions by replacing the network service with the TCP wrapper service before the communication can be completed. The IP addresses for TCP wrappers are located in the hosts.allow and hosts.deny. For example, before any IP address can connect to a particular service/port on a system using TCP wrappers, the TCP wrappers utility first checks to see if the requesting IP address is approved to access the service/port. If TCP wrappers deems that the IP address is allowed, by checking the hosts.allow and hosts.deny files, the requesting IP address is allowed to continue to access the service and port. Note that even though the IP address is allowed to access the service/port, the IP address will still need to carry out any authentication requirements for the service. Figure 5.12 shows the TCP-wrappers process.

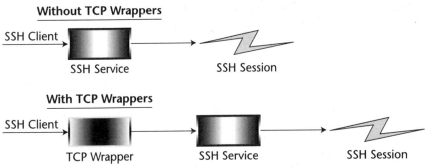

Figure 5.12   TCP wrappers with SSH.

A good way to think of TCP wrappers is simply as a set of access-control lists applied to specific TCP ports on a Unix operating system. For example, once an SSH management server is set up to administer sensitive servers and/or devices, there may be a need to secure the access to the SSH server to only the firewall admin group's subnet, or the backup operator's subnet, or any machine located in the management network. Furthermore, if the admin-level subnets or IP addresses are known on a network, there is no limitation or reason not to place TCP wrappers on SSH servers. TCP wrappers will prevent unauthorized internal and external employees from simple brute-force SSH attacks by complexly eliminating any possibility of the unauthorized IP addresses to connect to the SSH management server.

The SSH application/process can use TCP wrappers to prevent unautho-rized users from connecting to the SSH server, while permitting valid groups, such as firewall-management groups. To use TCP wrappers on an SSH server using SSH Communications' Unix SSH server, complete the following steps:

1. Change directories to your SSH2 configuration folder using the follow-ing syntax:

   ```
   #cd /usr/local/bin/ssh-3.2.3
   ```

2. Configure and make the SSH server with the libwrap binary using the following syntax:

   ```
   #./configure -with-libwrap
   #make
   #make install
   ```

3. Once the SSH server has compiled correctly, change directories to the /etc directory using the following syntax:

   ```
   #cd /etc
   ```

4. Edit the two TCP wrapper files, called hosts.allow and hosts.deny. The TCP wrappers daemon always reads IP addresses or hostnames in hosts.allow first. If it sees a match in hosts.allow, it will permit the IP address or hostname. If it does not see a match in hosts.allow, it will read the hosts.deny. This being the case, you want to put a "deny all rules" in hosts.deny. If neither the hosts.allow nor hosts.deny file contains information, all IP addresses and hostnames will be allowed. The following is the format required for the hosts.allow and hosts.deny files, as well as examples of each:

```
Format     .    daemon : IP.address or hostname
Hosts.allow
sshd2: 10.1.0.

Hosts.deny
sshd2:ALL
```

5. The hosts.allow file would allow access to any IP address coming from 10.1.0.0 to 10.1.0.254. The hosts.deny file would deny access to every other IP address.

SSH Connection Filters

Connection filters are available with VanDyke Software's VShell SSH server. Unlike Unix TCP wrappers, connection filters are a simple access-control list applied to the TCP/IP interface that the SSH service is listening on. It is not a separate process, nor does it in any way intercept the SSH client request; rather, it accepts or rejects SSH connections based on the source IP address located in the TCP header of an IP packet. To view the Connection Filters screen in the VShell SSH server, complete the following steps:

1. Select Start ➪ Programs ➪ VShell ➪ VShell.

2. Highlight the Connection Filters section.

The VShell Connection Filters screen (see Figure 5.13) shows two separate sections: the Filter entries section and the Test filter section. The Filter entries section is where the filters would actually be set. Notice the default filter to allow access to all IP addresses, denoted by 0.0.0.0/0.0.0.0. The Test filter section tests the connection to any IP address specified.

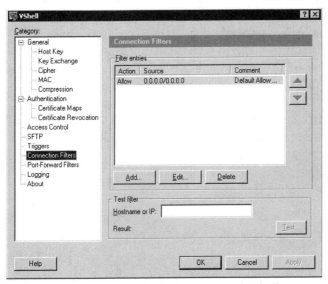

Figure 5.13 The Connection Filters screen of VShell's SSH server.

Let's say you want to deny access to the SSH server from the users' network (172.16.1.0/24) but permit access to the SSH server from the management network (10.1.0.0/24). Complete the following steps to add the appropriate connection filters:

1. Select the Add button.

2. Select Netmask for the Filter type.

3. Enter **172.16.1.0** for the Network.

4. Enter **255.255.255.0** for the Mask.

5. Enter **Users' network** for the comment.

6. Select the Deny radio button under the Action section on the left side.

7. Select OK.

8. Select the Add button.

9. Select Netmask for the Filter type.

10. Enter **10.1.0.0** for the Network.

11. Enter **255.255.255.0** for the Mask.

12. Enter **Management network** for the comment.

13. Select the Allow radio button under the Action section on the left side.

14. Select OK.

15. Highlight the default filter, Allow 0.0.0.0/0.0.0.0, which allows all IP addresses to connect, and move the filter to the bottom using the downward arrow key on the right-hand side. The filters are read from top to bottom. When a client attempts to connect, the top filter will be read first. If a match is identified, the other filters are not read and the matched filter is executed. When placing several filters on the VShell SSH server, it is probably good practice to make a final Deny filter that denies any IP address that does not match any of the filters before it.

You're done. Now any IP address on the 172.16.1.0/24 network will be restricted, and all addresses on the 10.1.0.0/24 network will be permitted (as shown in Figure 5.14).

SSH Host Restrictions

Host restrictions are available with SSH Communications' Windows SSH server. SSH host restrictions are very similar to VShell's connection filters. Both are a simple access-control list applied to the TCP/IP interface on which the SSH service is listening. To view the Host Restrictions screen in SSH Communications' SSH server, complete the following steps:

1. Select Start ⇨ Programs ⇨ SSH Secure Shell Server ⇨ Configuration.

2. Highlight the Host Restrictions section.

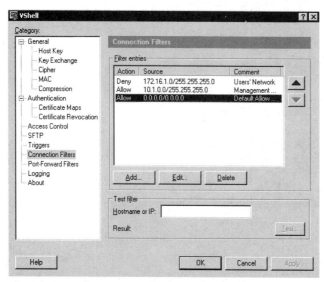

Figure 5.14 The new set of access filters.

The SSH Communications' Host Restrictions screen (see Figure 5.15) shows two separate sections: the Allow login from hosts and the Deny login from hosts.

Let's say you want to deny access to the SSH server from the users' network (172.16.1.0/24), but permit access to the SSH server from the management network (10.1.0.0/24). Both Allow and Deny fields use special syntax, denoted with the \ symbol, to include variables, so each IP address does not need to be entered. Complete the following steps to add the appropriate connection filters:

1. Move the mouse inside the Allow login from hosts.

2. Type **10\.1\.0\..***.

3. Move the mouse inside the Deny login from hosts.

4. Type 172\.16\.1\..

5. Select Apply.

You're done. Now any IP address on the 172.16.1.0/24 network will be restricted and all addresses on the 10.1.0.0/24 network will be permitted (as shown in Figure 5.16).

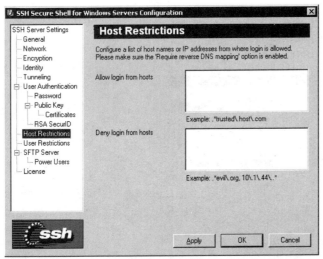

Figure 5.15 The Host Restrictions screen of SSH Communications' SSH server.

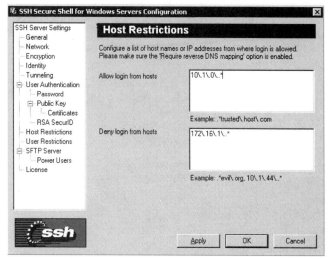

Figure 5.16 The new set of host restrictions.

Summary

In this chapter, I introduce several options that SSH can provide to deploy and maintain secure-management processes and procedures. Management methods are often targeted by attackers as an attack vector, creating a false sense of security for many administrators who overlook management processes and procedures.

Secure management involves sure-management networks, but also secure management services on devices. I cover the use of SSH services in atypical environments such as network devices/network hardware. Various types of devices, including routers, switches, load balancers, storage appliances, VPN servers, and firewalls, can provide SSH services on their respective network hardware, eliminating the need for insecure protocols such as Telnet and greatly improving the management of these devices. For example, a VPN server that controls access to the internal network for external users and is managed remotely with HTTP or Telnet negates many of the security issues of the VPN server itself (encryption). Furthermore, storage devices that hold and protect critical company data may use a clear-text protocol for management, making admin-level access to the machine more vulnerable.

This chapter demonstrates how SSH can secure both network devices and management methods with the use of native SSH services on network devices and the integration of SSH with other operating-system tools such as Chroot and TCP Wrappers. The next chapter covers port forwarding and how an SSH can be utilized as a remote-access solution rather than just a secure-management solution. The next chapter expounds upon the definition of SSH and how it can be utilized in so many ways.

Remote Access
Solutions

SSH Port Forwarding

We have discussed several features, utilities, and benefits that SSH provides with a single service or subsystem, but one of the most useful and powerful features is port forwarding. Since port forwarding is such a strong feature of SSH, two chapters are dedicated to it. This chapter addresses the basics of port forwarding, such as what it is, how to set it up, and some of its basic requirements. The next chapter discusses the advanced usages of port forwarding and how to use it in network architecture in order to optimize it.

Port forwarding is the ability of an SSH client to connect to an SSH server and then forward other ports within the established SSH connection. Port forwarding is also referred to as SSH tunneling, where alternative TCP traffic is sent over an encrypted SSH tunnel. The great part about port forwarding is that it requires few to no changes on the SSH server, besides being enabled, and it is fully functional on most default SSH2 installations.

For example, if an SSH connection is established between an SSH server and an SSH client, another protocol/port, such as IMAP (port 143), could be tunneled within the SSH connection over port 22. Since port forwarding uses only the existing SSH tunneling for communication, usually on port 22, only one firewall rule is required to permit an unlimited number of ports to be tunneled through the existing SSH session. SSH port forwarding not only requires fewer firewall rules, which reduces the required number of ports allowed into the internal network; it allows several insecure protocols to be secured, such as mail (IMAP, POP3, and SMTP), file transfer (SMB, FTP, CIFS, and NFS), and management (Telnet, VNC, and pcAnywhere). Figure 6.1 shows an example of the tunneling process.

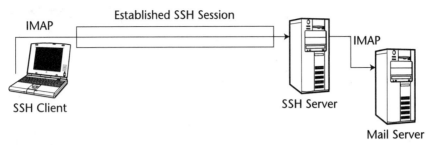

Figure 6.1   An established SSH connection with the IMAP protocol tunneled.

Before discussing port forwarding, let's examine two of the three types of port forwarding: local and remote, also referred to as outgoing and incoming, respectively.

NOTE Dynamic port forwarding is discussed in Chapter 9, under the "Dynamic Port Forwarding and SOCKS" section.

Local port forwarding is when an SSH client makes any type of connection to a local port on its localhost, presumably the loopback interface (127.0.0.1), and the connection is tunneled outbound through the established SSH connection to another computer (either the SSH server or a computer that the SSH server can make a connection to).

Remote port forwarding does the opposite of local port forwarding. It forwards communication coming from a remote port on a remote server, such as the SSH server, to a local port on the SSH client (or a machine that the SSH client has access to).

A good example of local port forwarding is the use of internal Web intranet pages. Let's say that business travelers need to access the internal intranet page at least three times a day. The business travelers are usually connecting from inside customer networks and/or hotel dial-up connections. The use of a VPN device does not satisfy the business travelers' needs. IPSec VPNs cannot traverse firewall devices over Network Address Translation (NAT). Furthermore, remote access is required from other customer networks and hotel environments, where networking configuration will always be an unknown. Let's say the corporate network contains only three servers and an unlimited number of business travelers. The network contains a firewall, protecting the perimeter of the network; an SSH server, for established SSH connections; and an internal intranet Web server, which holds the intranet Web page. The following five simple steps are the only ones required in order to allow business travelers secure access to the intranet from all different types of networks:

1. Install an SSH server listening on port 22.

2. Install a single rule on the firewall that allows connections on port 22 to reach the SSH server.

3. Set up the SSH client to locally port forward port 80 to the intranet Web server when a connection has been requested on its lookback interface (127.0.0.1).

4. Connect to the SSH server with the SSH client, with the port-forward rules enabled.

5. Open a Web browser and enter the lookback IP address (127.0.0.1); the intranet Web site should be displayed.

Figure 6.2 shows the example architecture.

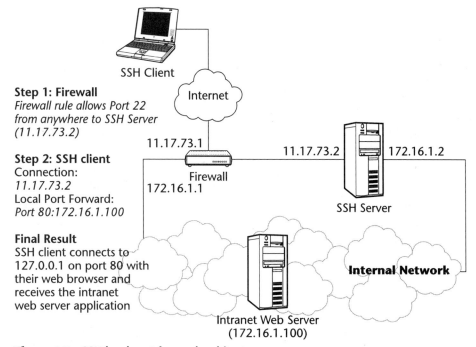

Figure 6.2   SSH local port-forward architecture.

A good example of remote port forwarding is the use of public FTP servers. Although using FTP and port forwarding is a very tricky procedure, due to the use of active FTP, it still can be done. Let's say that both internal employees and external customers need to get files from an organization's public FTP server. While the FTP server contains public information for the customers to download, it also contains private information for employees to use. The network contains an FTP server, an SSH server, and an unlimited number of employees and customers who need to access the FTP server. The use of SFTP is a good alternative by the organization, but the organization does not want to make its customers use SFTP, since SFTP clients do not come on most operating systems by default (it would be really nice if they did). The only requirement is that internal employees cannot use clear-text protocols to access sensitive company information. To prevent the private information from being sent over the Internet in clear-text, a remote port-forwarding session can be set up. The following five simple steps are the only ones required in order to allow customers to download information with FTP as well as to allow internal users to download information with the use of encryption (shown in Figure 6.3):

1. Install an SSH server that listens on port 22.

2. Install an SSH client on the FTP server.

3. Set up the SSH client on the FTP server for a remote port-forwarding session. Set up the session so that when the SSH client (the FTP server) establishes a connection to the SSH server, a remote port-forwarding session will be established that will make the SSH server listen on port 21 and redirect any connections to port 21 (on the SSH server) to port 21 on the FTP server.

4. Internal employees should FTP to the SSH server on port 21, which will be forwarding to the FTP server on port 21 over the established SSH session.

5. External public customers should make a regular FTP connection to the FTP server on port 21, which will not be encrypted with SSH.

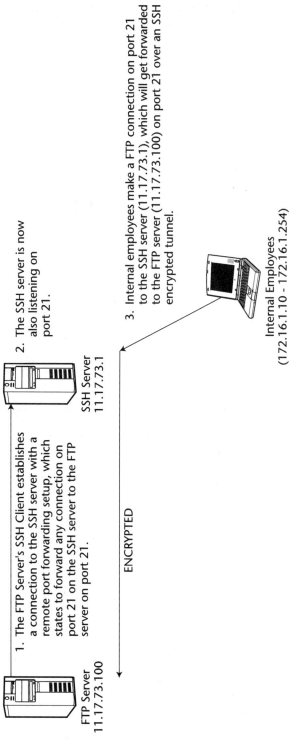

1. The FTP Server's SSH Client establishes a connection to the SSH server with a remote port forwarding setup, which states to forward any connection on port 21 on the SSH server to the FTP server on port 21.

FTP Server
11.17.73.100

2. The SSH server is now also listening on port 21.

SSH Server
11.17.73.1

3. Internal employees make a FTP connection on port 21 to the SSH server (11.17.73.1), which will get forwarded to the FTP server (11.17.73.100) on port 21 over an SSH encrypted tunnel.

ENCRYPTED

Internal Employees
(172.16.1.10 - 172.16.1.254)

Figure 6.3   SSH remote port-forward architecture.

SSH port forwarding is simple and straightforward. The theory behind port forwarding is much like the process of simple TCP relaying. A TCP relay is the ability to accept connections on a particular port and redirect them somewhere else. For example, every connection on port 80 on a machine's loopback address (127.0.0.1) is relayed to port 80 on 172.16.1.100. The only difference with SSH port forwarding is that the connection is redirected through an established SSH session first and then replayed to the remote machine. Some basic requirements must be met in order for port forwarding to work, such as a valid connection from the SSH server to the remote server (the server receiving the relayed connection); however, that is not a separate configuration step but an assumed requirement.

A key point to keep in mind regarding port forwarding is that protocols such as IMAP, SMTP, and POP3 being tunneled are terminated at the SSH server. For example, if a client is connecting to an SSH server and then port forwarding SMTP and IMAP over SSH to receive e-mail securely, the mail protocols will be tunneled from the SSH client to the SSH server; then the mail protocols will be sent over their native protocols from the SSH server to the mail server. The communication from the SSH server to the mail server will not be under an SSH session. Figure 6.4 shows further details.

Notice in Figure 6.4 that the IMAP and SMTP protocols are protected from the SSH client to the SSH server by the port-forwarding tunneling process; then they communicate with their native protocols without any tunnels from the SSH server to the mail server.

This chapter examines some of the basics of SSH port forwarding, specifically the following topics:

- Networking basics of port forwarding for clients
- Networking basics of port forwarding for servers

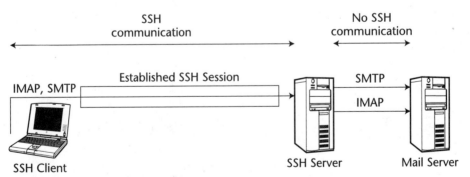

Figure 6.4 Where an SSH session would be terminated.

Also, configuring local and remote SSH port forwarding on the following SSH clients is explored:

- SSH command-line client (OpenSSH and commercial versions)
- SSH Communications' SSH client
- SecureCRT SSH client

Lastly, enabling SSH port forwarding on the following SSH servers is examined:

- OpenSSH (Unix and Windows)
- SSH Communications' SSH server (Unix and Windows)
- VanDyke's Software SSH server (Windows)

Networking Basics of Port Forwarding for Clients

Before discussing how to configure port forwarding on clients, you should understand the basic networking concepts of port forwarding, especially in terms of what it is, how it works, and what is happening behind the scenes. A deep understanding of the core concepts of port forwarding will eliminate a lot of confusion later in the advanced sections.

The first basic concept is the established SSH session. Each SSH client and SSH server will have an authenticated and established SSH session. The actual session can be used for terminal access, SFTP/SCP access, or no access, if both the terminal session and SFTP/SCP are restricted.

NOTE An SSH session can still be established if terminal or SFTP/SCP access is not granted.

The restriction of terminal and SFTP access usually means that the user has the right to use the SSH session for port forwarding through the SSH server but not for gaining access to the SSH server. Once the SSH session is established, any port-forwarding options on the SSH client will be applied; however, any port-forwarding rules need to be configured before the SSH session has been established. If port-forwarding options are configured during or after the SSH session has been established, the options will not be effective until the session is fully re-established.

The second major concept of port forwarding is that most, if not all, configuration of port forwarding is conducted on the client, not on the server. For example, if port forwarding is required between an SSH client and an SSH server, the configuration for the incoming or outgoing SSH rules will be on the client. In the port-forwarding architecture, the server needs to allow port forwarding, but no specific configuration is required on the server.

> **NOTE** Many SSH server installations allow port forwarding by default, requiring no configuration at all after a default installation of the SSH server.

The port-forwarding rules applied to the SSH client will vary, depending on whether the rules are local (outgoing) or remote (incoming) on the SSH client. The use of local (outgoing) rules provides a practical and more advantageous option than remote port forwarding. So you will probably use local port forwarding more often than remote port forwarding.

Local port-forwarding rules redirect connections on local ports—that is, ports local to the operating system that the SSH client is running on—to a specified port and server on the other side of the SSH established connection, which can be the SSH server itself or a machine that the SSH server can access.

When configuring local port forwarding, the user is given the option to specify the IP address to use for local forwarding as well as the port number. For example, if the SSH client is installed on a machine that has an IP address of 172.16.10.21, the options for the local IP address will be 172.16.10.21 or 127.0.0.1, which is the loopback interface of the computer. A loopback is basically an IP address that identifies the local machine using TCP/IP. In most cases, you will want to use the loopback address, 127.0.0.1, for local port forwarding.

Furthermore, using the real IP address, such as 172.16.10.21, is a security risk, since other machines could connect to your IP address (172.16.10.21) and use your established SSH connection to tunnel communication. That being said, that may be your intended usage, so proceed with caution.

Once you have chosen the loopback address, 127.0.0.1, for the IP address to use for local port forwarding, you will have to choose which port you would like to connect to. You can choose any port you like, as long as the operating system allows you to access that port. (Some operating systems do not allow sharing of services on a single port, such as port 445 on Windows.) The best option for a port is to use the standard port for the protocol that will be forwarding. For example, if Web communication will be forwarded, which uses HTTP and HTTPS, you will probably want to use ports 80 and 443 with the lookback interface. Keep in mind that if you use a port that is not standard, such as port 1173, you will have to tell your client application, such as your Web browser, to use port 1173 instead of port 80 or 443 (for example, http://127.0.0.1:1173).

Now that you have chosen your local IP address and local port, you need to choose which remote server you want to redirect any connections made to your specified local address and port. For example, if the remote server is the internal Web server for an organization, which holds the company's intranet application, you need to choose the IP address of the internal Web server. Keep in mind that the SSH server must be able to communicate with this machine natively, without any firewall, router ACLs, or networks preventing it from communicating with the remote machine. If the IP address of the internal Web server is 192.168.12.15, that will be the IP address of the remote server. After the IP address of the remote server is specified, the remote port has to be selected also. Unlike the local-port option, the remote-port option is dictated by the remote server. For example, if the intranet Web application uses HTTP, which is port 80, you must specify port 80 and the remote port. Furthermore, if the remote server is a mail server and you are forwarding mail protocols, you have to choose SMTP and POP3, which are ports 25 and 110.

Now that you have your local IP address (127.0.0.1), local port (80), remote server IP address (192.168.12.15), and remote port (80), selected for your local port-forwarding rule, you are ready to forward the HTTP protocol through the SSH connection. The following steps walk you through the process of using the local port-forwarding session by using an SSH server with two IP addresses: one that faces externally to the Internet, 12.15.10.21, and one that faces internally to the internal network, 192.168.12.1:

1. Having established your local port-forwarding rules, establish an SSH connection to the SSH server on its external IP address (12.15.10.21) using the required authentication options (see Figure 6.5).

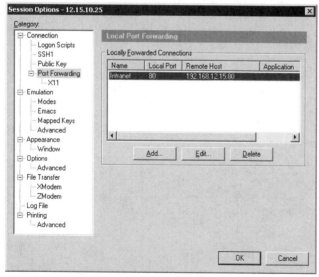

Figure 6.5   Local port-forwarding rules in an SSH client.

2. The SSH session is now established with the local port-forwarding rules enabled. (To confirm, you can type **netstat –an** on a command shell, and your lookback IP address, 127.0.0.1, should be listening on port 80.) Next, open your Web browser. In the URL section of your Web browser, type **127.0.0.1** (see Figure 6.6).

3. Once your Web browser attempts a connection to your lookback address, 127.0.0.1, on port 80 (by default, Web browsers connect on port 80), your port-forwarding rules will be triggered. The rules will dictate that all connections to 127.0.0.1 on port 80 should be redirected through the established SSH connection to 192.168.12.15 on port 80.

4. Assuming your SSH server can communicate with 192.168.12.15, the connection is forwarded beyond your SSH server to the internal Web server, on port 80. The internal Web server sends the results, probably the intranet's home page, to the SSH client's Web browser. See Figure 6.7.

Note that the local port-forwarding connection from your SSH client to the SSH server is fully encrypted with SSH, but the connection from the SSH server to the local intranet server uses its native protocol, which would be HTTP. For an example of how this works, see Figure 6.8.

Figure 6.6 A Web browser pointing to a loopback address (127.0.0.1).

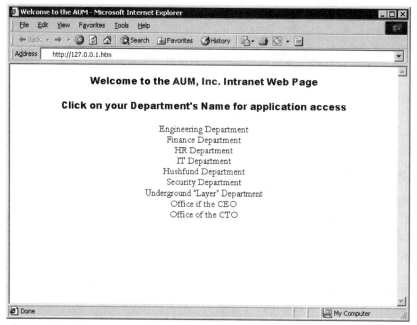

Figure 6.7 The company's intranet Web page to the remote SSH client, sent after requesting 127.0.0.1 on the URL of the Web browser.

Local Port Forwarding Rule:
Local IP: 127.0.0.1
Local Port: 80
Remote IP: 192.168.10.21
Remote Port: 80

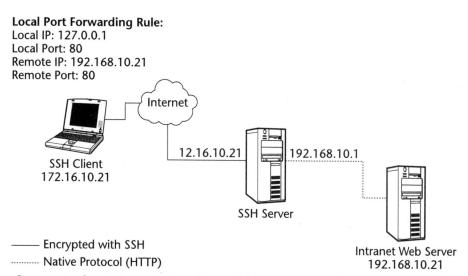

Figure 6.8 The SSH encrypted session and the native protocol (HTTP) session.

Remote port forwarding has functionality similar to local port forwarding; the specific steps, however, are actually quite different. Remote port forwarding redirects remote connections on the SSH server to local ports on the SSH client, that is, the operating system that the SSH client is running on, over an SSH established connection. When configuring remote port forwarding, the SSH client is given the option to specify the port to have the remote SSH server listen on. For example, if the SSH client chooses port 21, the SSH server will begin to listen on port 21 automatically once the SSH connection is established. Once the SSH client has chosen the port number for the SSH server and has established an SSH connection, any machine connecting to port 21 on the SSH server will be redirected to the SSH client over an encrypted SSH tunnel. The port number that is redirected from the SSH server to the SSH client is also determined by the SSH client. Unlike the SSH server, the SSH client's machine will not automatically start listening on that port; rather it is assumed that a service, such as FTP, is already running on that port, which would be the whole reason to set up the remote port-forwarding rule.

Now that the SSH client has chosen the remote port for the SSH server to listen on (port 21), the remote port-forwarding rule can be initialized. The following steps walk you through the process of using the remote port-forwarding session by using an SSH server with two IP addresses: one that faces externally to the Internet, 12.15.10.21, and one that faces internally to the internal network, 192.168.12.1:

1. Execute the remote port-forwarding rules, an established SSH connection to the SSH server on its external IP address (12.15.10.21), and the required authentication options. See Figure 6.9.

2. Now that the SSH session is established, the remote port-forwarding rules should be enabled. (To confirm, you can type **netstat –an** on the SSH server, and port 21 should be listening.)

3. Once an FTP client connects to the SSH server on FTP, the connection will be redirected to the SSH client on port 21, over the encrypted SSH session.

Note that the remote port-forwarding connection from the SSH client to the SSH server is fully encrypted with SSH but that the connection from the SSH server to the FTP client uses the native protocol, which would be FTP. For an example of how this operates, see Figure 6.10.

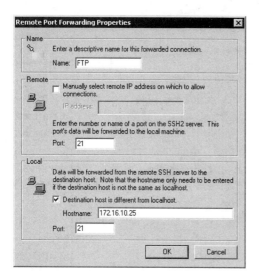

Figure 6.9   Remote port-forwarding rules in an SSH client.

Remote Port Forwarding Rule:
Local IP: 172.16.10.21
Local Port: 21
Local service: FTP
Remote Port: 21

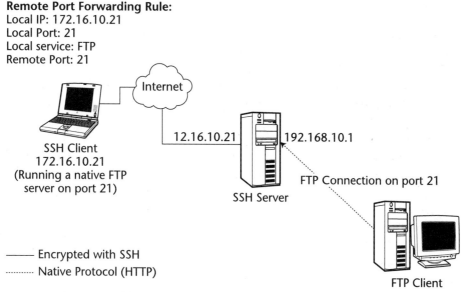

—— Encrypted with SSH
········· Native Protocol (HTTP)

Figure 6.10   Remote port forwarding using FTP.

Networking Basics of Port Forwarding for Servers

Unlike the networking concepts of port forwarding for SSH clients, the networking basics of port forwarding for SSH servers is quite simple. Port forwarding in SSH server environments does not require any type of special configuration for the client to use the specific feature. The only major requirement for the SSH servers is that the port forwarding feature be either enabled (allowed) for the clients or, if it is not desired, disabled (disallowed).

As with SSH clients, the first basic concept of networking for SSH servers is the established SSH session. Each SSH client and SSH server will have an authenticated and established SSH session. The SSH server can permit access to a terminal shell, SFTP/SCP access, or neither, thereby allowing only an established (authenticated) session. Once the SSH session is established and authenticated by the SSH server, any port-forwarding option can be applied that has been configured on the SSH client. Note that while many SSH servers allow port forwarding by default, port forwarding can be disabled by some SSH servers and can also be limited, restricting or permitting port forwarding on a designated set of servers or specified users and groups. This restriction or permission of port forwarding, port-forwarding ports, and port-forwarded servers is configured on the SSH server. If an SSH client attempts to port forward a port or attempts to port forward to a server that is restricted by the SSH server, the client will be denied access.

The port-forwarding rules applied on the SSH clients can either be outgoing (local) or incoming (remote). The type of port forwarding on the SSH client will determine the type of networking enabled on the SSH server.

If outgoing (local) port forwarding is being used on the SSH client, no specific networking changes are generated on the SSH server. For example, if an SSH client is port forwarding port 143 (IMAP) to an e-mail server that the SSH server is connected to, the SSH server will not change its networking configuration but will act as a conduit for the SSH connection between the SSH client and the e-mail server. In this architecture, the SSH client sends packets to the SSH server destined for the e-mail server on port 143. Once the SSH server receives the incoming packets from the authenticated SSH client on the established SSH session, the SSH server redirects or routes the packets to the e-mail server on port 143 on behalf of the remote SSH client. In this example, the SSH server is acting more as a router between the authenticated and established SSH client and the desired server; however, no networking changes or services are modified on the SSH server itself.

Similarly, if the SSH client is port forwarding to the SSH server, not to another server that the SSH server may be connected to, the SSH server still has no specific networking changes generated. For example, if the SSH server is also acting as an FTP server on port 21 and an SSH client port forwards FTP to the SSH server, there are no networking changes on the SSH server. Since the SSH client is port forwarding to an existing service (port) on the SSH/FTP server, the SSH server's networking configuration does not change but rather continues to act as an SSH server as well as an FTP server.

If incoming (remote) port forwarding is being used on the SSH client, networking changes on the remote SSH server are generated. For example, if an SSH client is using remote port forwarding on port 21 (FTP), the authenticated and established SSH session will generate and start a service on port 21 on the selected networking interfaces on the SSH server. In this architecture, the SSH client waits for redirect packets from the SSH server. In this example, a remote FTP client connects to the generated FTP service on the SSH server. Once the SSH server receives the incoming packets from the FTP client, the SSH server redirects and relays the packets to the SSH client's FTP service on port 21 on behalf of the FTP client. Slightly different from the preceding example, the SSH server is acting as a redirector on port 21 between the authenticated and established SSH client and the remote FTP client.

SSH Port Forwarding

Now that you have looked at some of the basic concepts of port forwarding, turn your attention to how to configure port forwarding in several SSH clients and SSH servers. The discussion in the paragraphs that follow provides the foundation for the material in the next chapter, which addresses advanced SSH port forwarding.

In the following discussion on SSH clients and servers, a common architecture will be used for each of the configuration examples. That common architecture is illustrated in Figure 6.11. The common architecture shows how to configure port forwarding for both SSH clients and SSH servers on their respective applications and systems.

Before proceeding to your exploration of the various configuration options, examine the individual components of the common architecture. Table 6.1 lists the different devices of the common architecture shown in Figure 6.11 and describes what they do.

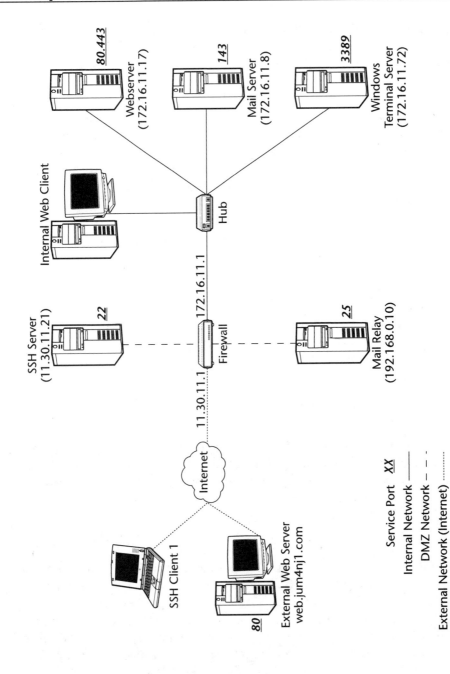

Figure 6.11 The common architecture used for the example configurations of port forwarding.

Table 6.1   Devices of the Common Architecture

DEVICE	DESCRIPTION
SSH Client 1	This device represents any stand-alone operating system with any SSH client loaded on the machine. This client can be connecting to the Internet from a DSL, Cable, T1, T3, or dial-up (modem) connection. Also, this client can either be using a NAT'd (RFC 1918) address, such as 10.0.0.172, or a publicly routable address, such as 203.28.38.44. Lastly, the client can be connecting from a residence, office, hotel, airport wireless, or business-partner location.
External Web Server SSH Client 2	This device represents the exact parameters of SSH Client 1; however, it is also running a Web server on port 80.
Internet	This is the information superhighway.
SSH Server	The SSH server that listens only on port 22 and with an IP address of 11.30.11.21, which is a publicly routable address.
Firewall	The firewall restricts all incoming traffic from the outside Internet to all destinations, except for any requests to the SSH server on port 22. A rough example of the firewall rules looks like the following: Allow (Pass) any connection from the internal network outbound. Allow (Pass) any connection from the outside (Internet) to the SSH server on port 22. Deny (Block) any connection from the outside (Internet) to the internal network or the DMZ network on any port. Allow (pass) any connection from the SSH server to the DMZ or internal network. These rules will restrict any type of traffic coming from the outside Internet, except for SSH connections to the SSH server. I will demonstrate how allowing only port 22 through the firewall will still allow services such as e-mail, intranet Web pages, and remote management to be provided in a secure manner. The firewall's external IP address is 11.30.11.1 and does not listen to any ports on its external interfaces.
Mail Relay	This device represents a mail-relay server. A mail-relay server is responsible for sending e-mail for individual e-mail clients. This server has an internal IP address of 192.168.0.10 and is using SMTP for the sending of e-mail, which listens on port 25.
Hub	This device represents a hub. It is used to connect the internal servers to the internal network. It does not have an IP address, nor does it listen on any port.

(continued)

Table 6.1   *(continued)*

DEVICE	DESCRIPTION
Internal Web Client	This device represents any operating system with a Web client. Since most operating systems contain a Web client by default, this device can represent every operating system on the internal network.
Web Server	This device represents the internal Web server of the organization. This server holds the organization's intranet Web page, which is used to manage many of the applications and systems that are internal to the network, such as time-entry applications, expense applications, internal bulletin-board pages, and so on. This server has an internal IP address of 172.16.11.17 and is listening on port 80 (HTTP) and port 443 (HTTPS).
Mail Server	This device represents the mail server for the organization. The mail server is used to receive incoming e-mail for individual e-mail clients. This e-mail server has an internal IP address of 172.16.11.8 and is using IMAP for incoming e-mail, which is listening on port 143.
Windows Terminal Server	This device represents the internal management server for the organization. It is used to manage internal operating systems and network devices. This is a Windows 2000 server with terminal services enabled. The server has an internal IP address 172.16.11.17 and is listening on port 3389.

Now that the common architecture has been described and defined, let's explore how to individually configure the SSH clients and SSH servers for port forwarding. The following SSH servers and SSH clients will be discussed:

- Command-line clients
  - OpenSSH client
  - SSH Communications'
  - VanDyke Software
- SSH Communications' GUI SSH client
- SecureCRT SSH client
- PuTTY
- OpenSSH server (Unix and Windows)
- SSH Communications' SSH server (Unix)
- SSH Communications' SSH server (Windows)
- VanDyke's Software SSH server (Windows)

Local Port Forwarding for SSH Clients

The paragraphs that follow describe basic configuration steps for SSH clients, according to the parameters in Figure 6.11.

Configuration for Command-Line Clients

OpenSSH, SSH Communications', and VanDyke Software provide a command-line client for SSH connections, as described in Chapter 3. OpenSSH's command line-client is called ssh. SSH Communications' SSH client is called ssh2. Lastly, VanDyke Software's SSH client is called vsh. We will be using the three terms, ssh, ssh2, and vsh, to represent the respective SSH clients.

Using SSH Client 1 as your starting point, use the -L switch to configure local (outgoing) port-forwarding options. The syntax for the local (outgoing) port-forwarding options is as follows:

```
-L listen-port:host:port (OpenSSH and SSH Communications')
-local localport:remotehost:remoteport (VanDyke Software)
```

The listen-port or localport option designates the port to have the local operating system listen on. The host or remotehost option is the IP address of the remote server that the SSH server is connected to. The port or remoteport option is the port that the remote server is listening on. The specific -L options to use, according to Figure 6.11, are the following for OpenSSH and SSH Communications:

```
-L 25:192.168.0.10:25
-L 80:172.16.1.117:80
-L 443:172.16.1.117:443
-L 143:172.16.11.8:143
-L 3389:172.16.11.72:3389
```

The specific -local options to use, according to Figure 6.11, are the following for VanDyke Software:

```
-local 25:192.168.0.10:25
-local 80:172.16.1.117:80
-local 443:172.16.1.117:443
-local 143:172.16.11.8:143
-local 3389:172.16.11.72:3389
```

NOTE Do not confuse the listen-port option with the port option. The listen-port option is the port that the SSH client's operating system will listen on, with the loopback (127.0.0.1) interface, in order to relay the connection. The port option is the port number on the remote server, which cannot be changed by the SSH client.

The listen-port option can be any port on the SSH client's operating system. For example, instead of using listen-port 80 for the local relay to the remote Web server, the SSH client can use port 79. The remote connection will still be on port 80, but the local forward will connect on port 79. In order to make the connection, the Web browser has to point to port 79 instead of the default 80, which is quite easy (for example, http://127.0.0.1:79). This flexibility works well if multiple remote Web servers will be locally port forwarded, since only one local port can be forwarded to one remote IP address. On the other hand, the flexibility of the listen-port option is available only if the connecting client application, such as a Web-browser client, is able to connect using a nonstandard port, such as 79. In some cases, such as with the Terminal Services client, the client application cannot be configured to use a different connection port; therefore, the local-port option must remain 3389 in order for the connection to work correctly.

To connect to your SSH server in Figure 6.11 and forward all the local ports, the following syntax should be used:

OPENSSH

```
ssh 11.30.11.21 -1 jum4nj1 -p 22 -L 25:192.168.0.10:25 -L
80:172.16.11.17:80 -L 443:172.16.11.17:443 -L 143:172.16.11.8:143 -L
3389:172.16.11.72:3389
```

SSH COMMUNICATIONS

```
ssh2 11.30.11.21 -1 jum4nj1 -p 22 -L 25:192.168.0.10:25 -L
80:172.16.11.17:80 -L 443:172.16.11.17:443 -L 143:172.16.11.8:143 -L
3389:172.16.11.72:3389
```

VANDYKE SOFTWARE

```
vsh 11.30.11.21 -1 jum4nj1 -p 22 -local 25:192.168.0.10:25 -local
80:172.16.11.17:80 -local 443:172.16.11.17:443 -local
143:172.16.11.8:143 -local 3389:172.16.11.72:3389
```

The first part of the syntax connects the SSH client to the SSH server (11.30.11.21) on port 22, designated by the -p option, with the username of jum4nj1, designated by the -l option. Once the SSH server's IP address and port number have been designated, the local port-forwarding options need to be set. As you can see, the syntax can be quite long if several port-forwarding options are used. Different configuration files are ideal when more than one port-forwarding option is required to be set. (Refer to the Unix Setup section in Chapter 3, "Secure Shell Clients," on how to set up different configuration files.) Once the SSH client is authenticated and the SSH session is established, the port-forwarding options will automatically be enabled. To confirm, type **netstat -an | more** and the port-forwarded ports should be listening on the loopback interface (127.0.0.1).

Once you have confirmed that the port-forwarded sessions are enabled, use your client application to connect to your port-forwarded session. For example, to use the Windows Terminal Services port-forwarding session, execute the terminal services client and enter **127.0.0.1** for the server IP address. Since 127.0.0.1 is listening on the SSH client's machine on port 3389, it will accept this connection request from the client application and forward it to 172.16.11.72 via the SSH connection and the SSH server. Similarly, other clients, such as mail clients and Web clients, will need to use the loopback interface (127.0.0.1) to connect to the remote server via the SSH session.

Configuration for SSH Communications' GUI SSH Client

SSH Communications also creates a GUI SSH client for Windows operating systems. Using SSH Client 1 from Figure 6.11 as the starting point, we can configure the local port-forwarding options quite easily using the following steps:

1. Start ⇨ Programs ⇨ SSH Secure Shell ⇨ SSH Client.
2. Click Profiles ⇨ Add Profile.
3. Name the profile SSH server or anything you wish.
4. Click Profiles ⇨ Edit Profile ⇨ SSH Server.
5. Select the Tunneling tab.
6. Under the Outgoing tab, select Add. At this point, you can add the specific local port-forwarding information.
7. Under Display Name, enter Mail Relay.
8. Leave the Type drop-down menu to **TCP**.
9. Enter **25** for Listen Port.
10. Enter **192.168.0.10** for Destination Host.
11. Enter **25** for Destination Port.
12. Select the OK button.

The final result should look similar to Figure 6.12, which shows the SSH client's outgoing tunnel configuration.

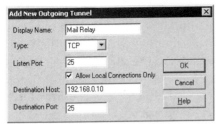

Figure 6.12   SSH Communications' GUI for local port-forwarding options.

Continue to enter the rest of the local port-forwarding options by repeating steps 7 through 11. Make sure the result looks like Figure 6.13.

Once all the outgoing tunnels have been entered, select OK. The outgoing port-forwarding tunnels for SSH Communications have now been entered. Once the connection is established, the local port-forwarding tunnels will be available.

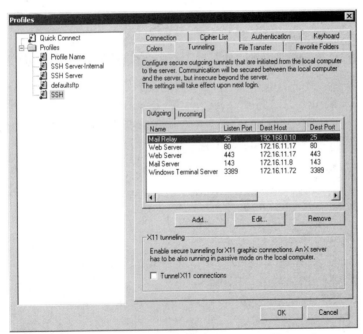

Figure 6.13   The complete list of local port-forwarding options.

Configuration for VanDyke Software's Secure CRT

VanDyke Software creates a GUI SSH client for Windows operating systems. Using SSH Client 1 from Figure 6.11 as the starting point, you can configure the local port-forwarding options quite easily using the following steps:

1. Start ⇨ Programs ⇨ SecureCRT ⇨ SecureCRT.
2. File ⇨ Connect ⇨ *Highlight a saved SSH connection.*
3. Right-click the select SSH connection and select Properties.
4. Highlight the Port Forwarding section.
5. Select the Add button. At this point, you can add the specific local port-forwarding information.
6. Under the Name section, enter **Mail Relay**.
7. Under the Local section, leave the Manually Select Local IP Address on Which to Allow Connections unchecked. Use the loopback interface IP address, 127.0.01, which is the default. If the "real" IP address of the SSH client is desired, such as 172.16.1.100 or 206.13.11.17, select this checkbox and enter the IP address. Again, for your purposes at this time, you will use the loopback interface, so leave the box unchecked.
8. Under the Local section in the Port textbox, enter **25**, since you will be connecting to your local port 25 to forward SMTP, which uses port 25.
9. Under the Remote section, check the box labeled Destination Host Is Different from the SSH Server, since your remote server is the mail-relay server, not the SSH server itself. If the remote port were on the SSH server, you could leave this box unchecked; however, in this case, it is not.
10. Under the Remote section in the Port textbox, enter **25**, since the remote mail server uses SMTP, which uses port 25.
11. Under the Application section, do not put anything. This section can be configured to automatically bring up an application, such as an e-mail client, once the SSH session has been established. Although this option is very useful, you will not be using it here. It is recommended, however, to use this option as needed to eliminate steps for the novice end-user. For example, if you were to locate the e-mail client's executable, such as Microsoft Outlook or Netscape Mail, once SecureCRT is used to authenticate the SSH session, the e-mail client would automatically start. To novice end-users, this process simplifies the steps for gaining access to e-mail, which is the single step of establishing the SSH connection. In addition, since so many novice users are used to one-step e-mail access, this option proves to be really useful.
12. Select the OK button at the bottom of the window.

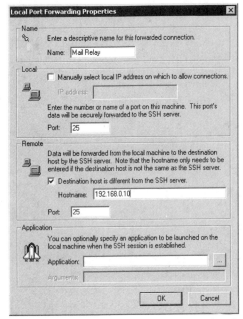

Figure 6.14   SecureCRT SSH client for local port-forwarding options.

Figure 6.14 shows the final result of the local port-forwarding options from the preceding steps.

Continue to enter the rest of the local port-forwarding options by repeating steps 6 through 12. Make sure the result looks like Figure 6.15.

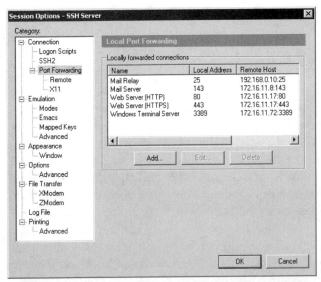

Figure 6.15   The complete list of local port-forwarding options on SecureCRT.

Once all the outgoing tunnels have been entered, select OK. The outgoing port-forwarding tunnels for SecureCRT have now been entered. Once the connection is established, the local port-forwarding tunnels will be available.

Configuration for PuTTY

PuTTY is a freeware SSH client for Windows operating systems. Using SSH Client 1 from Figure 6.11 as the starting point, you can configure the local port-forwarding options quite easily using the following steps:

1. Double-click "putty.exe."

2. Browse to Connection ⇨ SSH ⇨ Tunnels.

3. Highlight Tunnels.

4. Skip the X11 forwarding section, since this area does not apply to your example. If you wanted to forward X11 sessions from an X11 server, this would be the option to select.

5. Under the Port Forwarding section, leave Local Ports Accept Connections from Other Hosts unchecked. This option mandates the listen ports to be accepted only from the local machine. If you need to have other hosts connect to the SSH client machine to forward ports, check the checkbox.

6. Under the Port Forwarding section, leave Remove Ports Do the Same unchecked. This option is for remote (incoming) port forwarding, which allows other hosts to connect to the remote port on the SSH server.

7. Under the Port Forwarding section, enter **25** for the Source port textbox.

8. Under the Port Forwarding section, enter **192.168.0.10:25** for the Destination textbox. Be sure to enter the option with the following format: IPAddress:port.

9. Under the Port Forwarding section, select the Local radio button.

10. Under the Port Forwarding section, select Add.

Figure 6.16 shows the final PuTTY configuration from the preceding steps.

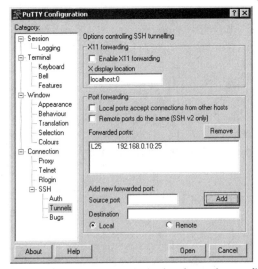

Figure 6.16 PuTTY with the local port-forwarding option.

Continue to enter the rest of the local port-forwarding options by repeating steps 7 through 10. Make sure the result looks like Figure 6.17.

Once all the outgoing tunnels have been entered, select Open. The outgoing port-forwarding tunnels for PuTTY have now been entered. Once the connection is established, the local port-forwarding tunnels will be available.

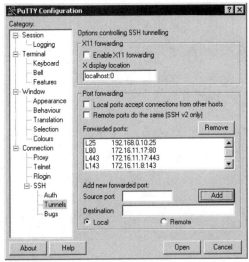

Figure 6.17 The complete list of local port-forwarding options on PuTTY.

Remote Port Forwarding for SSH Clients

Thus far, the discussion has examined only local (outgoing) port forwarding to and from the SSH clients. In the paragraphs that follow, the discussion will explore the use of remote (incoming) port forwarding in accordance with Figure 6.11.

As discussed earlier, remote port forwarding is the opposite of local port forwarding, allowing remote ports on the SSH server to be forwarded to local ports on the SSH client or even other ports/servers via the SSH client. In the example illustrated in Figure 6.11, web.jum4nj1.com is a Web server that also contains an SSH client. In order to allow the internal Web client in Figure 6.11 to connect to the remote Web server using the SSH client, remote port forwarding needs to be enabled. In order to accomplish this, the Web server (web.jum4nj1.com) needs to use an SSH client and set up a remote forward to the SSH server. The remote forward can be configured to have the SSH server listen on port 80 and redirect any connections on port 80 (on the SSH server) to the SSH client on port 80, over an encrypted SSH tunnel. This will allow the internal Web client to connect to the SSH server on port 80 and gain encrypted access to web.jum4nj1.com. The following sections demonstrate how to configure remote port forwarding on web.jum4nju1.com, according to the preceding example and Figure 6.11.

Configuration for OpenSSH Client (Unix and Windows)

The Web server in Figure 6.11, web.jum4nj1.com, can have a routable IP address (206.13.7.1) or a nonroutable IP address (172.16.7.1) in order to set up remote port forwarding. The fact that both internal and external addresses can be used with remote port forwarding makes remote port forwarding the perfect utility to side-step firewalls. I highly recommend not using remote port forwarding to side-step firewalls, but I should state that using internal IP addresses with SSH clients can allow outbound connections on ports not usually allowed through the firewall rules (discussed more in the next chapter). Using OpenSSH, the following command should be issued on web.jum4nj1 .com to enable remote port forwarding:

```
#ssh 11.30.11.21 -R 80:localhost:80
```

Once the SSH connection is made with the remote port-forwarding settings, the internal Web client should open his or her favorite Web browser and point to the following URL: http://11.30.11.21:80. Also, on the SSH server itself, the following URL can be used: http://127.0.0.1:80. This will display the Web site on web.jum4nj1.com to both the internal Web client and the SSH server on the encrypted SSH connection.

Configuration for SSH Communications' Command-Line Client (Unix and Windows)

As with OpenSSH commands, SSH Communications' command-line clients can be used for remote forwarding sessions. To connect to the Web server in Figure 6.11 with SSH Communications' SSH, the following command should be issued on web.jum4nj1.com:

```
#ssh2 11.30.11.21 -R 80:localhost:80
```

Once the SSH connection is made with the remote port-forwarding settings, the internal Web client should open the Web browser and point to the following URL: http://11.30.11.21:80. Also, on the SSH server itself, the following URL can be used: http://127.0.0.1:80. This will display the Web site on web.jum4nj1.com to both the internal Web client and the SSH server on the encrypted SSH connection.

Configuration for SSH Communications' GUI SSH Client (Windows)

SSH Communications' GUI clients can also be used for remote forwarding sessions. To connect to the Web server in Figure 6.11 using SSH Communications' SSH GUI client, the following steps should be issued on web.jum4nj1.com:

1. Select Start ⇨ Programs ⇨ SSH Secure Shell ⇨ Secure Shell Client.
2. Choose Profiles ⇨ Edit Profiles.
3. Select the appropriate profile for the remote SSH server (11.30.11.21).
4. Click the Tunneling tab.
5. Select the Incoming tab.
6. Press the Add button.
7. Enter **WEB** for Display Name.
8. Choose TCP for Type.
9. Select 80 for the Listen Port. (This is the port that the SSH server will listen on.)
10. Enter **localhost** for Destination Host.
11. Enter **80** for Destination Port. (This is the port that the SSH client machine will be accepting connections on.)
12. Select OK.

Figure 6.18 shows the result of the preceding steps.

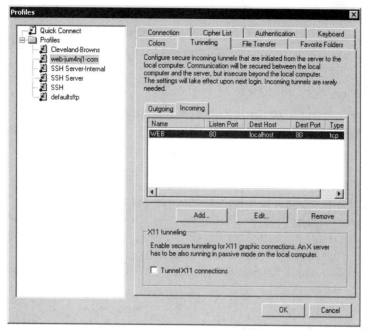

Figure 6.18   The Remote port-forwarding configuration.

Once the SSH connection is made with the remote port-forwarding settings, the internal Web client should open the Web browser and point to the following URL: http://11.30.11.21:80. Also, on the SSH server itself, the following URL can be used: http://127.0.0.1:80. This will display the Web site on web.jum4nj1.com to both the internal Web client and the SSH server on the encrypted SSH connection.

Configuration for VanDyke Software's SecureCRT

VanDyke Software's SecureCRT SSH client can also be used for remote forwarding sessions. To connect to the Web server in Figure 6.11 using SSH Communications' SSH GUI client, the following steps should be issued on web.jum4nj1.com:

1. Select Start ⇨ Programs ⇨ SecureCRT ⇨ SecureCRT.
2. Select File ⇨ Connect.
3. Right-click the appropriate IP address or hostname and select Properties.
4. Browse to Connection ⇨ Port Forwarding ⇨ Remote.
5. Select Add.

6. In the Name section, type **WEB** for the Name field.

7. In the Remote section, check the checkbox Manually select remote IP address on which to allow connections and type **11.30.11.21** for the IP address.

8. In the Remote section, type **80** for the Port field.

9. In the Local section, type **localhost** for the Hostname field.

10. In the Local section, type **80** in the Port field.

11. Select OK.

Figure 6.19 shows the result of the preceding steps.

Once the SSH connection is made with the remote port-forwarding settings, the internal Web client should open the Web browser and point to the following URL: http://11.30.11.21:80. Also, on the SSH server itself, the following URL can be used: http://127.0.0.1:80. This will display the Web site on web.jum4nj1.com to both the internal Web client and the SSH server on the encrypted SSH connection.

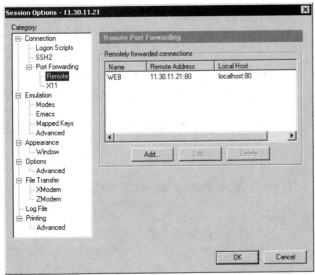

Figure 6.19 The Remote port-forwarding configuration with SecureCRT.

Port Forwarding for SSH Servers

The paragraphs that follow describe the basic configuration steps for SSH servers, according to the parameters in Figure 6.11. Unlike SSH clients, SSH servers require no special configuration or changes when the port-forwarding feature is used. Keep in mind, however, that while no special configuration is required, no restrictions are enabled by default, which allows all users, all ports, and all accessible internal servers to be potentially forwarded to. While the use of port forwarding is a very strong feature of SSH2 servers, allowing full port-forwarding access to all SSH users may not be desired. For example, since the SSH service is very flexible, the SSH server may be a remote-access solution (with port forwarding) for several users, a secure file server (SFTP) for other users, and/or shell access for other users. The ability to have all SSH accounts use the port-forwarding feature and access internal systems, such as the Windows Terminal server, may not be desired and could be a security issue. The following sections describe the use of port forwarding on the SSH server and any extra features the different implementations provide, such as port-forwarding filters.

Configuration for OpenSSH Server (Unix and Windows)

The SSH server in Figure 6.11, 11.30.11.21, has a routable IP address that can be accessible from both internal networks and external networks, such as the Internet. By default, port forwarding is enabled on many, if not all, SSH version 2 servers, including OpenSSH. Unfortunately, OpenSSH does not provide a native utility to restrict port forwarding to only authorized ports, servers, and/or accounts. If OpenSSH is being used, other methods can be used to restrict ports and servers, such as the firewall rules on 11.30.11.1 in Figure 6.11 or custom scripts. For example, using a firewall to restrict the SSH server to only authorized ports and servers and placing a "Deny" rule for all other internal servers is probably the best way to allow authorized access while denying access to the rest of the internal network.

Configuration for SSH Communications' SSH Server (Unix)

SSH Communications provides an SSH Server for Unix systems. The Unix SSH server is configured using the sshd2_config file located in /etc/ssh2, as described earlier in the SSH Communications' SSH server section in Chapter 2.

The SSH server in Figure 6.11, 11.30.11.21, has a routable IP address that can be accessible from both internal networks and external networks, such as the Internet. By default, port forwarding is enabled on SSH Communications' SSH server, so there is no special configuration needed on the SSH server after installation has been completed. (See Chapter 1 for details on how to install an SSH server.) SSH Communications provides the ability to restrict or permit port forwarding, also known as tunneling, on the SSH server. For example, if port forwarding is not desired, the tunneling settings can restrict access while still allowing terminal and/or SFTP access. In addition to permitting or restricting port forwarding, the ability to allow port forwarding for only a specified set of users and denying everyone else is possible. Furthermore, the ability to deny port forwarding for a set number of users and allow everyone else is possible. Lastly, in addition to allowing and denying specific users and/or groups, the SSH server can restrict port forwarding using ACLs based on IP addresses and port numbers. For example, if port forwarding is not desired to all internal machines but rather to a selected few, port forwarding ACLs can be set to allow only certain IP addresses on certain ports to be accessible to port forwarding SSH clients. To view the tunnel configuration options and configure these options on SSH Communications' SSH server, perform the following steps:

1. Change directories to /etc/sshd2:

   ```
   #cd /etc/sshd2
   ```

2. View the sshd2_config file, specifically, the tunneling section:

   ```
   #more sshd2_config
   ```

3. The tunneling section of the sshd2_config is as follows:

   ```
   ## Tunneling
   #     AllowX11Forwarding              yes
   #     AllowTcpForwarding              yes
   #     AllowTcpForwardingForUsers      sj1, cowboyneal@slashdot\.org
   #     DenyTcpForwardingForUsers       2[[:digit:]]*4,peelo
   #     AllowTcpForwardingForGroups     privileged_tcp_forwarders
   #     DenyTcpForwardingForGroups      coming_from_outside
   #
   # Local port forwardings to host 10.1.0.25 ports 143 and 25 are
   # allowed for all users in group users.
   # Note that forwardings using the name of this host will be allowed
   #  (if it can be resolved from the DNS).
   #
   #   ForwardACL allow local .*%users \i10\.1\.0\.25%(143|25)
   #
   # Local port forwardings requested exactly to host proxy.company.com
   # port 8080 are allowed for users that have 's' as first character
   # and belong to the group with group id 10:
   #
   #   ForwardACL allow local s.*%10 proxy\.company\.com%8080
   ```

```
#
# Remote port forwarding is denied for all users to all hosts:
#  ForwardACL deny remote .* .*
```

4. Uncomment the AllowTcpForwarding line by deleting the # symbol.

5. Uncomment the AllowTcpForwardingForUsers line by deleting the # symbol.

6. On the same line, delete the default entries (sjl, cowboyneal@ slashdot\.org).

7. Enter the following accounts to allow port forwarding: root, admin, and system@Aum-sshserver.com:

```
AllowTcpForwarding          yes
AllowTcpForwardingForUsers   root, admin, system@Aum-sshserver\.com
```

Notice that the \ is required before the .com. A \ is mandatory when using a symbol.

8. Continue to enter values, deny access to the backup, and test accounts while allowing the RemoteAccess group:

```
AllowTcpForwarding          yes
AllowTcpForwardingForUsers   root, admin, system@Aum-sshserver\.com
DenyTcpForwardingForUsers    backup, test
AllowTcpForwardingForGroups RemoteAccess
```

9. At this point, port-forwarding restrictions based on users have been applied.

In addition to restricting port forwarding to users and/or groups, specific IP address and ports can be granted/denied access from port-forwarded rules. This feature is very important in terms of security, since you may not want to allow port-forwarding access from the outside to every server on the inside or every server that the SSH server has access to. These filters can specifically state which servers should be accessible and automatically deny everything else. To set port- forwarding filters according to Figure 6.11, the following settings should be set in the sshd2_config file:

```
ForwardACL    allow    local.*%users \i192.\.168\.0\.10%(25)
ForwardACL    allow    local.*%users \i172.\.16\.11\.17%(80|443)
ForwardACL    allow    local.*%users \i172.\.16\.11\.8%(143)
ForwardACL    allow    local.*%users \i172.\.16\.11\.72%(3389)
```

These rules allow all users and groups to only port forward to 192.168.0.10 (port 25), 172.16.11.17 (port 80 and 443), 172.16.11.8 (port 143), and 172.16.11.72 (port 3389), while denying access to all other servers. Notice the syntax used for the port forwarding ACLs. A \i is required before the first octet of the IP address, and a \ is required before every following octet. The complete syntax is as follows:

```
ForwardACL argument  users   \iIP\.Address\.of\.server%(port|port|port)
```

DNS names can also be used for ForwardACL statements. For example, if Aum.terminalserver.com is the destination server, on port 3389, the following syntax can be used:

```
ForwardACL Allow .*%users Aum\.terminalserver\.com%3389
```

Note that once Allow rules are applied on the SSH server, all other servers and/or devices will not be granted port-forwarding access. For example, only the servers specifically allowed will be accessible by the SSH clients who are port forwarding. All other servers will be denied by default unless otherwise stated. (This denial makes any Deny rules redundant, since everything else besides the server that has been allowed is denied automatically.) Furthermore, any server port-forwarding filtering overrides any client port-forwarding rules on the SSH clients themselves.

Configuration for SSH Communications' SSH Server (Windows)

SSH Communications provides an SSH server for Windows as well as Unix. Unlike the Unix version, the Windows version is configured and enabled using a GUI, as described earlier in the "SSH Communications' SSH server" section of Chapter 2.

The SSH server in Figure 6.11, 11.30.11.21, has a routable IP address that can be accessible from both internal networks and external networks, such as the Internet. By default, SSH Communications' SSH server enables port forwarding, so there is no special configuration required on the SSH server after installation has been completed. (See Chapter 1 for how to install an SSH server.) SSH Communications provides the ability to permit or deny port forwarding, also known as tunneling, on the SSH server. For example, if port forwarding is not desired, tunnel settings can be denied completely while still allowing terminal and/or SFTP access. In addition to permitting or restricting port forwarding, SSH Communications' allows port forwarding for only a specified set of users and denial for everyone else. Furthermore, the ability to deny port forwarding for a set number of users and allow everyone else is possible. To view the tunnel configuration options and configure these options on SSH Communications' SSH server, perform the following steps:

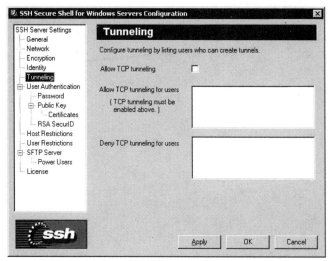

Figure 6.20   SSH Communications' Tunneling options.

1. Start ⇨ Programs ⇨ SSH Secure Shell Server ⇨ Configuration.

2. Under SSH Server Settings, browse to Tunneling. As shown in Figure 6.20, SSH Communications' Tunneling menu can allow or deny tunnels.

3. Check the Allow TCP Tunneling checkbox.

4. In the Allow TCP Tunneling for Users textbox, enter the usernames you would like to permit port forwarding to, such as the administrator account and other admin-level accounts (separated by a comma).

5. In the Deny TCP Tunneling for Users textbox, enter the usernames you would like to restrict port forwarding to, such as the guest account and other nonauthorized accounts (separated by a comma).

6. Select the Apply button.

7. Tunneling (port forwarding) restrictions have now been applied. As shown in Figure 6.21, tunneling restrictions and permissions are easy to apply.

The SSH server has now been configured with Terminal, SFTP/SCP, and port forwarding; port forwarding, however, is restricted to the administrator, chandradhar, and prabha accounts and is specifically denied to the guest, IUSR_SSH, and backup accounts.

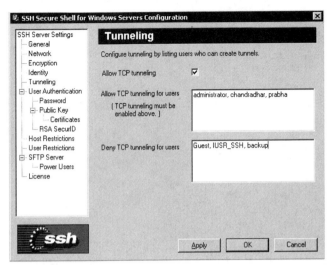

Figure 6.21   SSH Communications' Tunneling configuration options.

Configuration for VanDyke Software's VShell SSH Server

VanDyke Software provides an SSH server for Windows called VShell. The Windows version is configured and enabled using a GUI, as described earlier in the "VShell SSH Server" section of Chapter 2.

The SSH server in Figure 6.11, 11.30.11.21, also has a routable IP address that can be accessible from both internal networks and external networks, such as the Internet. Port forwarding is also enabled by default on the VShell server, so there is no special configuration needed on the SSH server after installation has been completed (see Chapter 1 for installing an SSH server). Similar to SSH Communications' SSH server, VShell also provides the ability to restrict or permit port-forwarding access, but it places the permissions and/or restrictions on the port-forwarded servers instead of on the users. For example, in Figure 6.11, port forwarding would be filtered by allowing the tunneling to the mail relay, mail server, Web server, and windows terminal server but then restricted to the other IP addresses on the internal network. In addition to permitting or restricting port forwarding by IP address, the ability to allow port forwarding for a specified hostname, network subnet (netmask), or domain can also be set. For example, if all servers in the 192.168.0.0 network were allowed to be port forwarded to, the entire network subnet could be set, instead of adding several hundred machines. Similarly, if all servers in the internal network are off limits and have the IP address range of 172.16.1.0-172.16.1.254, the entire subnet can be restricted. To view the filter-configuration options and configure these options on the VShell SSH server, perform the following steps:

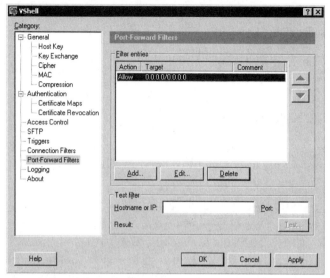

Figure 6.22 The VShell filtering options.

1. Start ⇨ Programs ⇨ VShell ⇨ VShell.

2. Browse to the Port-Forward Filters section (see Figure 6.22).

In order to configure the port-forwarding options according to Figure 6.11, use the following steps.

1. Notice the default rule that allows port forwarding to all machines. Delete this rule by highlighting the rule and selecting Delete.

2. Select Add to add filtering entries.

3. Select the drop-down box next to Filter Type to view the type options, including IP address, Hostname, Netmask, and Domain (see Figure 6.23).

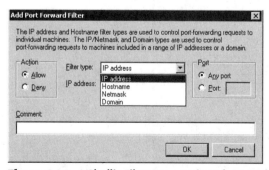

Figure 6.23 VShell's Filter Type options for port-forwarding filters.

4. In the Allow section, select the Allow radio button.

5. For the Filter type, select IP address.

6. In the IP address field, type **192.168.0.10**.

7. In the Port section, select the Port radio button and type **25** in the text box.

8. In the Comment field, type **Mail Relay**.

9. Select OK.

10. Repeat steps 7 through 11 for the other three servers. The final result should look like Figure 6.24.

Once Allow rules are applied on the VShell SSH server, only the servers specifically allowed will be accessible via port forwarding, all other servers and/or devices will not be accessible. This makes any Deny rules redundant, since everything else is denied automatically besides the server that has been allowed. Furthermore, any server port-forwarding filters override any client port-forwarding rules on the SSH clients themselves.

If the entire network were allowed to port forward, except for a few specified servers, both Allow filters and Deny filters would be required. For example, if the internal network had an IP range of 172.16.1.1-172.16.1.254 and the only server restricted was 172.16.1.100, the VShell port-forwarding filtering would need to look like Figure 6.25, where the 172.16.1.0 network is permitted and the 172.16.1.100 server is specifically denied.

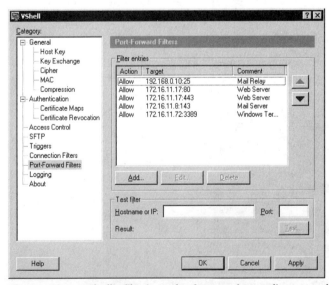

Figure 6.24 VShell's filtering rules for port-forwarding according to Figure 6.11.

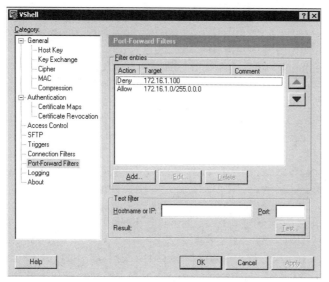

Figure 6.25   Access to the internal network, except for one server.

Make sure the Deny filter comes before the Allow filter, since filters are read from top to bottom and are executed immediately once there is a match.

Advantages to SSH Port Forwarding

The strong benefits of port forwarding involve its advanced usage, with little to no added complexity. While many organizations spend thousands of dollars and architectural resources to deploy IPSec VPNs, restrictions on the IPSec, such as NAT-enabled networks, often limit the type of access that remote users may utilize. While SSH port forwarding also has its limitations, the use of port forwarding, combined with its ease of use, its low overhead for setup, and its simplicity, makes port forwarding a very attractive remote-access solution.

You also probably notice that unlike other client/server architectures, most of the configuration of port forwarding is required on the SSH client, not on the SSH server. Most, if not all, SSH2 servers have SSH port forwarding enabled by default. This allows any client to take full advantage of the features after a basic default install of any SSH server. No special configuration or options are required after the initial installation of the SSH server is completed; however, additional configuration options can be enabled on certain SSH servers after installation. As stated before, the SSH client requires most, if not all, the configuration attention. In order to forward ports from the client to a remote server or vice-versa, the options need to be configured on the SSH client and enabled before the SSH connection has been established. While this effort is relatively low and usually required only once, many new users are not accustomed to the fact that no server-side configuration is required, only client-side configuration. The concept, while being relatively simple, confuses many new SSH users, thinking that in addition to client-side configuration, some magical tricks need to be configured on the SSH server also, which could not be farther from the truth. Once the port-forwarding configuration has been enabled on the SSH client, the port-forwarding tunnels should be fully functional.

The use of different SSH clients with port forwarding are also described in this chapter. While many of the SSH clients provide similar, if not the same, features as one another, there are some subtle differences that should be reviewed in order to select the best SSH client for your situation or organization.

While providing different functionality and usage, both local and remote port forwarding offer benefits to the entire SSH architecture. The fact that most TCP ports can be tunneled over an encrypted SSH session gives port forwarding and SSH a whole new identification. Instead of SSH being a solution for only encrypted Telnet, SSH now becomes a viable solution for any insecure TCP ports, especially mail protocols, such as POP3, IMAP, SMTP, intranet protocols, such as HTTP, and remote-management protocols, such as VNC, Windows Terminal server, X11, and pcAnywhere. Also, the most popular usage of SSH, which is encrypted terminal access, becomes a completely secondary feature. SSH is often deployed only for its port-forwarding capabilities, ignoring any terminal or SFTP access it may provide. Lastly, with its completely flexible architecture, combined with its fully encrypted communication, SSH port forwarding provides the ability to access almost any machine over any hostile or untrusted network with the full assurance of the safety and security of the remote session. The fact that the SSH session is fully encrypted, provides two-factor authentication options, and still grants virtually full access to the desired remote server or network makes SSH more flexible than other standard encryption applications.

Summary

This chapter discusses some of the networking basics of one of the more powerful features of SSH. Details on the port-forwarding architecture from both an SSH-client and an SSH-server perspective are introduced and demonstrated. From the initial discussion in the early sections of this chapter, you learn that not only does port forwarding allow SSH to secure weak protocols, such as mail protocols, file transfer protocols, and remote management protocols, but that it also provides the same functionality that end-users are accustomed to. Both remote and local port forwarding give SSH and SSH users an abundance of flexibility in current network architectures, due to their ability to adapt and co-exist with existing technologies, devices, and applications.

Once a framework is established regarding what port forwarding is, the chapter focuses on how to use it. The chapter discusses the configuration details of port-forwarding options on three SSH clients: OpenSSH, SSH Communications', and SecureCRT. Also, the chapter discusses the configuration details of three SSH servers: OpenSSH, SSH Communications', and VShell. Now that you know what port forwarding is and how to use it, how to optimize it with its basic and advanced features can be addressed. In the next chapter, the focus shifts from the theory, setup, and basic installation of port forwarding on clients and servers to the advanced uses of port forwarding, such as remote-access solutions. Many of the concepts discussed in this chapter are fully utilized in the next one, but with an added demonstration of their full flexibility and optimal usage. When deploying a remote-access solution for an organization or a backup VPN solution for a particular department/entity, it is important to understand the many uses of resources, such as port forwarding.

Secure Remote Access

Remote access solutions in various organizations need to meet strict requirements in order to satisfy the needs of their end-users, which can range from road warriors working from hotel rooms to technical administrators working from home. While remote access solutions need to be available, functional, and flexible, security concerns often get overlooked. For example, how many remote users in your network use the following items to get access to company resources?

- SMTP and POP/IMAP to retrieve e-mail
- Dialup modems when inside Network Address Translated (NAT'd) Local Area Networks
- SMB or NFS for remote file access
- PPTP, VNC, or pcAnywhere for remote management

If your organization does have several people who do access internal resources with any of these items, especially with the second option, you probably could use SSH as a partial or full remote access solution. I cannot discuss the topic of remote access solutions without bringing up IPSec as the standard remote access solution. While IPSec might be the favorable solution for many remote access architectures, it might have limitations that may not make it the best solution for you. For example, its cost requirements, its setbacks in NAT'd networks, and its significantly larger deployment requirements might not make it the optimal solution for you.

Following up from the previous chapter, in this chapter I examine the advanced usage of port forwarding in the context of remote access, specifically:

- Secure e-mail with SSH
- Secure File Transfer (SMBand NFS) with SSH
- Secure management (pcAnywhere, VNC, Terminal Services) with SSH
- Secure VPN with SSH (PPP over SSH)

Secure E-mail with SSH

The use of common e-mail protocols, such as SMTP, POP3, and IMAP, greatly increases the security exposures in an organization's e-mail architecture. Nevertheless, while there may be the availability of SSL-enabled POP3 and IMAP, the use of SMTP still allows outgoing e-mail exchanges to go over clear-text. While the use of clear-text protocols for any type of application, including e-mail, management, and file transfer, is just a bad idea, the use of clear-text protocols on the Internet is an even worse idea. The use of SSH can help mitigate some of the issues with clear-text e-mail protocols by using port forwarding with an SSH server to tunnel the SMTP and POP3/IMAP protocols over the Internet inside an SSH tunnel. This not only prevents unauthorized users from sniffing and reading other people's e-mail but also offers the ability to enforce two-factor authentication with the SSH connection, thus increasing the overall security of the e-mail architecture.

In this section, I demonstrate how to implement an SSH architecture with port forwarding to support secure e-mail. The architecture I will be using is shown in Figure 7.1.

Figure 7.1 shows an SSH server, listening on port 22 (SSH), and a mail-relay server, listening on port 25 (SMTP), in the Internet DMZ off the perimeter firewall. The corporate e-mail server is located inside the internal network, which is listening on port 110 (POP3).

The first example will assume that the SSH server is a Unix machine running OpenSSH, that the SSH client is SecureCRT running on a Windows platform for the road warriors, and that the e-mail client is Outlook Express. The mail relay and the e-mail servers can be any application, since no changes are required on either of these devices.

NOTE Any SSH server, SSH client, or e-mail client can be used for the secure e-mail architecture. My example is a random selection from the different SSH applications I have discussed thus far.

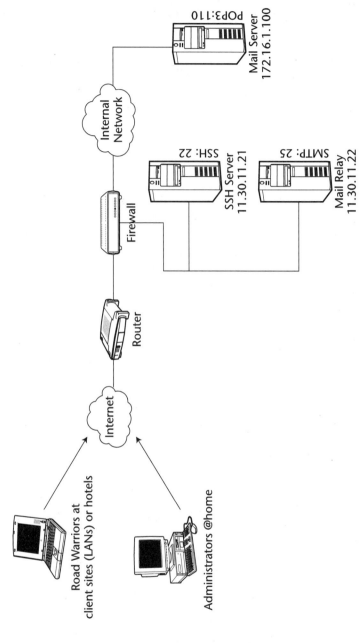

Figure 7.1   Secure e-mail architecture.

Setting Up the SSH Server

Since I am using the OpenSSH on a Unix, no special changes are required. The service will automatically port forward all connections to and from the SSH server. That being said, some specific rules need to be on the adjacent firewall to ensure that port-forwarding communications will be allowed. First, the firewall's external interface (the interface that faces the Internet) must allow connections from the outside Internet to the SSH server, specifically port 22 on IP address 11.30.11.21. Second, on the firewall's DMZ interface (the interface that connects to the SSH server and mail relay), connections from the SSH server must be allowed to the internal mail server, specifically allowing IP address 11.30.11.21 on any source port to port 110 on IP address 172.16.1.100. Lastly, connections from the SSH server to the mail relay inside the DMZ network need to be allowed, specifically from 11.30.11.21 on any source port to port 25 on IP address 11.30.11.22.

After the SSH server has been completely installed and the firewall rules are in place, the SSH server is ready for the secure e-mail architecture.

Setting Up the SSH Client

Once the SSH server has been set up, the SSH client on the road-warrior laptops should be configured. Using SecureCRT 4.0 or above, configure as follows:

1. Select Start ➪ Programs ➪ SecureCRT ➪ SecureCRT.
2. Choose File ➪ Quick Connect.
3. Select SSH2 as the Protocol field.
4. Enter **11.30.11.21** for the Hostname field.
5. Enter **22** to the Port field.
6. Enter the correct username, such as Kusum, in the Username field.
7. Make sure the "Save session" box is checked.
8. Select "Connect" and log in to the SSH server with the appropriate password.
9. After the session has been established, disconnect the session, File ➪ Disconnect.
10. Select File ➪ Connect and highlight the 11.30.11.21 option.
11. Right-click 11.30.11.21 and the select properties.
12. Highlight the Port Forwarding section.

Now that the setup is complete, you can add the local port-forwarding options:

13. Select Add to display the Port Forwarding options.

14. Enter **Mail Relay** for the Name field.

15. In the Local subsection, make sure "Manually select local IP address on which to allow connections" is unchecked.

16. In the Local subsection, enter **25** for the Port field.

17. In the Remote subsection, make sure "Destination host is different from the SSH server" is checked.

18. Enter **11.30.11.22** for the Hostname field.

19. In the Remote subsection, enter **port 25** for the Port field.

20. Do not enter anything for the Application subsection.

21. Select OK.

Now that the Mail Relay local port-forwarding option is set up, the Mail Server local port-forwarding option can be set:

22. Select Add to display the Port Forwarding options.

23. Enter **Mail Server** for the Name field.

24. In the Local subsection, make sure "Manually select local IP address on which to allow connections" is unchecked.

25. In the Local subsection, enter **110** for the Port field.

26. In the Remote subsection, make sure "Destination host is different from the SSH server" is checked.

    a. Enter **11.30.11.22** for the Hostname field.

27. In the Remote subsection, enter port **110** for the Port field.

28. In the Application subsection, enter the path for Outlook Express. Once the SSH session has been established, this option will open Outlook Express automatically, requiring no interaction from the end-user. While this option may seem trivial, requiring one fewer step for novice end-users is significant. This option virtually allows one-step execution for secure e-mail.

    a. "c:\Program Files\Outlook Express\msimn.exe"

29. Select OK.

The result should look like Figure 7.2.

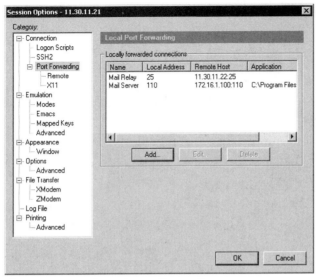

Figure 7.2 Local port-forwarding settings.

After the SSH client has been completely installed, the e-mail client is ready for the secure e-mail architecture.

Setting Up the E-mail Client

Once the SSH client has been set up, the e-mail client on the road-warrior laptops should be configured. Using Microsoft Outlook Express 4.0 or above, configure as follows:

1. Start ⇨ Programs ⇨ Outlook Express.

2. Select Tools from the menu bar and select Accounts.

3. Select the Mail tab.

4. Select the Add button and choose mail option.

5. For Display name, enter the name you would like to have displayed for your e-mail account, such as Mohandas Gandhi. Select Next.

6. For E-mail address, enter your e-mail address given to you by your e-mail administrator, such as gandhi@bharat.com. Select Next.

7. The next screen should be the E-mail Server Names. There are four steps to complete here:

   a. If you are using POP3, select POP3 for your incoming mail server (if you are using IMAP, make sure IMAP is selected for your incoming server).

  b. For the Incoming mail server, enter **127.0.0.1**. Remember, you have already set up your our port-forwarding steps in the prior section. Once the SSH session has been established, local ports will listen on port 25 and 110. When Outlook Express attempts to connect to 127.0.0.1 on 110, it will be redirected by the SSH client to the e-mail server of the SSH tunnel.

  c. For the Outgoing mail server, enter **127.0.0.1**.

  d. Select Next.

 8. Enter your account name given to you by your e-mail administrator, such as Gandhi.

 9. Enter your password, if you would like; however, I recommend you leave this blank and allow the application to prompt you for authentication every time you log in. Select Next.

 10. Click Finish. The e-mail client for secure e-mail has been completed.

 11. To verify, highlight 127.0.0.1 in the account field and choose the Properties button on the right. Figures 7.3, 7.4, and 7.5 show how the General, Servers, and Advanced tabs should look on your e-mail client.

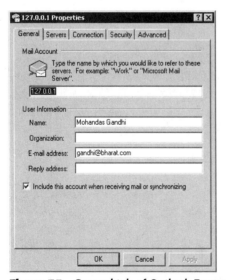

Figure 7.3 General tab of Outlook Express.

Figure 7.4 Servers tab of Outlook Express.

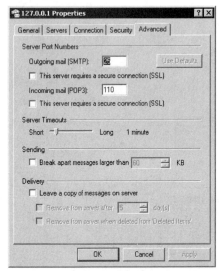

Figure 7.5 Advanced tab of Outlook Express.

Once you have verified your setting, select OK and Close. You have completed the e-mail client setup for SSH.

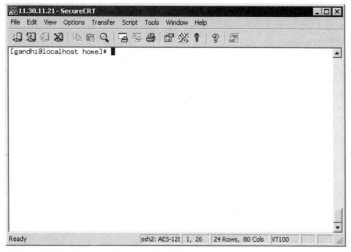

Figure 7.6   Connection to the SSH server.

Executing Secure E-mail

At this point, you have completed the necessary steps for secure e-mail. You have configured your SSH server and appropriate firewall rules, configured your SSH client for port forwarding, and configured your e-mail client to use your loopback address.

In order to start using the secure e-mail architecture, open SecureCRT and connect to the SSH server, as shown in Figure 7.6.

To verify the port-forwarding tunnels, type **netstat –an** on the command line, and both port 25 and port 110 should be listening on the IP address 0.0.0.0, as shown in Figure 7.7.

```
Active Connections

  Proto  Local Address          Foreign Address        State
  TCP    0.0.0.0:25             0.0.0.0:0              LISTENING
  TCP    0.0.0.0:110            0.0.0.0:0              LISTENING
  TCP    0.0.0.0:135            0.0.0.0:0              LISTENING
  TCP    0.0.0.0:445            0.0.0.0:0              LISTENING
  TCP    0.0.0.0:1025           0.0.0.0:0              LISTENING
  TCP    0.0.0.0:1027           0.0.0.0:0              LISTENING
  TCP    0.0.0.0:1029           0.0.0.0:0              LISTENING
  TCP    0.0.0.0:1031           0.0.0.0:0              LISTENING
  TCP    0.0.0.0:1160           0.0.0.0:0              LISTENING
  TCP    0.0.0.0:1169           0.0.0.0:0              LISTENING
```

Figure 7.7   Local port-forwarding connections listening on ports 25 and 110.

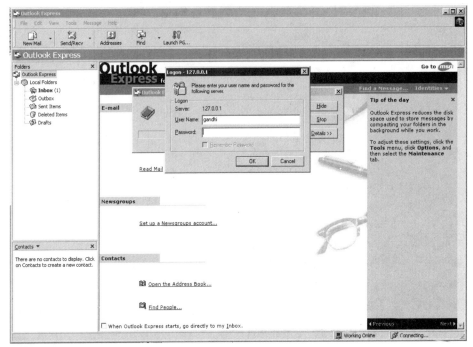

Figure 7.8   Outlook Express.

Once the SSH server has been established, Outlook Express should automatically open. You should automatically be prompted to log in with your correct password, as shown in Figure 7.8.

Once you have authenticated, your e-mail should be downloaded from the e-mail server over the encrypted SSH tunnel.

Note that the e-mail communication will be going through its native protocols, such as SMTP and POP3, to and from the SSH server on the internal network; however, the e-mail communication will be encrypted in the SSH tunnel from the SSH server, over the Internet, to the e-mail client.

Congratulations! You have just implemented a secure e-mail architecture over the Internet.

Secure File Transfer (SMB and NFS) with SSH

Common file transfer protocols such as SMB (Server Message Block), and NFS (Network File System) are often used in many network environments to share files to and from file servers. For example, Windows networking relies heavily on NetBIOS with SMB for file transfers to and from Windows servers and clients. While the need for SMB is quite important, the attack threats of SMB and NetBIOS greatly increase the security exposures in many Windows networks. While use of NetBIOS with SMB may be appropriate for internal networks, exposure of SMB file sharing to remote users and hostile networks, such as the Internet, is not. Nevertheless, although SMB over the Internet is not appropriate, remote users still need access to corporate file servers, including Windows file servers. Secure remote access is where SSH can be used for secure file access.

In addition to SMB, NFS (over TCP) also is exposed to many security threats in an organization. NFS is a clear-text protocol. Authentication information, as well as payload information, can be sniffed from this protocol. Also, as with SMB, NFS is dangerous to use in hostile networks such as the Internet. NFS vulnerability attacks are abundant; therefore, any use of this protocol can significantly increase the security risk of your organization. Nevertheless, as with SMB, the security vulnerabilities with NFS do not make the desire to gain remote file access over hostile networks any less demanding. While the security threats may be high with this protocol, the demand for remote file access needs to be met. This is also where SSH can be used for secure file access.

The use of SSH can help mitigate some of the issues with vulnerable or clear-text file transfer protocols by using port forwarding with an SSH server to tunnel the SMB and NFS protocols over the Internet inside an SSH tunnel. This not only protects against security attacks and unauthorized sniffing but also offers the ability to enforce two-factor authentication with the SSH connection, thus increasing the overall security of the file transfer architecture.

In this section, I will demonstrate how to implement an SSH architecture with port forwarding to support secure file transfer. The architecture I will be using is shown in Figure 7.9.

Figure 7.9 shows an SSH server, listening on port 22 (SSH), and two internal file servers. The two file servers include a Windows 2000 file server, listening on port 445 (SMB over TCP), a Sun Solaris NFS file server, listening on port 2049 (NFS over TCP) and port 1026 (mountd). The SSH server is located in Internet DMZ off the perimeter firewall, segmented from the internal network. The corporate file servers are located inside the internal network, fully accessible to internal employees for file access.

The second example will assume that the SSH server is a Windows machine running VanDyke Software's VShell SSH server, that the SSH client is SSH Communications' SSH2 client running on a Unix platform for the road warriors, and that the file transfer clients are smbclients for SMB and mount for NFS. Any SSH server or SSH client can be used. The example is a random selection from the different SSH applications I have discussed thus far.

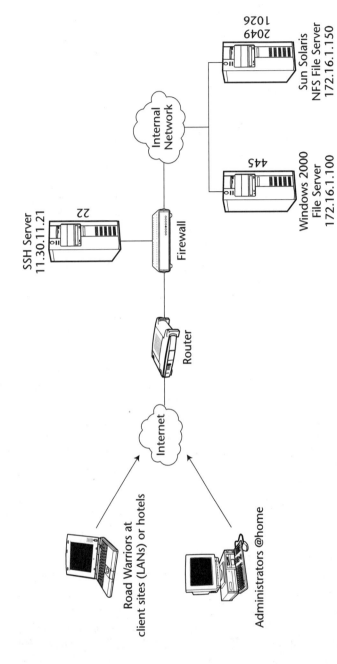

Figure 7.9 Secure file-sharing architecture.

Table 7.1 Firewall Rules That Need to Be Enabled

RULE NUMBER	SOURCE	DESTINATION	SERVICE	ACTION
1	Any	SSH-Server	Port 22	Allow
2	SSH server	Windows File Server	Port 445	Allow
3	SSH server	Solaris NFS file server	Port 2049 Port 1026	Allow
4	Any	Any	Any	Deny

Setting Up the SSH Server

Since I am using the VShell SSH server on a Windows platform, no special changes are required. The service will automatically port forward all connections to and from the SSH server. Nevertheless, similar to the first example, there needs to be some specific rules on the adjacent firewall to ensure that port forwarding communications will be allowed. First, on the firewall's external interface (the interface that faces the Internet), connections must be allowed from the outside Internet to the SSH server, specifically port 22 on IP address 11.30.11.21. Second, the firewall's DMZ interface (the interface that connects to the SSH server), needs to allow connections from the SSH server to the internal file servers. Specifically, the rules need to allow the SSH server (11.30.11.21) on any source port to port 445 on the Windows file server (172.16.1.100) and allow the SSH server (11.30.11.21) on any source port to port 2049 and 1026 on the Solaris NFS file server (172.16.1.150). Table 7.1 shows an example of the firewall rules.

After the SSH server has been completely installed and the firewall rules are in place, the SSH server is ready for the secure file transfer architecture.

Setting Up the SSH Client

Once the SSH server has been set up, the SSH client on the road-warrior Unix laptops should be configured. Using SSH Communications' SSH server version 3.0 or above, configure as follows:

1. Change directories to your home directory.
2. Since you would like to connect to both file servers, you will have local port-forwarding options for each of them with the use of the –L option

on a single command. You need to have three local port-forwarding options to set, specifically 445 for SMB and 2049 and 1026 for NFS/Mountd.:

```
-L 445:172.16.1.100:445
-L 2049:172.16.1.150:2049
-L 1026:172.16.1.150:1026
```

3. Type the appropriate SSH command with local port forwarding:

```
#ssh 11.30.11.21 -p 22 -l <username> -L 445:172.16.1.100:445 -L
2049:172.16.1.150:2049 -L 1026:172.16.1.150:1026
```

4. Since typing that very long command will become tedious over time, create a configuration file for your local port-forwarding options:

   a. Open a blank file (using Vi or Emacs, whichever you like. I recommend Vi, but you Emac lovers are outnumbering us Vi lovers).

   b. Enter the following lines into the file. These lines specify the local port-forwarding options:

   ```
   LocalForward        "445:172.16.1.100:445"
   LocalForward        "2049:172.16.1.150:2049"
   LocalForward        "1026:172.16.1.150:1026"
   ```

   c. Save the file in your home directory as Config.

5. Type the appropriate SSH command, referencing the new config file:

```
#ssh 11.30.11.21 -p 22 -l <username> -F Config
```

That's it! To verify that the SSH connection has executed the port forwards, type **netstat –an** on port 445, 2049, and 1026 should be listening on the local interface, as shown in Figure 7.10.

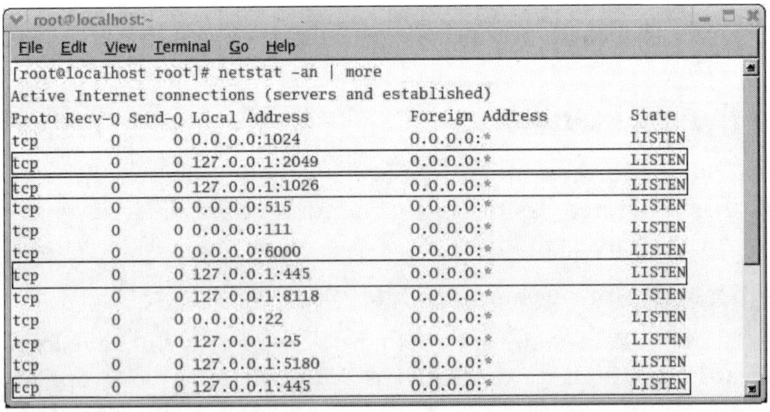

Figure 7.10 Ports 445, 2049, and 1026 listening on the road warrior's Unix system.

After the SSH client has been completely configured, the file server clients are ready for the secure file server architecture.

Setting Up the File Server Clients

As with the SSH server, no special configuration is required for the file transfer clients. Each client, including smbclient and mount, is a stand-alone command-line client that can be used seamlessly with SSH. As with the e-mail client in the first example, all connections, instead of directing things to the real servers, will be directed locally to the loopback interface, specifically 127.0.0.1, to connect to the local port forwards set up by the SSH connection, which will then take those connections and forward them to the appropriate servers over the SSH connection.

Executing Secure File Transfer

At this point, you have completed the necessary steps for secure file transfer. You have configured your SSH server and appropriate firewall rules, configured your SSH client for port forwarding, and configured your file transfer client to use your loopback address.

In order to start using the secure file transfer architecture, execute SSH Communications' SSH client and connect and authenticate to the VShell SSH server, as shown in Figure 7.11.

After authenticating, verify the port-forwarding tunnels on the SSH connection by typing **netstat –an** on the command line. Ports 445, 2049, and 1026 should be listening on the loopback address. (See Figure 7.12.)

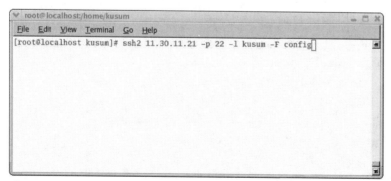

Figure 7.11   Connection to the SSH server.

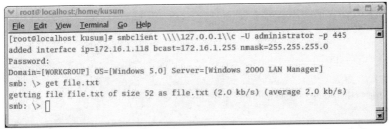

```
root@localhost:~                                                        _ □ X
File  Edit  View  Terminal  Go  Help
[root@localhost root]# netstat -an | more
Active Internet connections (servers and established)
Proto Recv-Q Send-Q Local Address          Foreign Address        State
tcp       0      0 0.0.0.0:1024            0.0.0.0:*              LISTEN
tcp       0      0 127.0.0.1:2049          0.0.0.0:*              LISTEN
tcp       0      0 127.0.0.1:1026          0.0.0.0:*              LISTEN
tcp       0      0 0.0.0.0:515             0.0.0.0:*              LISTEN
tcp       0      0 0.0.0.0:111             0.0.0.0:*              LISTEN
tcp       0      0 0.0.0.0:6000            0.0.0.0:*              LISTEN
tcp       0      0 127.0.0.1:445           0.0.0.0:*              LISTEN
tcp       0      0 127.0.0.1:8118          0.0.0.0:*              LISTEN
tcp       0      0 0.0.0.0:22              0.0.0.0:*              LISTEN
tcp       0      0 127.0.0.1:25            0.0.0.0:*              LISTEN
tcp       0      0 127.0.0.1:5180          0.0.0.0:*              LISTEN
tcp       0      0 127.0.0.1:445           0.0.0.0:*              LISTEN
```

Figure 7.12   Local port-forwarding connections listening on ports 445, 2049, and 1026.

Secure File Sharing with SMB and SSH

Once the SSH connection has been established, you can attempt to log in to the Windows SMB file server. To transfer files to and from the c share on the Windows file server, type the following command on the Unix SSH client:

```
#smbclient  \\\\127.0.0.1\\c -U <username> -p 445
```

smbclient has very simple syntax: -U is for the username; -p is for the port number. This command will connect to the local port on 445 and then be forwarded by the SSH session. After the connection reaches the Windows file server, you should be prompted for a password. Use your Windows file server password given to you by your Windows administrator and log in. After you have entered the correct password, you will now be able to upload and download files from the Windows file server using simple Get and Put commands. The results should look like Figure 7.13.

```
root@localhost:/home/kusum                                            _ □ X
File  Edit  View  Terminal  Go  Help
[root@localhost kusum]# smbclient \\\\127.0.0.1\\c -U administrator -p 445
added interface ip=172.16.1.118 bcast=172.16.1.255 nmask=255.255.255.0
Password:
Domain=[WORKGROUP] OS=[Windows 5.0] Server=[Windows 2000 LAN Manager]
smb: \> get file.txt
getting file file.txt of size 52 as file.txt (2.0 kb/s) (average 2.0 kb/s)
smb: \> []
```

Figure 7.13   The results of file sharing with SSH with SMB and smbclient.

Notice a couple of things about Figure 7.13. First, observe that the connection is to the loopback interface. Second, check out the password prompt by the remote Windows file server, which is still over the SSH tunnel. (This solves problems of NTLM weaknesses also, which will not be discussed here.) Lastly, mark the get file.txt command, which downloads the file called file.txt from the remote Windows file server to the local Unix laptop, all over the encrypted SSH session.

NOTE An SSH client on Windows will not be able to forward local connections on port 445, since Windows networking does not allow SMB over TCP and another service to share port 445; thus, the SSH forward will be denied access to that local port.

This scenario allows you to use SMB over an encrypted SSH tunnel over the Internet.

Secure File Sharing with NFS and SSH

To use SSH with NFS, one additional step needs to be completed on the NFS server. The /etc/exports file, the file that holds the lists of authorized clients, needs to add the SSH server's IP address to this file. Since SSH clients will be using the SSH server to access the NFS server, it must be authorized to do so. Edit the /etc/exports file in the NFS server to the following:

```
/home 11.30.11.21 (rw, root_squash)
```

Once the change has been made and the services have been restarted, establish the session with the SSH server. Once the session has been established, you can attempt to log in to the Solaris NFS file server. To transfer files to and from the /home NFS share on the Solaris NFS file server, type the following command:

```
#mount -t nfs -o tcp,port=2049 ,mountport=1026 127.0.0.1:/home /nfsmount
```

Mount is the actual protocol to access the NFS server, using port 1026 in this example. The mount command has very simple syntax, where the IP address of the NFS server is separated by a colon to the NFS share, followed by the local path to mount the remote NFS share, such as /nfsmount in this example. This command will connect to the local port on 2049 and 1026 and then be forwarded by the SSH session. After the connection reaches the Solaris NFS file server, the NFS server will verify that you are allowed to mount this NFS share. After it verifies you, the remote NFS share should be mounted to /nfsmount on your local Unix operating system.

This scenario allows you to use NFS over an encrypted SSH tunnel over the Internet.

NOTE All file sharing in the preceding examples, including SMB and NFS, will use the native protocols from the SSH server to the file servers; however, the file transfer protocols (SMB and NFS) will be encrypted in an SSH tunnel over the Internet.

Congratulations! You have just implemented a secure file transfer architecture over the Internet.

Secure Management with SSH

The use of common management protocols, such as VNC, pcAnywhere, and Windows terminal services, which uses the RDP protocol, greatly increases the security exposures in an organization's remote management architecture. While the security exposures of the preceding applications vary, all four popular remote management applications have had security vulnerabilities associated with the application, the encryption used for the communication between the server and client, or the authentication process itself. The use of the common remote management protocols may be the attack vector for an unauthorized user or attacker to compromise an internal system from the outside. If the remote management applications are deployed in a secure, fully patched fashion, many of them only require a username and password to authenticate. As a general rule of thumb, your internal networks and servers should never be accessible with just a single username and password, whether it is a VPN (PPTP) password or a terminal services password.

The use of SSH can help mitigate some of the issues with remote management applications, poor encryption algorithms used with management protocols, and single username/password requirements. SSH can use port forwarding with an SSH server to tunnel the management protocols over the Internet inside an SSH tunnel. Doing so not only protects unauthorized users from attacking the management applications and protocols but also offers the ability to enforce two-factor authentication with the SSH connection, thus increasing the overall security of the management architecture.

In this section, I will investigate how to implement an SSH architecture with port forwarding to support secure management. The architecture I will be using is shown in Figure 7.14.

Figure 7.14 shows an SSH server, listening on port 22 (SSH) in the Internet DMZ off the perimeter firewall. Inside the internal network are three management servers, including a Windows Terminal server, listening on port 3389 (RDP), a Linux VNC server, listening on port 5901, and a pcAnywhere server, listening on ports 5631 and 5632.

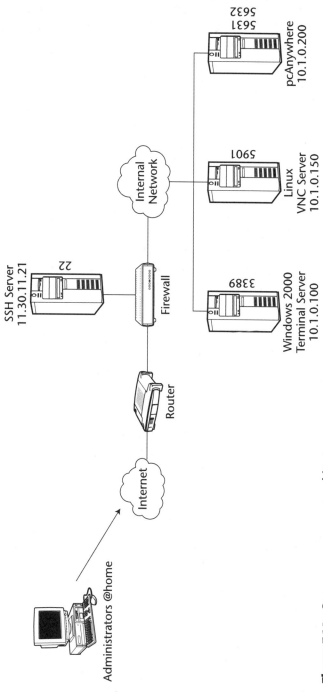

Figure 7.14   Secure management architecture.

The third example will assume that the SSH server is a Unix machine running SSH Communications' SSH server, that the SSH client is SecureCRT running on a Windows platform for the remote administrators, and that the management clients are a Terminal Services client, VNC client, and a pcAnywhere client.

NOTE Any SSH server and SSH client can be used; my example is a random selection from the different SSH applications I have discussed thus far.

Setting Up the SSH Server

Since I am using the SSH Communications' SSH server on a Unix platform, no special changes are required. The service will automatically port forward all connections to/from the SSH server. Nevertheless, as with the first example, some specific rules need to be implemented on the adjacent firewall to ensure that port-forwarding communications will be allowed. First, the firewall's external interface (the interface that faces the Internet) must allow connections from the outside Internet to the SSH server, specifically port 22 on IP address 11.30.11.21. Second, the firewall's DMZ interface (the interface that connects to the SSH server) needs to allow connections from the SSH server to the internal management servers. Specifically, the rules need to allow the SSH server (11.30.11.21) on any source port to port 3389 on the Windows Terminal server (10.1.0.100), allow the SSH server (11.30.11.21) on any source port to port 5901 on the Linux VNC server (10.1.0.150), and allow the SSH server (11.30.11.21) on any source port to port 5631 and 5632 on the pcAnywhere server 10.1.0.200). Table 7.2 shows an example of the firewall rules.

After the SSH server has been completely installed and the firewall rules are in place, the SSH server is ready for the secure management architecture.

Table 7.2 Firewall Rules That Need to Be Enabled

RULE NUMBER	SOURCE	DESTINATION	SERVICE	ACTION
1	Any	SSH server	Port 22	Allow
2	SSH server	Windows Terminal server	Port 3389	Allow
3	SSH server	Linux VNC server	Port 5901	Allow
4	SSH server	pcAnywhere server	Port 5631 Port 5632	Allow
5	Any	Any	Any	Deny

Setting Up the SSH Client

Once the SSH server has been set up, the SSH client for the remote administrators should be configured. Using SecureCRT 4.0 or above, configure as follows.

1. Select Start ⇨ Programs ⇨ SecureCRT ⇨ SecureCRT.
2. Choose File ⇨ Quick Connect.
3. Select SSH2 for the Protocol field.
4. Enter **11.30.11.21** for the Hostname field.
5. Enter **22** for the Port field.
6. Enter the correct username, such as Shreya, in the Username field.
7. Make sure the Save Session box is checked.
8. Select Connect, and log in to the SSH server with the appropriate password.
9. After the session has been established, disconnect the session by choosing File ⇨ Disconnect.
10. Select File ⇨ Connect and highlight the 11.30.11.21 option.
11. Right-click 11.30.11.21 and then select properties.
12. Highlight the Port Forwarding section.

Now that the setup is complete, you can add the local port-forwarding options.

13. Select Add to display the Port Forwarding options.
14. Enter **Terminal Server** for the Name field.
15. In the Local subsection, make sure "Manually select local IP address on which to allow connections" is unchecked.
16. In the Local subsection, enter **3389** for the Port field.
17. In the Remote subsection, make sure "Destination host is different from the SSH server" is checked.

    a. Enter **10.1.0.100** for the Hostname field.

18. In the Remote subsection, enter port **3389** for the Port field.
19. In the Application subsection, you can either leave it blank or enter the path for the Terminal Services client. If you decide to put in the path, it will execute the Terminal Services client automatically. If you leave it blank, you will have to execute the Terminal Services client manually.
20. Select OK.

Now that the terminal services local port-forwarding option is set up, the Linux VNC server local port-forwarding option can be set.

21. Select Add to display the Port Forwarding options.

22. Enter **VNC Server** for the Name field.

23. In the Local subsection, make sure "Manually select local IP address on which to allow connections" is unchecked.

24. In the Local subsection, enter **5901** for the Port field.

25. In the Remote subsection, make sure "Destination host is different from the SSH server" is checked.

    a. Enter **10.1.0.150** for the Hostname field.

26. In the Remote subsection, enter **port 5901** for the Port field.

27. In the Application subsection, you can either leave it blank or enter the path for the VNC client. If you decide to put in the path, it will execute the VNC client automatically. If you leave it blank, you will have to execute the VNC client manually.

28. Select OK.

Now that the VNC local port-forwarding option is set up, the pcAnywhere local port-forwarding option can be set.

29. Select Add to display the Port Forwarding options.

30. Enter **pcAnywhere** for the Name field.

31. In the Local subsection, make sure "Manually select local IP address on which to allow connections" is unchecked.

32. In the Local subsection, enter **5631** for the Port field.

33. In the Remote subsection, make sure "Destination host is different from the SSH server" is checked.

    a. Enter **10.1.0.200** for the Hostname field.

34. In the Remote subsection, enter **port 5631** for the Port field.

35. In the Application subsection, you can either leave it blank or enter the path for the pcAnywhere client. If you decide to put in the path, it will execute the pcAnywhere client automatically. If you leave it blank, you will have to execute the pcAnywhere client manually.

36. Select OK.

Since pcAnywhere requires two ports, you will have to add a second local port forward.

37. Select Add to display the Port Forwarding options.

38. Enter **pcAnywhere2** Server for the Name field.

39. In the Local subsection, make sure "Manually select local IP address on which to allow connections" is unchecked.

40. In the Local subsection, enter **5632** for the Port field.

41. In the Remote subsection, make sure "Destination host is different from the SSH server" is checked.

    a. Enter **10.1.0.200** for the Hostname field.

42. In the Remote subsection, enter port **5632** for the Port field.

43. You can leave the Application subsection blank.

44. Select OK.

The result should look like Figure 7.15.

After the SSH client has been completely installed, the management clients are ready for the secure management architecture.

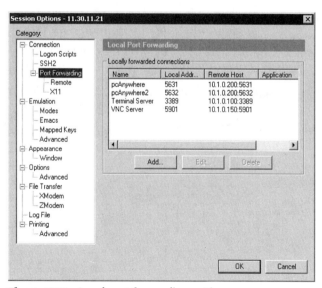

Figure 7.15 Local port-forwarding settings.

Setting Up the Management Clients

As with the SSH server, no special configuration is required on the management clients. Each client, including the Terminal Services client, the VNCviewer, and the pcAnywhere client, is a standalone command-line client that can be used seamlessly with SSH. As with the e-mail client in the first example, instead of directing things to the real servers, all connections will be directed locally to the loopback interface, specifically 127.0.0.1, to connect to the local port forwards established by the SSH connection, which will then take those connections and forward them to the appropriate servers over the SSH connection.

Executing Secure Management

At this point, you have completed the necessary steps for secure management. You have configured your SSH server and appropriate firewall rules, configured your SSH client for port forwarding, and configured your management clients to use your loopback address.

To start using the secure management architecture, execute SecureCRT and connect and authenticate to the SSH Communications' SSH server, as shown in Figure 7.16.

After authenticating, verify the port-forwarding tunnels on the SSH connection by typing **netstat –an** on the command line. Ports 3389, 5631, 5632, and 5901 should be listening on the loopback address, as shown in Figure 7.17.

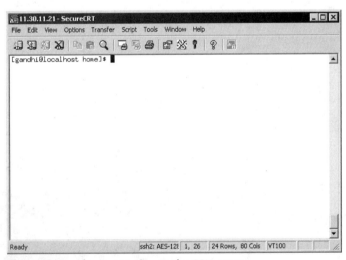

Figure 7.16   The connection to the SSH server.

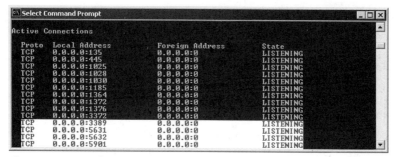

Figure 7.17   Local port-forwarding connections listening on port 3389, 5631, 5632, and 5901.

Secure Management with Windows Terminal Services and SSH

Once the SSH server has been established, you can attempt to log in to the Windows terminal server. To log in to the Windows terminal server, enter the following commands:

1. Select Start ⇨ Programs ⇨ Terminal Services Client.

2. Enter **127.0.0.1** for the Server.

3. Select Connect.

Once the Terminal Services client connects to the loopback address on port 3389, the SSH connection will forward that request to the Windows terminal server over the encryption SSH tunnel. After the connection reaches the Windows terminal server, you should see the login display and be prompted for your password, as shown in Figure 7.18.

Notice that the loopback interface is holding the connection by the designation of 127.0.0.1 in the upper left-hand corner in Figure 7.18. In order to log in, use your Windows terminal server or domain password given to you by your Windows administrator. After you have entered the correct password, you will view the desktop and have access to the operating system as if you were in front of the computer itself. You should load extra copy-and-paste utilities from Microsoft at the following Web address:

www.microsoft.com/windows2000/techinfo/reskit/tools/hotfixes/
    rdpclip-o.asp

Once the utilities are loaded, you will be able to drag and drop files from the terminal services session to your local machine over the SSH tunnel, making remote management and file transfer available with just one shot. The results should look like Figure 7.19.

Notice the 127.0.0.1 address in the upper left-hand corner in Figure 7.19. Also, notice the results of the 'ipconfig' command, which show the internal address of the Windows terminal server. At this point, any usage of the operating system can be done, including managing other operating systems, from this terminal, which occurs over a secure and encrypted SSH tunnel.

This scenario allows you to use Windows terminal services over an encrypted SSH tunnel over the Internet.

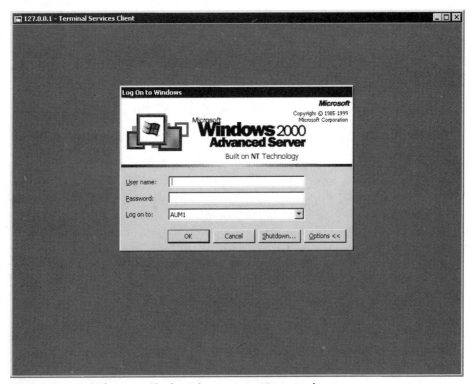

Figure 7.18   Windows terminal session over an SSH tunnel.

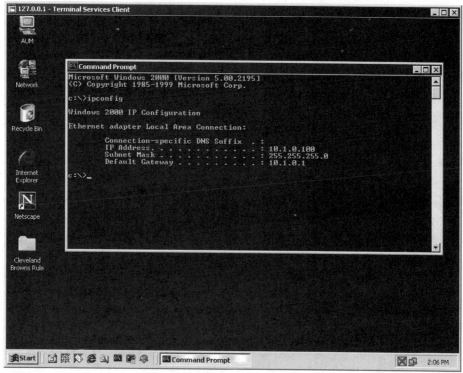

Figure 7.19   Results of Windows terminal services with SSH.

Secure Management with VNC and SSH

Once the SSH server has been established, you can attempt to log in to the Linux VNC server. To log in to the Linux VNC server, enter the following commands:

1. Change directories to the VNCviewer program (vncviewer.exe).

2. Type the following command:

   ```
   vncviewer localhost:1
   ```

   This command connects the vncviewer client on port 5901 to the local-host.

3. Select OK.

Once vncviewer connects to the loopback address on port 5901, the SSH connection will forward that request to the Linux VNC server over the encryption SSH tunnel. After the connection reaches the Linux VNC server, you should see the login display and be prompted for your session password, as shown in Figure 7.20.

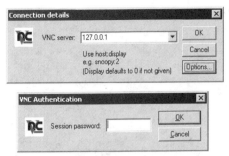

Figure 7.20 The vncviewer VNC client.

Notice that the loopback interface is used in Figure 7.20. In order to log in, you need to use your VNC server password given to you by your VNC administrator, shown at the bottom of Figure 7.20. After you have entered the correct password, you will view the desktop and have access to the operating system as if you were in front of the computer itself. The results should look like Figure 7.21.

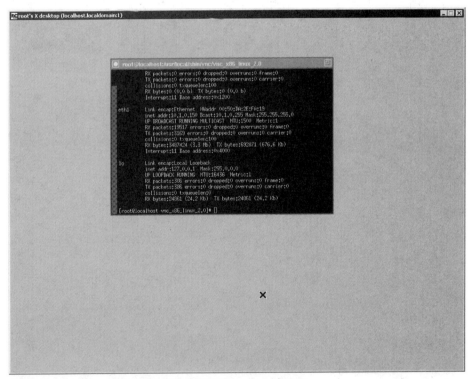

Figure 7.21 The results of the Linux VNC server with SSH.

Again, notice the localhost.localdomain:1 in the upper left-hand corner in Figure 7.21, designating that the connection is on the loopback interface (127.0.0.1). Also, notice the results of the 'ifconfig -a' command, which shows the internal address of the Linux VNC server. At this point, any usage of the operating system can be done, including managing other operating systems, from this terminal over a secure and encrypted SSH tunnel.

This scenario allows anyone to use a Linux VNC server over an encrypted SSH tunnel over the Internet.

Secure Management with pcAnywhere and SSH

Once the SSH server has been established, you can attempt to log in to the pcAnywhere server. The process to log in to the pcAnywhere Server is similar to the one used in the other two examples; however, a couple of changes need to be made on the pcAnywhere server. Since pcAnywhere uses TCP ports 5631 and 5632, there is no problem port forwarding both of those ports in one SSH session. Also, pcAnywhere uses UDP port 5632, which cannot be tunneled over the SSH session. Therefore, you must disable the use of UDP 5632 on the pcAnywhere server. To turn off UDP port 5632 on the pcAnywhere server, enter the following commands on the pcAnywhere server and the pcAnywhere client:

1. Open regedit, and select Start ⇨ Run ⇨ regedit.exe.

2. Browse to the following registry key:
   - HKLM\SOFTWARE\Symantec\pcANYWHERE\ CurrentVersion\System

3. Add a DWORD value with the following contents:
   - Value Name: TCPIPConnectIfUnknown
   - Value Data: 1

4. After making the registry changes on both the pcAnywhere server and pcAnywhere client, reboot both machines.

5. On the pcAnywhere client machine, open pcAnywhere. Enter Start ⇨ Programs ⇨ pcAnywhere.

6. Select the Remotes button.

7. Enter File ⇨ New.

8. Select the Setting tab.

9. Enter **127.0.0.1** for the "Network host PC to control or IP address:" option, as shown in Figure 7.22.

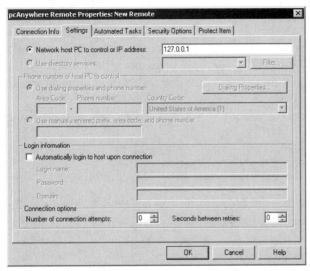

Figure 7.22   "Network host PC to control or IP address" option.

10. Select OK.

11. Name the session pcAnywhere Server.

12. Double-click the new pcAnywhere icon, and you should now be displaying the pcAnywhere connection over the secure SSH session.

Once the pcAnywhere client connects to the loopback address on ports 5631 and 5632, the SSH connection will forward that request to the pcAnywhere server over the encryption SSH tunnel. After the connection reaches the pcAnywhere server, you should see the login display and be prompted for your password. In order to log in, use your pcAnywhere server password given to you by your pcAnywhere administrator. After you have entered the correct password, you will view the desktop and have access to the operating system as if you were in front of the computer itself. The results should look like Figure 7.23.

Again, notice the results of the ipconfig command, which should be the internal address of the pcAnywhere server. At this point, any usage of the operating system can be done, including managing other operating systems, from this terminal over a secure and encrypted SSH tunnel.

This scenario allows us to use a pcAnywhere server over an encrypted SSH tunnel over the Internet.

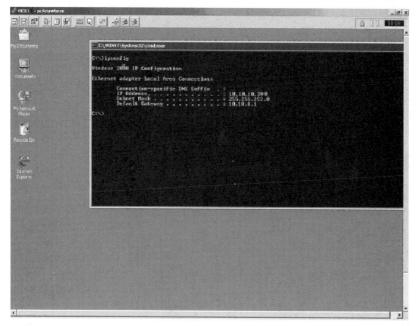

Figure 7.23 The results of the pcAnywhere server with SSH.

Secure VPN with SSH (PPP over SSH)

This section discusses the ability to use PPP (Point-to-Point Protocol) over an SSH connection as a fully functional virtual private networking (VPN) solution. If you look at traditional VPN implementations, such as IPSec implementations, PPP over SSH offers almost everything that other implementations do. For example, SSH offers strong encryption with 3DES, Point-to-Point (PPP) access, and the ability to provide multiple tunnels between two different networks. Furthermore, unlike other VPN solutions, PPP over SSH as a VPN solution does not require a significant cost for hardware appliances or software licensing, does not require significant support requirements, and has the ability to adapt to your existing network without any major re-architectural requirements. The advantages just mentioned, as well as many others, make PPP over SSH an ideal VPN solution for many small to mid-tier types of networks.

PPP over SSH does not involve port forwarding but instead uses simple PPP scripts. Figure 7.24 shows a typical PPP architecture with an SSH server.

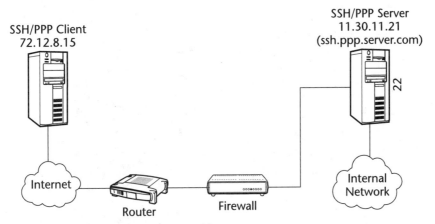

Figure 7.24   The SSH/PPP server architecture.

In the architecture shown in Figure 7.24, the SSH server is also the PPP server, which is a Linux RedHat 8.0 server running OpenSSH. Furthermore, the client in the example is a regular RedHat 8.0 client machine, with no services installed or running. No special changes are required on the firewall, except a rule that allows connections on port 22 to the SSH/PPP server. Once an SSH/PPP client makes that connection, it will have a VPN inside the internal network.

PPP Daemon on the Server

First, you must ensure the PPP daemon (pppd) is loaded and functional on your SSH server. If you are using Linux Redhat 8.0 or higher, the PPP daemon should work just fine out of the box. To confirm, type the following commands on the server:

```
#cd /usr/sbin
#pppd
```

If you see something similar to the following on the server, you know that the PPP daemon is working correctly. The PPP daemon spits out information to the screen that is not readable to end-users, but actually confirms that the PPP daemon is running correctly. The following is just an excerpt from the output of the PPP daemon:

```
~ }#_!}!}!} }4}"}&} } } } }%}&}"-1L}'}"}(}"e"~~ }#_!}!}!} }4}"}&} } } }
L}'}"}(}"e"~~ }#_!}!}!} }4}"}&} } } } }%}&}"-1L}'}"}(}"e"~~ }#_!}!}!}
}4}"}&} }} } }%}&}"-1L}'}"}(}"e"~~ }#_!}!}!} }4}"}&} } } } }%}&}"
1L}'}"}(}"e"~~ }#_!}!}!} }4}"}&} } } } }%}&}"-1L}'}"}(}"e"~~ }#_!}!}!}
```

VPN User and Sudo

Next, you must configure a user to run the pppd service. Many users choose to create a separate user account other than root, such as vpnmonkey, to execute the PPP daemon. The use of sudo ensures that remote VPN users will not have full root access to the PPP/SSH server, which would decrease the security posture of the remote access solution. If this is the route you are taking also, make sure you allow the vpnmonkey account to execute the pppd service by editing the sudoers file. Also, make sure you have set up the appropriate public-key authentication requirements for the vpnmonkey account, discussed in Chapter 4. However, to quickly refresh, make sure the public-key file (identity.pub) for the vpnmonkey account is in the authorized key file on the SSH/PPP server (/home/vpnmonkey/.ssh/authorized_keys). Furthermore, edit the sudoers file on the SSH/PPP server (/etc/sudoers) and allow vpnmonkey to start the PPP daemon. The contents of the sudoers file on the server should look like this:

```
Cmnd_Alias VPN=/usr/sbin/pppd
vpnmonkey ALL=NOPASSWD: VPN
```

To verify that su and sudo work correctly and have been configured appropriately, type the following commands on the server:

```
#su vpnmonkey
#sudo /usr/sbin/pppd noauth
```

If things are working correctly under sudo, you should see the following on the server, which is the PPP daemon spitting out information to the screen that is not readable to end-users, but actually confirms that the PPP daemon is running correctly. The following is just an excerpt of the output of the PPP daemon:

```
~ }#_!}!}!} }4}"}&} } } } }%}&}"-1L}'}"}(}"e"~~ }#_!}!}!} }4}"}&} } } }
L}'}"}(}"e"~~ }#_!}!}!} }4}"}&} } } } }%}&}"-1L}'}"}(}"e"~~ }#_!}!}!}
}4}"}&} }} } }%}&}"-1L}'}"}(}"e"~~ }#_!}!}!} }4}"}&} } } } }%}&}"
1L}'}"}(}"e"~~ }#_!}!}!} }4}"}&} } } } }%}&}"-1L}'}"}(}"e"~~ }#_!}!}!}
```

Client Script

Next, you must configure a script on the VPN client to use SSH for the PPP connection. This script was originally created on www.linuxorg.org by authors of that site.

Before editing the script, you must define the variables that will need to be customized according to the architecture. According to Figure 7.24, your server hostname will be ssh.ppp.server.com, your server username will be vpnmonkey, your server IP address will be 11.30.11.21, and your client IP address will be 72.12.8.15. The specific entries to modify are SERVER_HOST-NAME, SERVER_USERNAME, SERVER_IFIPADDR, and CLIENT_IFIPADDR.

Now that you have established the variables, you can use these variables in the script, as the following script shows in bold:

```
#!/bin/sh
# /usr/local/bin/vpn-pppssh
#
# This script initiates a ppp-ssh vpn connection.
# see the VPN PPP-SSH HOWTO on http://www.linuxdoc.org for more
information.
#
# revision history:
# 1.6 11-Nov-1996 miquels@cistron.nl
# 1.7 20-Dec-1999 bart@jukie.net
# 2.0 16-May-2001 bronson@trestle.com


#
# You will need to change these variables...
#


# The host name or IP address of the SSH server that we are
# sending the connection request to:
SERVER_HOSTNAME=ssh.ppp.server.com

# The username on the VPN server that will run the tunnel.
# For security reasons, this should NOT be root. (Any user
# that can use PPP can intitiate the connection on the client)
SERVER_USERNAME=vpnmonkey

# The VPN network interface on the server should use this address:
SERVER_IFIPADDR=11.30.11.21

# ...and on the client, this address:
CLIENT_IFIPADDR=72.12.8.15


# This tells ssh to use unprivileged high ports, even though it's
# running as root. This way, you don't have to punch custom holes
# through your firewall.
LOCAL_SSH_OPTS="-P"


#
# The rest of this file should not need to be changed.
#
```

```
PATH=/usr/local/sbin:/sbin:/bin:/usr/sbin:/usr/bin:/usr/bin/X11/:

#
# required commands...
#

PPPD=/usr/sbin/pppd
SSH=/usr/bin/ssh

if ! test -f $PPPD  ; then echo "can't find $PPPD";  exit 3; fi
if ! test -f $SSH   ; then echo "can't find $SSH";   exit 4; fi


case "$1" in
  start)
     # echo -n "Starting vpn to $SERVER_HOSTNAME: "
     ${PPPD} updetach noauth passive pty "${SSH} ${LOCAL_SSH_OPTS}
${SERVER_HOSTNAME} -l${SERVER_USERNAME} -o Batchmode=yes sudo ${PPPD}
nodetach notty noauth" ipparam vpn ${CLIENT_IFIPADDR}:${SERVER_IFIPADDR}
     # echo "connected."
     ;;

  stop)
        # echo -n "Stopping vpn to $SERVER_HOSTNAME: "
        PID=`ps ax | grep "${SSH} ${LOCAL_SSH_OPTS} ${SERVER_HOSTNAME} -
l${SERVER_USERNAME} -o" | grep -v ' passive ' | grep -v 'grep ' | awk
'{print $1}'`
        if [ "${PID}" != "" ]; then
          kill $PID
          echo "disconnected."
        else
          echo "Failed to find PID for the connection"
        fi
     ;;

  config)
    echo "SERVER_HOSTNAME=$SERVER_HOSTNAME"
    echo "SERVER_USERNAME=$SERVER_USERNAME"
    echo "SERVER_IFIPADDR=$SERVER_IFIPADDR"
    echo "CLIENT_IFIPADDR=$CLIENT_IFIPADDR"
   ;;

  *)
    echo "Usage: vpn {start|stop|config}"
    exit 1
    ;;
esac

exit 0
```

Save the script as wee-pee-en, or whatever you wish, and make it executable (chmod a+x wee-pee-en). After the script is executable, enter the following command on the client to use the wee-pee-en script and access the SSH/VPN server over a trusted VPN connection:

```
#wee-pee-en start
```

If all goes well, you should see the following on the client:

```
Using interface ppp1
Connect: ppp1 <--> /dev/pts/1
local IP address 11.30.11.21
remote IP address 72.12.8.15
```

To disable the VPN, type the following on the client:

```
#wee-pee-en stop
```

That's it! This scenario allows anyone to use a PPP over an encrypted SSH connection to create a secure VPN session over the Internet.

Summary

Using some of the basic techniques discussed in the last chapter, combined with some advanced techniques described in this chapter, has allowed us to use SSH as a fully fledged remote access solution that can support popular remote access demands, such as e-mail, file transfer, and management. While the configurations of each of these remote access demands slightly differ, the basic principles of port forwarding apply to each of them.

Port forwarding is a powerful and very useful feature of SSH that almost overshadows the terminal access that it provides. In fact, many SSH solutions deployed in networks today are being deployed more for their port-forwarding capabilities than for their remote terminal access capabilities. Furthermore, the flexibility of SSH, which allows it to be used from both NAT'd networks and non-NAT'd networks, makes it a very attractive remote access solution that can support end-user security in any type of network environment, whether it is from a hotel room, a home office, a customer site, a data center, or even a wireless network at your local coffee shop.

The use of other applications, such as Outlook Express, Netscape Messenger, and Eudora, with SSH allows SSH to mitigate and solve security concerns in other entities. In addition to securing other applications, the use of SSH with existing, required, or standard protocols, such as SMB and NFSallow, allow it to interoperate with existing networks quite easily with little to no effect on the end-user. Lastly, its ability to support GUI applications allows SSH to provide a truly secure remote management solution for the remote administrator.

Basic port forwarding and advance techniques allow SSH to be a fully functional and very inexpensive remote access solution that cannot be matched with any other service, device, or protocol. Now that you fully understand port forwarding, I will shift gears to other uses of SSH, such as general protocol replacement. In the next chapter, I will discuss how SSH should be used instead of various other dangerous protocols, such as insecure "R" protocols.

Protocol Replacement

SSH Versatility

SSH is a very versatile utility. Aside from all the uses I have discussed thus far, SSH also provides the following functionality in a secure manner:

- Terminal access
- File transfer (SFTP)
- Secure chat
- Secure backups

This chapter discusses many of the versatilities of SSH. Some of the utilities previously listed are basic and come installed with a default installation of SSH, such as terminal access and file sharing with the Secure File Transfer Protocol (SFTP). SSH can be used in conjunction with other utilities listed previously that are common in many network architectures but not necessarily secure, such as chat and backups.

This chapter demonstrates how SSH can be used to replace several other protocols, many of which are insecure protocols that greatly decrease the security posture of a network environment. For example, SSH can be used to replace the dangerous protocols listed in Table 8.1.

Table 8.1 Protocols That SSH Can Replace for Stronger Security

SSH UTILITY	PROTOCOL
SSH (Terminal Access)	RSH, Rlogin, Rexec
SFTP	FTP, SMB, NFS, RCP
SSH with Chat	IRC
SSH with Backups	RSync

Terminal Access

One of the most basic uses of SSH that I have only implied thus far is SSH terminal access. One of the primary reasons to install SSH is to provide secure terminal access. In order to replace the dangerous Berkeley R-protocols such as RSH and Rlogin, SSH needs to be used. Furthermore, if other terminal emulators such as Telnet are used in addition to the Berkeley R-protocols, the level of security across a network environment will be greatly reduced. SSH not only provides the same level of access that RSH, Rlogin, and Telnet do, but it does so in a secure manner through two-factor authentication, advanced authorization, and strong encryption.

SSH is often deployed for its secure terminal access, aside from the other features such as port forwarding and SFTP discussed in the next section. When dealing with remote management issues across the Internet or even insecure internal networks, Telnet, RSH, rexec, and Rlogin can and will cripple an organization's security infrastructure by allowing any passive user from gaining access to sensitive information, such as usernames, passwords, directory structures, and so on.

For example, RSH, Rlogin, and Rexec are clear-text protocols that provide some type of remote terminal emulation or remote execution service. All three of these protocols can be sniffed with any traffic analyzer that can reveal authentication and authorization information to an unauthorized user. This can potentially allow unauthorized users to gain access to sensitive authentication information and either log in to systems and/or devices or execute remote commands in an unauthorized fashion.

The following examples show a traffic analyzer program that will sniff the connections among four protocols: RSH, Rlogin, Rexec, and finally the SSH connection. The examples show how the use of three insecure protocols basically provides no security and how the use of SSH not only brings a great deal of security, but also provides the same level of functionality. The architecture for the example is shown in Figure 8.1.

Compromising a System with Remote Shell (RSH)

The first example will address RSH (Remote Shell). This section will not go into the specifics of RSH, because you will never use it after reading this section, but some basics need to be covered. RSH is the client end of a client-server relationship, which works with an RSH server (rshd), usually listening on port 514. RSH executes a remote command on a remote RSH server as if the command came from the machine itself. The RSH client uses a username and password that he or she must have on the server running the RSH server. For example, all usernames and passwords in the Unix password file, /etc/passwd or /etc/shadow, will be allowed to authenticate to the RSH server with their system credentials. This issue with RSH, as I have already discussed, is that the RSH protocol is clear-text, so anyone sniffing the wire can obtain username and password information of the user's account on the system. Once an unauthorized user obtains the information, the system is virtually compromised. See Figure 8.2 for a sniffer program that captures the RSH connection.

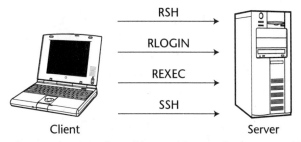

Figure 8.1 Sample architecture for terminal access with RSH, Rlogin, Telnet, and SSH.

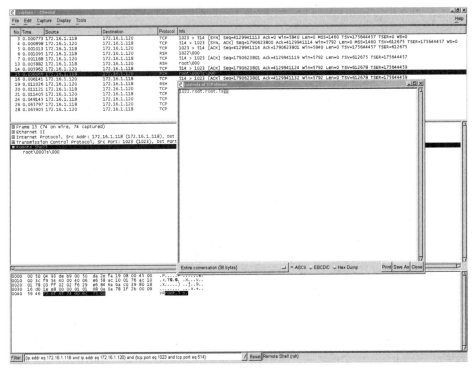

Figure 8.2 Sniffer capturing an RSH connection.

Compromising a System with Remote Login (Rlogin)

Remote Login (Rlogin) is also a client/server technology wherein the client, Rlogin, connects to an Rlogin server (Rlogind), usually listening on port 513. Rlogin starts a remote terminal session on a system, usually an operating system or device, running the rlogin server. Rlogin also uses the username and password information from the Unix password file, such as /etc/passwd or /etc/shadow. In addition to using the password file, Rlogin uses the rhosts file, which has a list of IP addresses that are authorized to log in to the server. As with RSH, Rlogin has connections that are in clear-text, which allows a passive attacker to sniff the connection and access the username, password, and IP address in order to make a valid connection. Once an unauthorized user obtains the information, the system is virtually compromised. See Figure 8.3 for a sniffer program that captures the Rlogin connection.

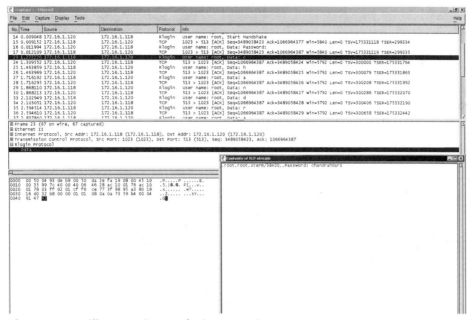

Figure 8.3   Sniffer capturing an Rlogin connection.

Compromising a System with Remote Execution (Rexec)

Remote Execution (Rexec) is also a client/server technology wherein the client, Rexec, connects to a rexec server (Rexecd), usually listening on port 512. Rexec executes a remote command on a remote Rexec server as if the command came from the machine itself. Rexec also uses the username and password information from the Unix password file, such as /etc/passwd or /etc/shadow. As with RSH, Rexec has connections that are in clear-text, which allows a passive attacker to sniff the connection and access the username and password information on the remote operating system or device. Once an unauthorized user obtains the information, the system is virtually compromised. See Figure 8.4 to view a sniffer program that captures the Rexec connection where a user has to log in to the rexec server with a username of root, a password of shreya, and a command of 'ls'.

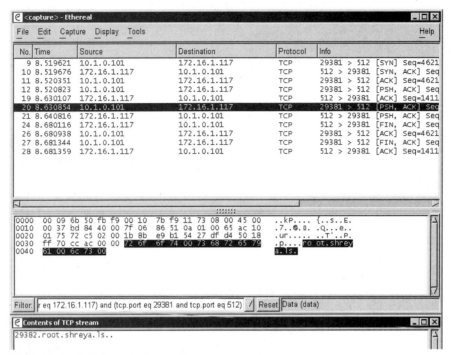

Figure 8.4 Sniffer capturing an Rexec connection.

Why Access via SSH Is Better

After learning about the insecurities of RSH, Rlogin, and Rexec, you should now understand why utilities such as SSH were developed and widely adopted. The use of RSH, Rlogin, and Rexec in any hostile environment, whether it be the Internet, an internal network, a DMZ environment, an extranet, or even a local network, will cause a lot of security issues for a given network. In order to protect against the basic flaws of the protocols mentioned previously, SSH should be used. While RSH, Rlogin, and Rexec provide moderately different functions, all three of the utilities' primary functions is to provide the execution of a command on a remote server, either through a local terminal session or a remote execution service. SSH can eliminate the need for all three of these utilities by providing the same, if not better, remote execution service or terminal sessions with an encrypted and secure connection. Unlike RSH, Rlogin, and Rexec, SSH is not a clear-text protocol, so if passive attackers were sniffing the network, they would not be able to gain or view any useful information, such as username and passwords. The connection is completely encrypted, from the time the user is authenticated to the time the session is closed. See Figure 8.5 to view a sniffer program that captures an SSH connection.

Notice how Figure 8.5 is quite different from Figures 8.4, 8.3, and even 8.2. While all four utilities (RSH, Rlogin, Rexec, and SSH) offer the same type of access, the protocols they use are quite different. Furthermore, the end result of all four utilities is a remote execution. There are no added advantages to using Rlogin over SSH, aside from the fact that some end-users may be used to the older insecure protocol. Furthermore, if a remote terminal session is not desired, just remote execution, both RSH and Rexec can be used with SSH in order to secure the connection. The use of remote commands instead of a remote terminal session may be required for night backup processes; therefore, Rexec with SSH, which will be discussed later in this chapter, is also a stronger alternative than Rexec alone.

Figure 8.5 Sniffer program that captures an SSH connection.

File Transfer with Secure File Transfer Protocol (SFTP)

File sharing over a network has been a standard capability in organizations for a great deal of time. Standard protocols such as FTP (File Transfer Protocol), Microsoft's SMB (Server Message Block), and NFS (Network File System) are probably the most popular methods of transferring files within most organizations. Despite the popularity of these three protocols, all have many security problems. FTP and NFS are clear-text protocols that have several security issues, including clear-text transmission of authentication (username/password) information.

Unlike the last section, this section will not discuss the issues with FTP, NFS, or SMB, but rather discuss how to use SSH's file transfer subsystem (Secure File Transfer) and a secure file-sharing method. I assume that you are somewhat aware of the security problems with FTP, NFS, and SMB and proceed with how to develop a secure solution.

Secure File Transfer Protocol (SFTP) is a subsystem used with SSH. SFTP is very similar to FTP; however, it offers the ability to transfer files to and from an SFTP server (SSH server) to or from an SFTP client over a secure encryption connection. SFTP and FTP both use client/server architecture, but SFTP carries with it a performance penalty that you will endure, as the packets are encrypted before they are sent over the wire. Often, however, this performance penalty may be negligible, especially when the extra security gained in using SFTP is factored in.

Each installation of SSH version 2 has the SFTP subsystem available and functioning by default. There are no extra steps required on the SSH server in order to start the SFTP subsystem after a default installation; the SFTP subsystem is built right into the service and will respond on the selected port chosen for SSH, such as port 22. Despite the fact that all three major providers of SSH, including OpenSSH, SSH Communications, and VanDyke Software, enable the SFTP subsystem by default, there are different features of each installation that may affect your decision-making process. The following section discusses the different SFTP installations, as well as the specific features of each in regard to four main uses of SFTP:

- General setup and use of SFTP
- SFTP for management purposes
- SFTP for corporate file-sharing (file access controls)
- SFTP for authorized system users (user access controls)

This overview will allow you to understand the general uses of SFTP and also allow your decision-making process to be as informed as possible, depending on your business and security requirements for SFTP.

SFTP with the OpenSSH SFTP Server

The OpenSSH SFTP subsystem is a great solution when requiring the secure transfer of file and folders from one machine to the next. As stated earlier, the use of the SFTP subsystem is enabled by default on the OpenSSH server; no special or additional steps are required. To ensure that the SFTP subsystem has been enabled, open the sshd_config file on the SSH server and scroll all the way to the bottom of the file. The SFTP subsystem information should be at the very end. Enter the following command to view the SFTP subsystem information in OpenSSH's configuration file:

```
#cd /etc/ssh/
#more sshd_config
```

The following syntax should be at the end of the sshd_config file:

```
# override default of no subsystems
Subsystem     sftp    /usr/libexec/openssh/sftp-server
```

If the SFTP is not desired and only the use of the SSH service (shell or port forwarding access) is desired, the SFTP subsystem can be easily disabled by commenting out the "Subsystem SFTP" line. For example, in order to disable the SFTP subsystem in OpenSSH, make sure the last two lines of your sshd_config file look like the following:

```
# override default of no subsystems
# Subsystem sftp    /usr/libexec/openssh/sftp-server
```

Since you want to use the SFTP subsystem, make sure it is enabled (uncommented) in your /etc/ssh/sshd_config file. Now that you understand how to enable/disable the SFTP subsystem, examine the different ways you can use it with OpenSSH.

Using OpenSSH for Management Purposes

First, I will discuss OpenSSH in terms of management purposes. Using any SFTP client, such as the command-line version that comes with OpenSSH (sftp), you can make a connection to an SFTP server to download files in a secure fashion. For example, if you want to copy the file called Commodore-Vic20.txt from the SFTP server, which has an IP address of 172.16.11.17, enter the following commands with your OpenSSH SFTP client:

```
#sftp 172.16.11.17 -p 22 -l <username>
#get CommodoreVic20.txt
#exit
```

Similarly, to upload a file to the SSH server, such as a file called Pitfall.txt, enter the following commands:

```
#sftp 172.16.11.17 -p 22 -l <username>
#put Pitfall.txt
#exit
```

As with FTP, the command-line SFTP client will download or upload files to and from the clients' local directory; however, it will be conducted over an encrypted session. In this case, OpenSSH is a very strong alternative for general management purposes for most organizations. Root-level users cannot only log in to an OpenSSH server for command-line access, but they can use the SFTP subsystem to transfer important and sensitive files and directories in a secure and easy fashion.

Using OpenSSH for File Sharing

To provide the use of the SFTP subsystem in a complementary fashion to SSH, valid accounts have to be made on the operating system, since SSH uses operating-system accounts, not their own specific SSH accounts. That being the case, having an account on the operating system means the account has the right to the system's files also, such as /etc/, /usr/sbin, /var, and so on. Even if the purpose of the account is to transfer files securely to/from /tmp/share, the account, because it is an operating-system account, has inherent rights to the operating system itself.

In a file-server situation, you may not want to expose the operating system directories or the entire directory architecture for SFTP access, but rather a folder or two for general organization-wide file sharing. For example, you may not want all users to download a copy of /etc/passwd but only files in a specified directory, such as their home directory or a directory called /tmp/share. In this case, the use of file access controls should be used.

By default, there are no access control permissions on the SFTP subsystem; all file access permission relies on the native operation system permission. In the Unix world, all access control permissions for SFTP will be controlled by the Read/Write/Execute values placed by the files and folders themselves. In the Windows world, the file access permissions for SFTP will be controlled by the NTFS access controls.

You need to place appropriate access control permission on the operating system, not just rely on the SFTP subsystem. If proper access controls are not placed on either operating system, an SFTP client might be capable of traversing outside the desired SFTP folder through the use of symbolic links on the system or just plainly having those rights inertly form the operating system itself.

No matter whether SSH is used for management purposes or for file-sharing purposes, file access controls should be in place to restrict users to only their home directory or a defined SFTP folder. To place appropriate file access controls, you need to use operating-system utilities as opposed to SSH utilities. Tools such as chmod for Unix and Cacls.exe for Windows can be used to place permission on individual files and folders. As you may have already guessed, this endeavor can be an exhaustive challenge, since all the sensitive files for an entire operating system need to be protected. Furthermore, some files, such as /etc/passwd, need to be readable to all accounts on the system, whether they are root-level accounts or just regular user accounts, which may not be the ideal situation.

Since there is no function with OpenSSH to restrict SFTP access to a limited number of files, aside from the operating system's access control, OpenSSH is a very moderate solution for general file sharing for low-level or non-root/non-admin level users. Since file-sharing servers will need to provide access to several users and protect the operating system itself from these users, using OpenSSH's SFTP subsystem will be a cumbersome process.

Authorizing Users with OpenSSH

Lastly, I will discuss OpenSSH in terms of authorized system users. In all OpenSSH installations, all users on the operating system, such as the list of users in the /etc/passwd file, will be allowed to log in to the service, unless specifically denied. With OpenSSH, specific accounts can be allowed to log in or they may simply be denied access, despite having an account in /etc/passwd. This limitation allows the OpenSSH architecture to restrict the users who have SSH/SFTP access to a specific list of accounts. This list can include all accounts in /etc/passwd, which is the default, or just a subset of the accounts.

For example, if there are 500 accounts that have access to a machine running OpenSSH, possibly by using an NIS architecture, but only 80 of those accounts need access to the operating system itself, OpenSSH can allow or deny SSH/SFTP access by specifying account names and/or account variables that are authorized to log in.

If the purpose of the SFTP subsystem is to allow all users in the Engineering Department to access, upload, and download files to and from the operating system, adding the group 'Engineering' as the only group that can use SSH or SFTP is a relatively easy process. Furthermore, if the Engineering accounts only need access to their home directory, without using the SFTP subsystem as a file server but rather as a complementary tool to SSH terminal access, OpenSSH is a strong alternative.

For example, say the Engineering Department regularly needs to transfer files, such as compiled binaries, source code, or configuration files, to and from the home directory. If they are using SSH for secure terminal access, transferring files with NFS, FTP, or even remote copy (RCP) would be counterproductive. The security they would gain from the encrypted SSH connection would be cancelled out by the insecurity of the NFS, FTP, and RCP sessions. In this scenario, the OpenSSH SFTP subsystem is a great alternative to NFS, FTP, and RCP. Unlike the SFTP file-server model, SFTP does not add insecurity to the operating system, since all the accounts on the system are using the operating system itself, which includes all the directories, binaries, and configuration files, not just accounts that should have access to one folder on the system, which is more difficult to restrict. In other words, all these accounts are authorized to roam around the operating system according to their account type, which includes viewing files from the command line or transferring files from SFTP.

OpenSSH on Windows and Cygdrive

Using OpenSSH on Windows is similar to, if not the same as, using OpenSSH on Unix. OpenSSH with Windows carries the same general recommendations as OpenSSH with Unix, specifically a strong solution for management purposes and authorized system-user purposes. But transferring files on OpenSSH for Windows is not a good idea, because of permission issues of sensitive operating system files and/or directories. That being said, one item I need to mention is the use of cygdrive as an SFTP root directory. In order to specify a directory that is not the default for the root of the SSH or SFTP subsystem, the use of the term cygdrive is required. For example, if the root directory e:\ is desired on a Windows operating system that has a C, D, and an E drive, your passwd file in your Program Files\OpenSSH\bin will look like the following:

```
Administrator::/cygdrive/e::
```

While all SFTP users are redirected to the e:\ volume, which may be the core SFTP directory, they are not restricted to e:\. This means that while the users' SFTP shell will begin at e:\, if they specify that they would like to access c:\ with their SFTP client, they will be allowed access to c:\, given that they have the NTFS permissions to do so. This reason, among several others, is why the author of the OpenSSH port to Windows stresses the fact that it should only be used for administrative purposes, since file-system security is enforced not by the OpenSSH SFTP subsystem but by the native NTFS permissions on the operating system.

SFTP with VanDyke Software VShell

VanDyke's VShell SSH server is an excellent solution when requiring the use of the SFTP subsystem. As with OpenSSH's SFTP subsystem, no extra steps are required to enable the SFTP subsystem on the VShell SSH server. Unlike with OpenSSH, with Vshell there is no direct on/off switch for the SFTP server; instead, two methods are used to enable or disable it. By default, the SFTP subsystem is enabled and allows everyone unrestricted access. In order to disable it, two items must be configured: access control and SFTP options. You can disable SFTP access for specific users on access control and you can limit access to SFTP folders with SFTP options. Both options don't really disable the SFTP subsystem, but restrict it to specific users. These options provide more granularity when configuring VShell's SFTP subsystem. To verify that VShell's SFTP subsystem has been enabled, complete the following steps:

1. Go to Start ➪ Programs ➪ VShell ➪ VShell.
2. Highlight the Access Control section.
3. Select the Allow checkbox in the SFTP row for the appropriate account(s).
4. Select Apply.
5. Highlight the SFTP section.
6. Ensure the appropriate users are enabled to have access to appropriate accounts. The default is to allow everyone to have full access to all files and directories.
7. Select Apply.

Now that the SFTP subsystem has been enabled, examine VShell in terms of management, file transfer, and authorized user access.

Using VShell for Management Purposes

First, I will discuss VShell in terms of management purposes. Using any SFTP client, such as VanDyke Software's SecureFX or SSH Communications' SSH client, you can make a connection to an SFTP server to download files in a secure fashion. For example, if you want to copy the file called Neeraja.txt from the SFTP server, which has an IP address of 172.16.6.12, you will complete the following commands with your SSH Communications' SSH client:

1. Start ➪ Programs ➪ SSH Communications ➪ Secure File Transfer Client.
2. Select Quick Connect.
3. Type **172.16.6.12** for the Host Name.
4. Type the name of the appropriate account for the User Name field.

5. Specify the port number in the Port Number field; the default is 22.

6. Select Password for the Authentication Method.

7. Select Connect.

8. Enter the correct password when prompted by the SFTP client.

9. That's it! You can now drag and drop files to/from the SFTP server with a Windows Explorer type of client. All files transferred from the SFTP client to the SFTP server, using drag and drop, copy and paste, or the option in the menu bar, are all encrypted.

Similarly, to upload a file to the SSH server, you can use the drag-and-drop, copy-and-paste, or the menu bar options.

As with FTP GUI clients, the GUI SFTP client can download or upload files to and from the clients' local directory to and from the SSH server using a encrypted session. In this case, VShell's SFTP server is a very good solution for general management purposes for most organizations. Administrator-level users can log in to an SSH server for command-line access and also use the SFTP subsystem to transfer important and sensitive files and directories in a secure and easy fashion.

Using VShell for File Sharing

Next, I will discuss VShell in terms of file sharing. As with OpenSSH, operating system accounts are used with VShell to provide the use of the SFTP subsystem in a complementary fashion to SSH. Having an account on the operating system, even if the account is only going to be used for SFTP, means that the account may have the right to access, modify, or read sensitive files on the operating system according to the NTFS permissions, such as \winnt, \winnt\system32, and \winnt\repair.

If the purpose of the VShell SFTP server is file sharing only, all VShell accounts will still have rights to other parts of the operating system because they are operating-system accounts. In a file-server situation, you might not want to expose the operating system directories or the entire directory architecture for SFTP access; instead, you might want to expose just a root folder for general organization-wide file sharing. For example, you might not want all users to download a copy of \winnt\repair\sam; instead, you might want them to download only files in a specified directory such as d:\share. In this case, the SFTP access control features of VShell should be used. In order to allow access to only the d:\share folder, which can be the root directory on the corporate file server, to all accounts on the system, complete the following steps:

1. Go to Start ⇨ Programs ⇨ VShell ⇨ VShell.
2. Highlight the SFTP section.
3. Under SFTP options, select Add.
4. For the SFTP root field, type **d:\share or simply browse to it using the ... button**.
5. Type **CorpFileServer** for Alias.
6. Select Add on the right hand section.
7. Add the Everyone group.
8. Choose OK.
9. Select Apply.

Now all accounts on the operating system, or the domain, can have SFTP access to the D:\share directory. In order to ensure that access to the rest of the operating system is denied, complete the following steps:

1. Highlight the <Unrestricted> option in the SFTP section and select Edit.
2. Remove all accounts, including Everyone and any other accounts that exist.
3. Enter any accounts, such as the administrator account, that you would like to provide full SFTP access to the system. If no accounts need to be added, select OK.
4. Select Apply.

Now no accounts, or only the administrator account, have unrestricted access. Furthermore, every other account on the system or domain only has access to D:\share, despite whatever NTFS permissions that account has. The VShell access control lists override the NTFS permissions on the VShell server when using SSH or SFTP subsystem. Figures 8.6 and 8.7 show the final result.

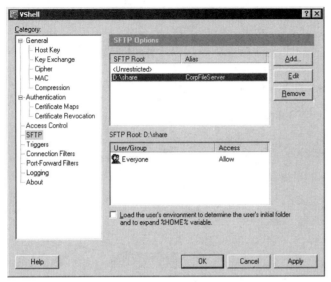

Figure 8.6 VShell SFTP file-server permission for the Everyone group.

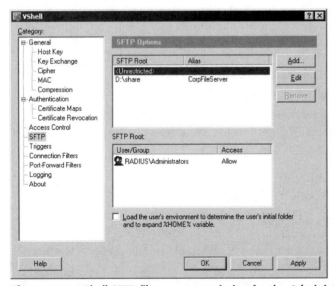

Figure 8.7 VShell SFTP file-server permission for the Administrators group.

In addition to restricting access to certain directories without the need for any operating system access control lists (ACLs), VShell can also permit/ restrict access to the SFTP subsystem to specific accounts. For example, if you want to allow everyone to have access to the SSH server as a corporate file server only, using the SFTP subsystem, but no command-line or port-forwarding access, this can be easily set with VShell by performing the following steps:

1. Choose the Access Control section.
2. Click Add.
3. Select the Everyone group and select OK.
4. Keep the Everyone group highlighted, and select Logon and SFTP for the Allow permissions.
5. Keep the Everyone group highlighted, and select Shell, Remote Execution, Port Forwarding, and Remote Port Forwarding under the Deny permissions.
6. Select Apply.

Now all accounts on the operating system or domain can access only the SFTP subsystem, with no access to the command prompt or port forwarding. Figure 8.8 shows the configuration settings.

As with the SFTP section, you can still allow the administrator account to have access to everything, if you want it to. Figure 8.9 shows the administrator account configuration settings.

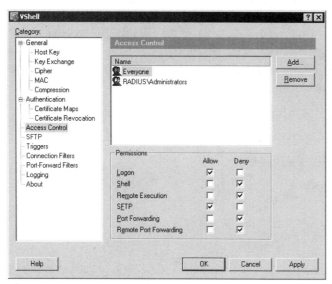

Figure 8.8   Access Control settings for the Everyone group.

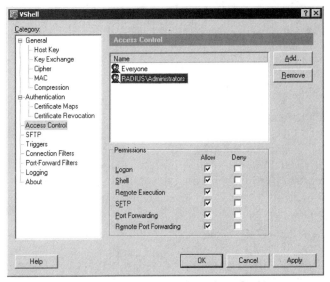

Figure 8.9   Access Control settings for the administrator account.

Using the preceding configuration, all users on the operating system or domain will only be able to securely transfer files with the corporate file server, while the administrator, or any equivalent accounts, will still have full access to the VShell server and underlying operating system.

Since VShell offers the ability to restrict operating-system accounts to only specific directories using SFTP, without the need for NTFS permissions, VShell is a very excellent alternative for general file sharing for all users or corporate file servers. In fact, using VShell's SSH server as a corporate file server is an excellent solution, because it offers the ability to conduct the following:

- FTP/Windows Explorer type of GUI access
- Drag-and-drop and copy-and-paste capabilities
- Easy file system security maintenance
- No NTFS permissions required, ensuring full security to the operating system and other directories
- Encryption
- Security

Since file-sharing servers need to provide access to several hundred accounts while not allowing any access to the operating system itself, use of VanDyke Software's SFTP subsystem offers a simple, straightforward, and very flexible solution. For more information on secure file servers, see Chapter 10.

Authorizing Users with VShell

Lastly, I will discuss VShell in terms of authorized system users. Typically, VShell installations allow all users on the operating system to log in to the service, which is the default. With VShell, however, specific accounts can be denied SSH/SFTP access, despite their having an account on the system, as shown in the previous example. A specific list of users who have access can include all accounts, which is the default, or a subset of the accounts.

To illustrate, suppose 500 accounts have access to a machine running VShell, possibly by using a domain architecture, but only 72 of those accounts need access to the operating system itself. VShell can allow or deny SSH/SFTP access by specifying account names and/or account variables that are authorized to log in. If the purpose of the SFTP subsystem is to allow all users in the Engineering Department to access, upload, and download files to and from the operating system, adding the group Engineering as the only one that can use SSH or SFTP is a relatively easy process. Furthermore, if the Engineering accounts only need access to the d:\share directory, VShell is a good solution. For example, say the Engineering Department needs to transfer files, such as compiled binaries, source code, or configuration files, to and from the d:\share directory. If they are using SSH for secure terminal access, using SMB or FTP for file transfer would be counterproductive. The security they gain from the encrypted SSH connection is cancelled out by the insecurity of the SMB or FTP sessions.

SFTP with SSH Communications' SSH Server

SSH Communications' SSH Server is also a great solution when requiring the use of the SFTP subsystem. No additional or extra steps are required to enable the SFTP subsystem on the SSH Communications' SSH server. By default, the SFTP subsystem is enabled. In order to verify that the SSH Communications' SFTP subsystem has been enabled, complete the following steps:

1. Go to Start ⇨ Programs ⇨ SSH Secure Shell Server ⇨ Configuration.
2. Highlight the SFTP server.
3. Ensure the appropriate directories are enabled, such as the users' home directory.
4. Select Apply.

Now that you have ensured that the SFTP subsystem is enabled, consider SSH Communications' SSH server in terms of management, file transfer, and authorized user access.

Using SSH Communications' SSH Server for Management Purposes

First, I will examine how SSH Communications' SSH server is used for management purposes. Using any SFTP client, such as VanDyke Software's SecureFX or SSH Communications' SSH client, a connection can be made to an SFTP server to download files in a secure fashion. For example, if you want to copy the file called Belwa.txt from the SFTP server, which has an IP address of 172.16.19.47, complete the following commands with your SSH Communications' SSH client:

1. Go to Start ⇨ Programs ⇨ SSH Communications ⇨ Secure File Transfer Client.

2. Select Quick Connect.

3. Type **172.16.1.19.47** for the Host Name.

4. Type the name of the appropriate account for the User Name field.

5. Specify the port number for the Port Number field, the default is 22.

6. Select Password for the Authentication Method.

7. Select Connect.

8. Enter the correct password when prompted by the SFTP client.

That's it! You can now drag and drop files to and from the SFTP server with a Windows Explorer type of client. All files that are transferred from the SFTP client to the SFTP server, using drag and drop, copy and paste, or the option in the menu bar, are encrypted. Similarly, to upload a file to the SSH server, you can use the drag-and-drop, copy-and-paste, or the menu bar options.

As with FTP GUI clients, the GUI SFTP client with the SSH Communications' SSH server can download or upload files to and from the clients' local directory to and from the SSH server using an encrypted session. In this case, SSH Communications' SFTP server is a very strong alternative for general management purposes for most organizations. Administrator-level users cannot only log in to an SSH server for command-line access; they can also use the SFTP subsystem to transfer important and sensitive files and directories in a secure and easy fashion.

Using SSH Communications' SSH Server for File Sharing

As with OpenSSH, with SSH, in order to provide the use of the SFTP subsystem in a complementary fashion to SSH, valid accounts have to be made on the operating system. They need to be made, as SSH Communications' SSH server also uses operating system accounts, not their own specific SSH accounts. That being the case, having an account on the operating system means the account has rights to all files on the operating system that NTFS permissions allow, such as \winnt, \winnt\system32, and \winnt\repair. If the purpose of the SFTP server is for file sharing only, all SSH accounts will still have rights to other parts of the operating system because they are operating-system accounts.

In a file-server situation, you may want users to have access to a root folder for general organization-wide file sharing but not want them to have exposure to the operating system directories or the entire directory architecture for SFTP access. For example, you may want users to be able to download files in a specified directory such as d:\share but not want everyone to be able to download a copy of \winnt\repair\sam. In this case, the use of the SFTP access control features of SSH Communications' SSH server should be used. In order to allow access to only the d:\share folder, which may be the corporate file server, to all accounts on the system, complete the following steps:

1. Start ⇨ Programs ⇨ SSH Secure Shell Server ⇨ Configuration.
2. Highlight the SFTP Server section.
3. Under Accessible directories options, select New (insert) icon.
4. Type CorpFileServer=D:\share (syntax is virtual dir=real dir).
5. Select Apply.

Now all accounts on the operating system, or the domain, can have SFTP access to the d:\share directory. All accounts will not have access to any other part of the operating system except the virtual directory that is listed. Furthermore, in addition to the virtual directories, the users' home directory can also be accessible, listed by the %D variable in the User home directory text box. In this example, the users' home directory is accessible, in addition to the corporate file server directory, as shown in Figure 8.10.

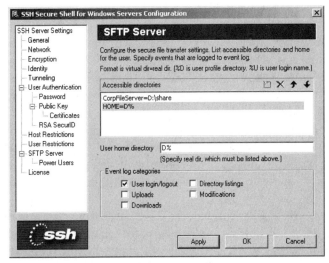

Figure 8.10   SFTP virtual directory.

Now all accounts only have access to d:\share using SFTP, despite their NTFS permissions. The SSH Communications' SSH server access control lists override the NTFS permissions on the SSH server when using SSH or SFTP subsystem. In addition to general user access, you may want to allow the administrator account, or equivalent power users, more access via SFTP. In order to provide power users with more access, while still restricting general SFTP users to the stated virtual directory, complete the following steps:

1. Highlight the Power Users section under SFTP server.

2. Select the Insert icon to add directories.

3. Type **C:=C:** and **D:=D:**.

4. Select Apply.

5. In the Power Users textbox, type administrator (or any other account you wish to grant further access).

6. Select Apply.

Now the administrator account has full SFTP access to the SSH server, while general users are still restricted to the d:\share directory, as shown in Figure 8.11.

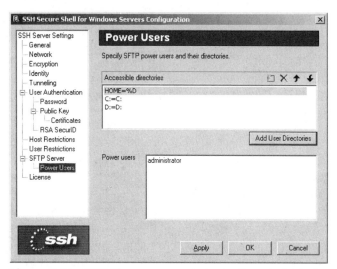

Figure 8.11 SFTP file-server permission to the administrator.

Unlike VShell, SSH Communications' SSH server does not provide such specific access to the SFTPsubsystem. For example, if you want to allow all users access to the SFTP subsystem only but no shell access, there is no obvious way to implement that with SSH Communications' SSH server version 3.2.3. While you can allow or deny user accounts or hosts via the SSH server, it is an all-or-nothing value, without specific options such as SFTP only. This makes SSH Communications' SFTP subsystem a little better than OpenSSH, but it offers less control than VShell. For example, using SSH Communications' SSH server, certain directories of the operating system can be exposed to SFTP users, thus restricting access to sensitive directories such as winnt\system32. Furthermore, advanced power users can have more access than the general accounts, granting a greater level of directory access. Nevertheless, in a corporate file-server model, command-line or port-forwarding access to the SSH server is highly undesirable and a security threat. Under the default installations of SSH Communications' SSH server, there is no easy way to restrict certain users to SFTP only while allowing others access to both SFTP and terminal sessions.

SSH Communications' SSH server offers the ability to restrict operating-system accounts to only specific directories using SFTP without the need for NTFS permissions. But it does not offer other restrictions on command-line or port-forwarding access. So, while it still may be a good solution for SFTP, maybe it is not the best for a file server. Nevertheless, it is a very excellent solution for general file sharing for all users or corporate file servers. For more information on secure file servers, see Chapter 10.

Authorizing Users with SSH Communications' SSH Server

In all SSH Communications' SSH server installations, all users on the operating system will be allowed to log in to the service unless specifically denied. With SSH Communications' SSH server, specific accounts can be allowed to log in or simply be denied, despite having an account on the system, shown in our last previous example. This allows the SSH Communications' SSH server architecture to limit the users who have SSH/SFTP access to a specific list of accounts. This list can include all accounts, which is the default, or a subset of the accounts. For example, if there are 500 accounts that have access to a machine running SSH, possibly by using a domain architecture, but only 88 of those accounts need access to the operating system itself, SSH Communications' SSH server can allow or deny SSH/SFTP access by specifying account names and/or account variables that are authorized to log in. If the purpose of the SFTP subsystem is to allow all users in the Engineering Department to access, upload, and download files to and from the operating system, adding the group 'Engineering' as the only group that can use SSH or SFTP is a relatively easy process. Furthermore, if the Engineering accounts only need access to the d:\share directory, SSH Communications' SSH server is a strong alternative. For example, say the Engineering Department needs to transfer files, such as compiled binaries, source code, or configuration files to and from the d:\share directory. If they are using SSH for secure terminal access, it would be counter-productive if they were using SMB or FTP for file transfer. The security they gain from the encrypted SSH connection is cancelled out by the insecurity of the SMB or FTP sessions. In this scenario, the SSH Communications' SSH server SFTP subsystem is a great alternative to SMB and FTP.

Comparison of the Three SFTP Solutions

Table 8.2 summarizes the three SFTP solutions that have been discussed. The table holds the different vendors on the x-axis and the list of available features/utilities on the y-axis. As described earlier, despite the fact that all three major providers of SSH, including OpenSSH, SSH Communications, and VanDyke Software, enable the SFTP subsystem by default, there are different features of each installation that will affect your decision-making process. This following table summarizes the previous discussion.

Table 8.2 SFTP Comparison Chart

	GENERAL SETUP	**MANAGEMENT**	**FILE SHARING**	**AUTHORIZED USERS**
OpenSSH	Installed by default	Ability to upload/ download files securely	• Full SFTP access. • Operating system file level security required. • No capabilities to only restrict users to SFTP. • No capabilities of restricting users to certain directories only.	Ability to allow or deny desired accounts only
VanDyke Software VShell server	Installed by default	Ability to upload/ download files securely	• Full SFTP access. • No operating system file level security required. • Restriction of only SFTP available. • Capable of restricting users to certain directories only.	Ability to allow or deny desired accounts only
SSH Communications' SSH server	Installed by default	Ability to upload/ download files securely	• Full SFTP access. • No operating system security required. • No capabilities to only restrict users to SFTP. • Capable of restricting users to certain directories only.	Ability to allow or deny desired accounts only

Secure Chat

The use of chat is becoming an increasingly popular tool in network environments. While chat was first used for local office gossip with a neighbor, it is now being used to communicate legitimate corporate information among employees. Chat offers great flexibility by allowing employees to work with one another in an easy, simple, and, most important, quick fashion to get more work done.

Now that chat is more of a mainstream tool for business operations, the traversing of sensitive information between employees over an insecure channel is not acceptable. For example, if a group of engineers is working on a piece of code and participants need to send sample snippets of code to one another using chat, an unauthorized user has the ability to capture that data, because most chat programs use clear-text communication. Furthermore, chat can also be used to transfer account information such as passwords, network information such as an IP address, and other sensitive information that should not be disclosed to unauthorized users.

To use chat in organizations without affecting the integrity of the data, consider using SSH with chat. Chat with SSH will not be addressing popular instant messaging programs such as AOL, MSN, or Yahoo!, since these programs use their own TCP ports that can just be port-forwarded over SSH for security. Just like e-mail, file transfer, and management can be port-forwarded, as you see in Chapters 6 and 7, any protocol, such as that used with AOL, MNS, or Yahoo!, can also be port-forwarded in a similar manner. The discussion in this section will be limited to the use of chat in internal networks without the need for port forwarding. In the architecture for this example, IRC servers run on common Unix shells and use that server as the chat interface. Figure 8.12 shows the example architecture.

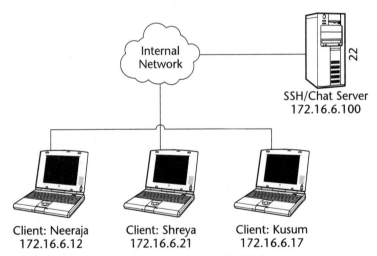

Figure 8.12 SSH architecture to be used with chat.

Secure chat with SSH uses the SSH server as the chat server also. So when users connect to the SSH server and gain access to a shell, they can execute their IRC client on the SSH shell and be connected to the IRC server, which is running locally on the SSH server. Once the user is connected, he will have a chat session under his SSH shell, which is all encrypted over the network. Complete the following steps to create a secure chat solution with SSH and your favorite IRC server:

1. Install SSH on 172.16.6.100.

2. Install your favorite IRC server on 172.16.6.100.

3. Create accounts for all three users on the chat server, including Kusum, Shreya, and Neeraja.

NOTE In larger networks, NIS+ can be used instead of creating local accounts for every IRC client.

4. With any of the three user accounts listed previously, connect to the SSH server using an SSH client.

5. Once authenticated, use an IRC client on the SSH server to connect to the local IRC services on the system.

Once you have logged in to the IRC server with the IRC client, running on the SSH server via your SSH client, you now have the ability to use IRC security with SSH. Your SSH terminal will show your IRC session with other accounts.

While this example is short and sweet, it is used to illustrate how an operating system running insecure services that are command-line-based, such as most IRC servers, can deploy an instance of SSH to make the connection secure. While the insecure service will still be available locally to all users, connections to and from the service will be allowed only with SSH, thus securing the connection over the network but still allowing access to the program locally. Figure 8.13 shows the two architectures.

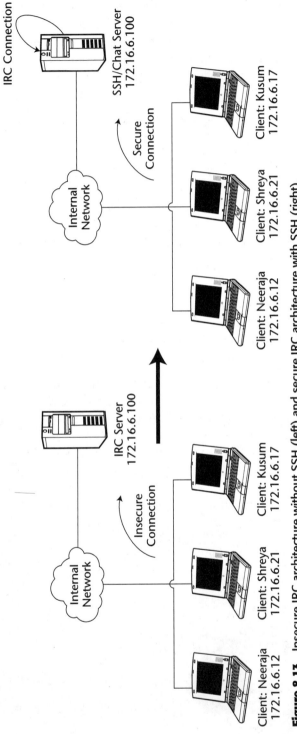

Figure 8.13 Insecure IRC architecture without SSH (left) and secure IRC architecture with SSH (right).

Secure Backups

Conducting backups in a network environment can be a very tricky item in terms of security. Many organizations deploy encryption on data networks such as SSH, IPSec, or SSL in order to protect sensitive data. The same organizations, however, may then conduct their backup architecture over a clear-text protocol. In fact, many organizations forget to realize that backup networks may be more sensitive than data networks, since they are direct repositories for data, without the need to compromise a single server.

A popular method for backing up data in a network environment is Rysnc. Rysnc is a protocol that offers an incremental file transfer and update process (backup) from one entity to the next. Rsync offers the ability to transfer only the differences of files between two entities in a given network, using a checksum process. These two items, combined with many others, make Rsysnc a very attractive tool in a backup architecture.

While there are many benefits to using Rsync in a backup architecture, Rsysnc is a clear-text protocol with limited authentication requirements. An unauthorized user can capture the Rsysnc process and gain access to data, account information, or even passwords. Therefore, in order to deploy a secure backup architecture, SSH should be used in combination with Rsync. Rsync with SSH will provide all the efficiencies and features that make Rsync so attractive, but will also provide encryption and public-key authentication, mitigating two of the top-most security concerns with Rsync, which are clear-text communication and limited authentication. The use of SSH with Rsync will not only encrypt all communication between two entities, eliminating the ability for an unauthorized user to compromise and steal the Rsync communication process, but also implement public-key authentication, making it very difficult for an unauthorized client to compromise the weak authentication requirements of Rsync. The following section discusses the procedures to implement a secure backup solution with Rsync and SSH.

Figure 8.14 shows the Rsysnc/SSH architectural example I will be using for this section. The two servers are both Unix machines using OpenSSH. Notice that there are two servers, one used for productions and one used for backups. The production machine will be using Rsync with SSH to transfer files to the backup server, which has an Rsysnc daemon listening on it.

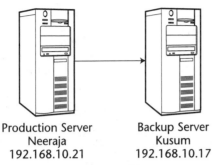

Production Server   Backup Server
Neeraja   Kusum
192.168.10.21   192.168.10.17

Figure 8.14 Backup architecture.

Complete the following steps to set up secure backup with Rsync and SSH:

1. Ensure that OpenSSH and Rsync are installed on the backup server. Ports 22 (SSH) and 873 (Rsync) should be listening on the backup server, if both daemons have been started.

2. Create a public and private-key pair on your backup server. You will be using public and private keys to authenticate to the backup server, instead of using usernames and passwords. Because this backup procedure will be automated, do not enter a passphrase for the private keys. You will be creating a DSA key pair (-t option), using 1024 bits (-b option), with a blank passphrase (-N option):

    ```
    [root@kusum]#ssh-keygen -t dsa -b 1024 -N ""
    ```

3. When asked to enter the file in which to save the key, enter **backup**.

4. Once the key has been created, you should have a backup.pub and backup file.

5. Copy backup.pub from the backup server to the production server, specifically in the production server's root directory (the user must be root to do this). Make an .ssh folder and concatenate the contents of the backup.pub file to the authorized keys files. (Chapter 4 discusses in detail public-key authentication with SSH.) The following are the contents:

    ```
    [root@neeraja]#cd /root
    [root@neeraja]#mkdir .ssh
    [root@neeraja]#cat backup.pub > ./ssh/authorized_keys
    [root@neeraja]#chmod 600 .ssh
    ```

6. The basics have now been set up! Now the rsync command can be used to conduct the backups. The —e option is a flag with Rsync to use SSH as the encryption communication between the two entities. Unlike other SSH usages, you don't need to use a subsystem or port forwarding with Rsysnc, but it is actually built in as an optional tool. Be sure to

preserve the permissions on the files being backed up by using the –p option. To back up from /usr from the production server (neeraja) to the backup server (kusum) using SSH, enter the following command:

```
[root@neeraja]#rsync -p -a -e ssh /usr kusum:/usr
```

7. Secure backup has now been implemented with SSH. In order to automate the process, enter a Cron job (automated scheduler) to execute the secure backup procedure:

```
[root@neeraja]#crontab -e
10 * * 0 /usr/bin/rsync -p -a -e ssh/usr kusum:/usr
```

8. In addition to Rsync, tar can be used to back up files via SSH by using a slightly different format. For example, to back up users' home directory on the production server (neeraja) to the backup server (kusum) using tar, enter the following command:

```
[root@neeraja]#ssh kusum "tar cfz - /home" > /tmp/home.tar.gz
```

Summary

This chapter discusses the versatility of SSH. Whether you are using SSH for secure terminal access, in order to replace RSH or Rlogin, for secure file transfer, in order to replace FTP, SMB, or NFS, for secure chat, in conjunction with IRC, or as a secure backup solution, in conjunction with Rsync, there is no doubt that SSH is a very versatile tool. Consider that other utilities or protocols such as RSH, Rlogin, SMB, FTP, NFS, Rsync, and IRC have very little in common; however, all of those protocols can be replaced with a single installation of SSH.

The versatility of SSH, combined with its strong encryption capabilities, its strong authentication capabilities, and even its strong authorization and integrity capabilities, makes it a powerful solution for several items, including terminal access, file transfer, chat, and backups. This chapter's focus is to demonstrate the flexibility of SSH using different vendor implementations, as well as to explore the lesser-known uses of SSH, such as secure chat and secure backup.

The core point to learn from this chapter is that the versatility of SSH can mitigate several of the security issues in your network while providing a solution for many core business functions, all with a single tool. While using a single version of SSH may not be desired due to capacity requirements, using a single application that serves several purposes can help your complex environment become simpler and thus more secure. The ability to patch, maintain, and support a single application across several systems is more manageable than to support several tools/utilities across multiple systems. Furthermore, the use of SSH as a backup solution, a file server, or for terminal access make it easier for users to learn, adopt, and optimize on a single solution.

Lastly, despite the fact that SSH has been so widely adopted by former RSH and Rlogin users, not only for its added security but also primarily because it is easy to use, it still has not carried over to other uses such as SFTP, chat, or backups. This chapter not only demonstrates what many users already know, that SSH is a strong alternative for RSH/Rlogin, but also that SSH is just as easy to use and deploy for other protocols such as FTP, chat, and backups. The use of SSH as a file server and backup solution is just as easy, if not easier, than its use as a secure terminal session. Either through default installations, which install the SFTP subsystem, or additional features such as Rsync, SSH can be a strong solution across multiple disciplines, not just for secure terminal access.

In the next chapter, I will shift the focus from SSH flexibility to SSH proxies and how to use an SSH proxy server to access several SSH servers, whether they are SSH terminal sessions or SFTP servers. Also, I will cover the uses of other tools, such as SOCKS and HTTP, in conjunction with SSH.

Proxy Technologies in a
Secure Web Environment

The use of proxy servers in any network environment can simplify the operating environment for end-users. A proxy server is an application that places a request on behalf of another entity. Most proxy servers in use today are Web proxies, where a client machine attempts to access a certain Web server but sends its request to the Web proxy server. The Web proxy server then sends the request to the real Web server on behalf of the client. Once the response is received from the Web server, the proxy server returns the request to the client.

The use of proxy technology can also be adapted to the SSH architecture. This chapter focuses on the use of SSH, as I have discussed it thus far, in combination with proxy servers, SOCKS, dynamic port forwarding, wireless networks, and secure Web browsing. These topics allow me to demonstrate another aspect of SSH while demonstrating the ability to optimize and utilize its flexibility. As a result of this chapter, the use of SSH will expand beyond a typical implementation into lesser-known methods of deployment, such as secure Web browsing and secure wireless networks.

Using SSH in combination with proxy technologies allows networks to optimize the strong security features from SSH with multiple devices and operating systems across an organization's architecture. The use of proxy technology allows normally insecure sessions to be secure, while providing a single repository for SSH communication. The focuses of this chapter are the following:

- SSH and SOCKS
- Dynamic port forwarding and SOCKS
- Secure Web browsing with SSH
- Securing wireless connections with SSH

SSH and SOCKS

The implementation of SOCKS proxy servers with SSH offers a great solution for network environments. Before I delve into SSH and SOCKS, I'll quickly examine SOCKS and its primary purposes. SOCKS is a generic proxy protocol able to plug into other protocols, such as SSH, in order to provide security across networking environments. SOCKS uses the typical client/server architecture, where a SOCKS client connects to a SOCKS server. The primary purpose of SOCKS is to allow a client on one end of a connection to access one or several hosts on the other end of a connection via the SOCKS server, without the client ever directly connecting to the desired host on the other side. Using this understanding, I will be using SOCKS to allow an SSH client to connect to multiple SSH servers by connecting to a single SOCKS server, which creates a secure communication channel between all clients and servers while reducing the complexity in the network architecture.

The primary purpose of installing a SOCKS proxy server is to allow a single entry point for SSH communication, which is then dispersed throughout the rest of the network. For example, let's say you have installed SSH on all your Web servers for secure remote management and would like to allow access to these Web servers, via SSH, to all your administrators from remote sites outside the confines of the internal network. Instead of allowing several SSH connections through your firewall, which could be 10 to hundreds of connections, you can set up a SOCKS proxy server that can proxy the SSH request to the SSH servers. Figure 9.1 shows the architecture in detail.

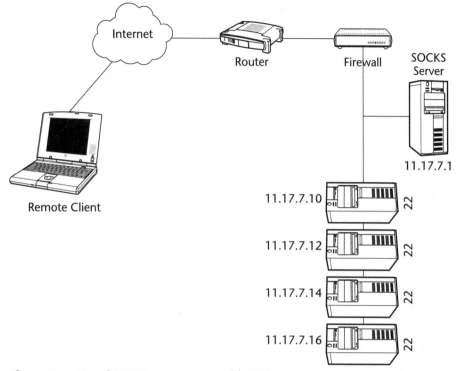

Figure 9.1 Use of SOCKS proxy servers with SSH.

Figure 9.1 shows a remote client outside the internal network. To allow a remote client to access multiple servers running SSH for management inside an internal network or DMZ networks, you could create a rule in the firewall that would allow access to every Web server or even to several hundred internal servers. Or you could use a SOCKS server to proxy all the requests from the remote clients to the SSH servers, which requires only a single rule in the firewall that would allow all remote clients to the SOCKS server on port 1080. Figure 9.2 shows how this operates.

Currently, there are many solutions for SOCKS servers, from large enterprise SOCKS servers, capable of handling many requests, to very small SOCKS servers, capable of only a limited capacity. For ease of illustration, consider how to install a very simple SOCKS server. The SOCKS server to be demonstrated is SOCKServ, version 2.0, which can be freely downloaded from www.geocities.com/SiliconValley/Heights/2517/sockserv.htm#intro. This is a version 4 SOCKS server. To complete the example described in Figure 9.1, a SOCKS server needs to be installed on 11.17.7.1, ensuring that SSH is listening on all destination servers, including 11.17.7.10, 11.17.7.12, 11.17.7.14, and 11.17.7.16; then SSH clients need to be configured to use SOCKS.

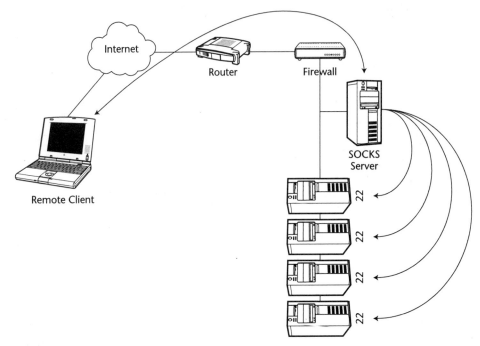

Figure 9.2 Use of SSH clients with a SOCKS proxy server.

To install SOCKServ, complete the following steps:

1. Unzip sockserv2.zip to any folder/directory.

2. Double-click on sockserv.exe.

3. Select the Configure button.

   a. Ensure that Listen Port is 1080.

   b. Ensure that Logging is enabled.

4. Select OK.

5. Select Start.

As shown in Figure 9.3, SOCKServ is now installed and ready for SSH connections.

To use the SOCKS server for SSH connections with SecureCRT, complete the following steps:

1. Confirm that a SOCKS version 4 or version 5 server is installed.

2. Open up SecureCRT. Start ⇨ Programs ⇨ SecureCRT ⇨ SecureCRT.

3. From the menu bar, select Options ⇨ Global Options.

4. Select the Firewall section.

5. For the Type field, select SOCKS version 4 or version 5, depending on what version you have installed, from the drop-down box.

6. For the Hostname or IP field, enter the IP address or hostname of the SOCKS server. In this example, it is 11.17.7.1.

7. For the port field, enter the port number you have selected for the SOCKS server. The default port is 1080.

8. Select OK.

The options should look like Figure 9.4.

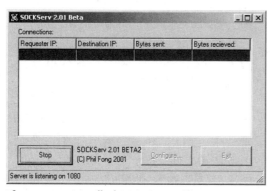

Figure 9.3   Installed SOCKServ utility.

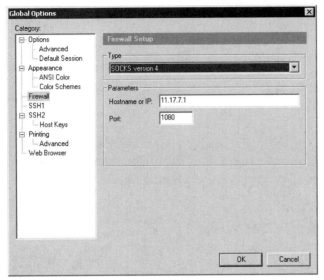

Figure 9.4   SecureCRT SOCKS options.

Now that you have SOCKS set up in your global options, you must configure each of your SSH connections to use the SOCKS firewall. Doing so will make your SSH request go to the SOCKS server first and will let the SOCKS server go to the server you requested on your behalf. To configure SSH connections to use the SOCKS server, compete the following steps:

1. Open SecureCRT, if it is not already open. Start ⇨ Programs ⇨ SecureCRT ⇨ SecureCRT.

2. For new connections, select File from the menu bar and select Quick Connect. For hostname, be sure to enter the hostname or IP address of the destination server you wish to reach, not the SOCKS server. For example, according to Figure 9.1, you could enter 11.17.7.10, 11.17.7.12, 11.17.7.14, or 11.17.7.16.

3. Select the checkbox that states Use firewall to connect.

4. For existing saved connections, select File from the menu bar and select Connect.

5. Highlight the connection you wish to edit; then right-click and select Properties. Be sure to select the connection of the destination sever you wish to reach, not the SOCKS server. For example, according to Figure 9.1, you could select 11.17.7.10, 11.17.7.12, 11.17.7.14, or 11.17.7.16.

6. The Connection section should have information about your saved connections.

7. In the right-hand pane, select the checkbox that states Use firewall to connect.

8. Select OK.

The options should look like Figure 9.5.

Again, be sure to keep the IP address and hostname fields to your desired destination server. Once the checkbox has been selected to use the firewall option, the SOCKS entry in your global settings will direct your connections to the SOCKS server, which will carry your request to the specified hostname or IP address that you have specified in your connection request. Once the setup has been completed, you should be able to use your SOCKS server, with a single firewall rule, to access any appropriate SSH enabled server.

To use the SOCKS server for SSH connections with SSH Communications' SSH client, complete the following steps:

1. Open the SSH Secure Client. Start ⇨ Programs ⇨ SSH Secure Shell ⇨ Secure Shell Client.

2. From the menu bar, select Edit ⇨ Settings.

3. Select the Firewall section.

4. For the Firewall URL field, enter the IP address or hostname of the SOCKS server, in the following format—socks://host:port. In this example, it is socks://11.17.7.1:1080.

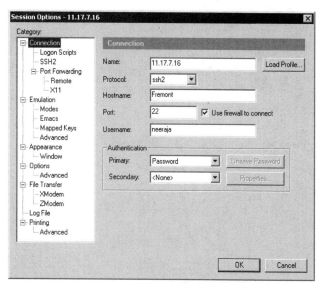

Figure 9.5 SecureCRT SOCKS options with saved connections.

5. For the SOCKS version field, select SOCKS version 4 or version 5, depending on what version you have installed, from the drop-down box.

6. Select OK.

The options should look like Figure 9.6.

Now that you have SOCKS set up in your global settings, you must config-ure each of your SSH connections to use the SOCKS firewall. Doing so will make your SSH request go to the SOCKS server first and will let the SOCKS server go to the server you requested. To configure SSH connections to use the SOCKS server, complete the following steps:

1. Open the SSH Secure Client, if it is not already open. Start ⇨ Programs ⇨ SSH Secure Shell ⇨ Secure Shell Client.

2. Select File ⇨ Profiles from the menu bar; then select Edit Profiles.

3. Highlight the profile you wish to edit. According to the example in Fig-ure 9.1, it would be the profile for 11.17.7.10, 11.17.7.12, 11.17.7.14, or 11.17.7.16. Be sure to select the connection of the destination server you wish to reach, not the SOCKS server. For example, according to Figure 9.1, you could select 11.17.7.10, 11.17.7.12, 11.17.7.14, or 11.17.7.16.

4. In the right-hand pane, select the checkbox that states Connect through firewall.

5. Select OK.

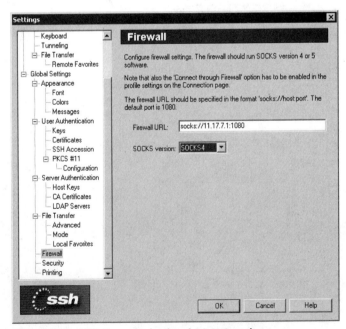

Figure 9.6 SSH Communications' SOCKS options.

The options should look like Figure 9.7.

Now that the SOCKS server is set up on 11.17.7.1 and the SSH clients are configured to use the SOCKS server to access the desired hosts, you can use the SOCKS/SSH architecture. Using your SSH client, SecureCRT, or SSH Communications' SSH client, connect to the desired host (11.17.7.16) with the use of the SOCKS server. (First, ensure that the firewall checkbox is selected.) When the SOCKS server receives the connection, it connects to 11.17.7.16 on your behalf and returns the connection to you. Once you have authenticated, you will have an SSH session via the SOCKS server. Furthermore, the connection between you and the SOCKS server and between the SOCKS server and the desired host is encrypted with SSH. After the session is enabled, you should see the connection in your SOCKServ utility, as shown in Figure 9.8.

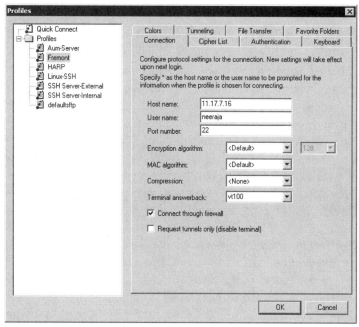

Figure 9.7 SSH Communications' SOCKS options under profiles.

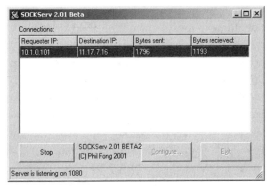

Figure 9.8 SOCKS connection with the SOCKServ utility.

Dynamic Port Forwarding and SOCKS

Dynamic port forwarding is another powerful feature of SSH in the port-forwarding architecture. Dynamic port forwarding offers the benefit of SOCKS proxy servers, described in the previous section, on a local port on an SSH client machine. Dynamic port forwarding uses a local port on the loopback address (127.0.0.1) that mimics a SOCKS server while performing the functions of a regular SOCKS service. For example, if an SSH connection has been established between an SSH client and an SSH server, instead of using the traditional local port-forwarding options, where each specific local port is matched to a specific port on the remote server, dynamic port forwarding can specify a local port to act like a SOCKS server that can be used by local applications, including mail, FTP, and Web clients. Many applications support the use of a SOCKS server; however, instead of specifying a real SOCKS server on a remote machine, you can specify the local machine (127.0.0.1) with the dynamic port-forwarding SOCKS server port, 1080 by default.

To set up dynamic port forwarding with SOCKS on an SSH client machine, complete the following steps:

1. From the SSH client, connect to the SSH server using the appropriate command-line client:

   ```
   OpenSSH      ssh <sshserver> -p <port> -l <username> -D 1080
   SSH          ssh2 <sshserver> -p <port> -l <username> -L socks/1080
   ```

2. On the SSH client; configure any relevant applications to use a SOCKS server for outbound connections. Enter the loopback address (127.0.0.1) for the IP address and port number 1080. Figure 9.9 and Figure 9.10 show example configurations of Internet Explorer and Netscape Messenger, respectively.

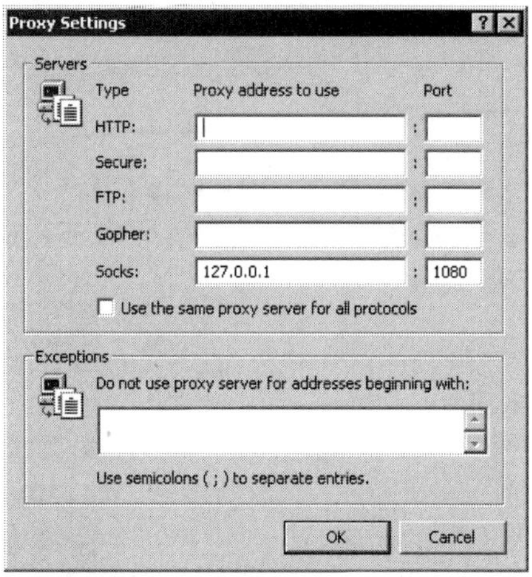

Figure 9.9   SOCKS configuration on Internet Explorer.

Figure 9.9 shows a SOCKS configuration on Internet Explorer. To reach this screen, open Internet Explorer ⇨ Tools ⇨ Internet Options ⇨ Connections ⇨ LAN Settings ⇨ Check Use Proxy Server ⇨ select Advanced ⇨ enter SOCKS information.

Figure 9.10 shows a SOCKS configuration on Netscape Messenger. To reach this screen, open Netscape Messenger ⇨ Edit ⇨ Properties ⇨ Advanced ⇨ Proxies ⇨ Manual Proxy Configuration ⇨ View. Then enter SOCKS information.

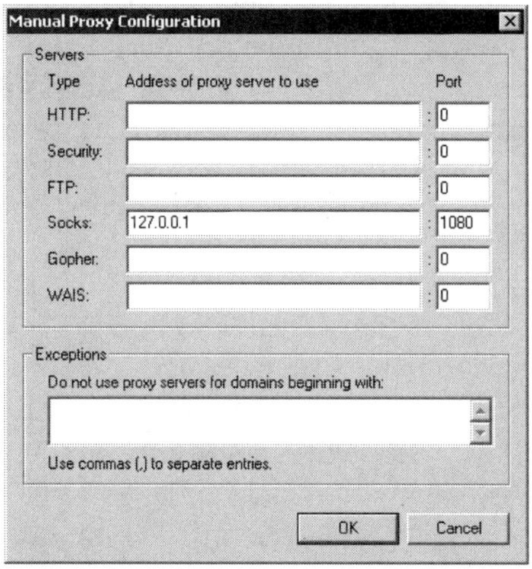

Figure 9.10   SOCKS configuration on Netscape Messenger.

All communication between the SSH client and the SSH server, no matter what applications are being used via the local SOCKS dynamic port-forwarding option, are encrypted.

NOTE DNS traffic to and from Web clients is not encrypted, since Web Clients are not SOCKS enabled; instead, they perform DNS lookup themselves over UDP port 53.

Dynamic port forwarding allows the flexibility of a local SOCKS server port to be used with all applications and the SSH client, while gaining the benefit of secure communications on any applications to/from the SSH server. Also, this model holds significantly less overhead than traditional local port forwarding by not requiring the use of specific local ports to match remote ports, but requiring only one local dynamic SOCKS port-forwarding option. Remember, unlike regular port forwarding, where all applications are configured to use the loopback address, dynamic port forwarding uses the real IP address for the desired server, not 127.0.0.1. For example, mail clients use the real IP address of the mail servers but use the SOCKS connection to access the real IP address. Furthermore, when configuring the e-mail client, you still use the real hostname or IP address for the mail server but use the loopback address only for the SOCKS menu. Figure 9.11 shows the dynamic port-forwarding architecture with Web browsers.

You may be asking yourself, with all the great uses for SSH and SOCKS, why there is still so much use of local port forwarding or why dynamic port-forwarding isn't more popular? These are great questions that have few answers. Many SSH users are well aware of local and remote port forwarding, but dynamic port forwarding still is not widely adopted. The following is a short list of some positives and negatives of dynamic port forwarding with SOCKS:

- Dynamic port forwarding can replace several local port-forwarding rules.
  - Consider that local port-forwarding options can grow to be 8 to 15 settings when using mail, file transfer, remote management, and Web browsing options. When using dynamic port forwarding, a single option just needs to be set on the SSH client and all applications need to be SOCKS enabled.
- Secure remote access (VPN architecture) becomes more manageable with SSH and the use of dynamic port forwarding.
- The use of secondary HTTP proxy servers or SOCKS servers is not required.

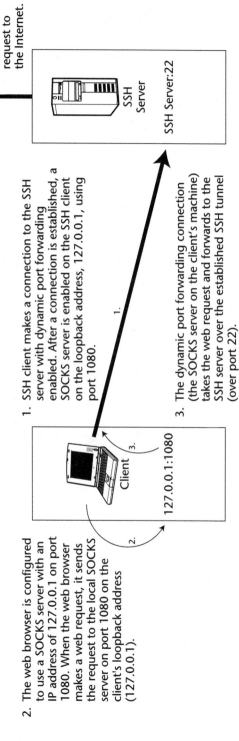

4. SSH server sends the request to the Internet.

SSH Server

SSH Server:22

1. SSH client makes a connection to the SSH server with dynamic port forwarding enabled. After a connection is established, a SOCKS server is enabled on the SSH client on the loopback address, 127.0.0.1, using port 1080.

3. The dynamic port forwarding connection (the SOCKS server on the client's machine) takes the web request and forwards to the SSH server over the established SSH tunnel (over port 22).

Client

127.0.0.1:1080

2. The web browser is configured to use a SOCKS server with an IP address of 127.0.0.1 on port 1080. When the web browser makes a web request, it sends the request to the local SOCKS server on port 1080 on the client's loopback address (127.0.0.1).

Figure 9.11   Dynamic port forwarding with SSH.

- Any insecure protocol or insecure network can be easily secure with only the need of an SSH server, SSH client, and SOCKS-enabled applications.
  - Most, if not all, Web, FTP, and e-mail applications are SOCKS aware.
- Dynamic port forwarding is available by default with most command-line SSH technologies.

Besides its advantages, dynamic port forwarding has some drawbacks. The following is a list regarding why dynamic port forwarding may not be usable for your particular organization:

- Relevant applications must support SOCKS.
  - Most Web clients and e-mail clients support SOCKS, but several applications and protocols, such as NFS and SMB, do not have SOCKS-enabled clients.
- Dynamic port forwarding requires additional configuration on client-side applications.
- Some SSH clients do not support dynamic port forwarding.

Secure Web Browsing with SSH

One of the most attractive features of SSH is the ability to surf the information superhighway in a secure fashion, despite the network you are sitting on (for example, the Internet), the protocol that the Web server is using (for example, HTTP), or the possibility that malicious users are sniffing your segment (for example, on wireless networks in coffee shops).

Secure Web browsing with SSH requires the use of an HTTP (Web) proxy server. Any proxy server will work, such as Microsoft's ISA proxy server, or SQUID, the Open Source proxy server. The installation and configuration of HTTP proxy servers is outside the scope of this section, so I assume that a proxy server has already been set up or can be set up in a relatively easy fashion (see www.squid-cache.org for Unix proxy servers and www.microsoft.com/isaserver/default.asp for Windows proxy servers). To use SSH's encryption capabilities with secure Web browsing, you need to implement port forwarding, discussed in Chapter 6, along with proxy servers. The architecture for the method you will be implementing is illustrated in Figure 9.12.

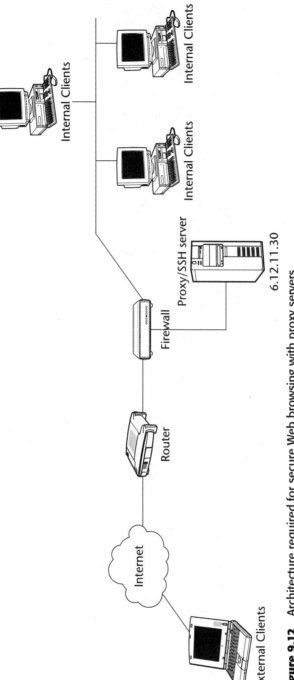

Figure 9.12   Architecture required for secure Web browsing with proxy servers.

Before you begin, briefly examine the architecture for proxy servers and Web browsing. If you use a proxy server for Web browsing in your organization, you probably have your Web browser point to your proxy server for requests. For example, with Internet Explorer, if you point to Tools ➪ Internet Options ➪ Connections ➪ LAN Settings and 'Use a proxy server' has a hostname or IP address, your Web browser is sending requests to your HTTP proxy server first, and the proxy server is reaching out to the real Web site on your behalf. With the use of SSH, the connection between the SSH client and the proxy server, which is also an SSH server, is secured, so any Web communication is protected.

The first step is to deploy a proxy server in your internal network. Many organizations have several proxy servers in their internal networks, either in their DMZ network or their internal network itself. Either location is fine, as long as all the internal clients can access the proxy server through firewalls or router-access control lists. The second step is to install an SSH server on the proxy server itself or to install an SSH server that has direct access to the proxy server. In your example, you will be installing an SSH server on the proxy server itself, but be aware that another server could be used solely for the SSH server as well. Once you have installed an SSH server on the proxy server, you should be ready to be setup for secure Web browsing. Assume that your proxy server, with an IP address of 6.12.11.30, is listening on port 8080 for all proxy requests. Also assume that your SSH server, also with an IP address of 6.12.11.30, is listening on port 22 for all SSH connections. Now that you have 6.12.11.30 listening on port 8080 (HTTP proxy) and port 22 (SSH), you are ready to begin.

The idea behind secure Web browsing is that the client will make a valid connection to the SSH server using any SSH client. The SSH client, however, will also be port-forwarding port 8080 on the SSH client to the SSH server. Therefore, any connection made to port 8080 on the local SSH client will be forwarded to the SSH server on port 8080 over the existing SSH tunnel. Since the SSH server will be listening for HTTP proxy connections on port 8080, any request made on the SSH client on port 8080 will be forwarded to the HTTP proxy server port, which is also port 8080, via SSH. As a result, the client's Web traffic will be tunneled through SSH from the client to the proxy server, securing your Web communications. In addition to setting up port forwarding, the client's Web browser will need to be configured to use port 8080 on its own loopback address (127.0.0.1) for any HTTP requests. The client must use itself (127.0.0.1) on port 8080 as its proxy server, which is really the port-forwarding tunnel of SSH. Once port forwarding has been set up for port 8080 and the Web browser has been configured (127.0.0.1) as the proxy server on port 8080, any requests from the Web browser will be sent to the proxy server over SSH as shown in Figure 9.13. Complete the following steps to set up SSH clients and the Web browser with secure Web communication on a Unix client:

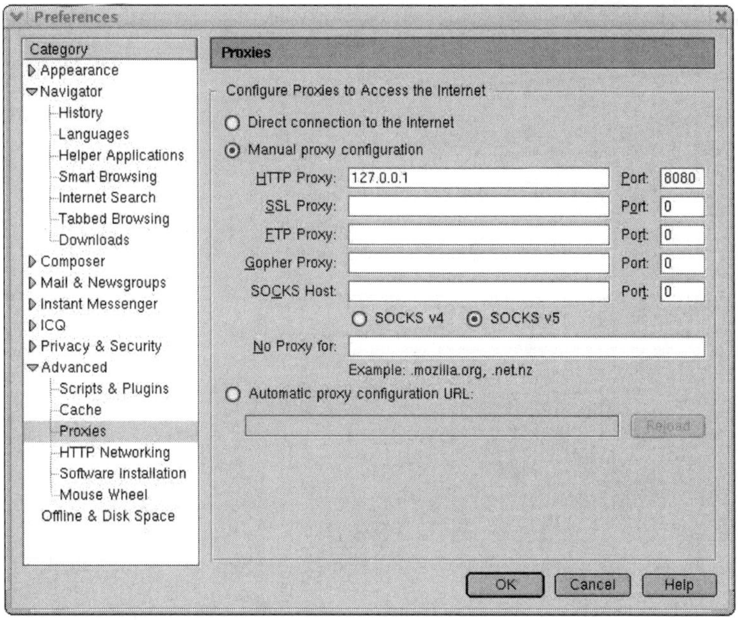

Figure 9.13 Proxy settings under Netscape for 127.0.0.1 on port 8080.

1. Connect to the SSH server, port-forwarding port 8080.

   ```
   #ssh 6.12.11.30 -p 22 -L 8080:6.12.11.30:8080
   ```

2. Open Netscape.

3. Select Edit from the menu bar and choose Preferences.

4. Expand the Advanced section in the left-hand pane.

5. Select Proxies under the Advanced section.

6. Select the Manual proxy configuration radio button.

7. For the HTTP Proxy: section, enter 127.0.0.1.

8. For the Port: section, enter 8080.

9. Select OK.

Complete the following steps to set up SSH clients and a Web browser with secure Web communication on a Windows client.

1. Open SecureCRT or SSH Communications' SSH client.

2. Configure sessions for the SSH server on 6.12.11.30, on port 22.

3. Enter the port-forwarding options to port forward all connections on port 8080 to 6.12.11.30. See Figures 9.14 and 9.15.

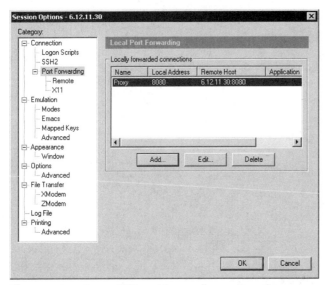

Figure 9.14   SecureCRT port-forwarding options for proxy connections over port 8080.

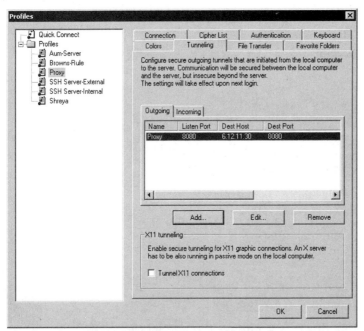

Figure 9.15   SSH Communications' SSH client's port-forwarding options for proxy connections over port 8080.

4. Save the sessions on the respective SSH clients and connect to the SSH server with the port-forwarding options enabled.

5. Open Internet Explorer.

6. Select Tools from the menu bar; then select Internet Options.

7. Select the Connections tab.

8. Select the LAN Settings button at the bottom of the section.

9. Select the Proxy server checkbox and enter 127.0.0.1 for the Address and 8080 for the Port.

10. Select OK. See Figure 9.16 for details.

Now that you have connected your SSH client to the SSH server (with your port-forwarding options enabled) and your proxy setting in your Web browser points to your own machine (127.0.0.1) on port 8080, you should be able to securely browse the information superhighway by encrypting all traffic from your client to your HTTP proxy server with SSH. Figure 9.17 shows the communication process.

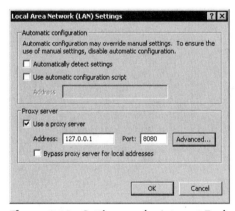

Figure 9.16   Settings under Internet Explorer for the proxy settings over port 8080.

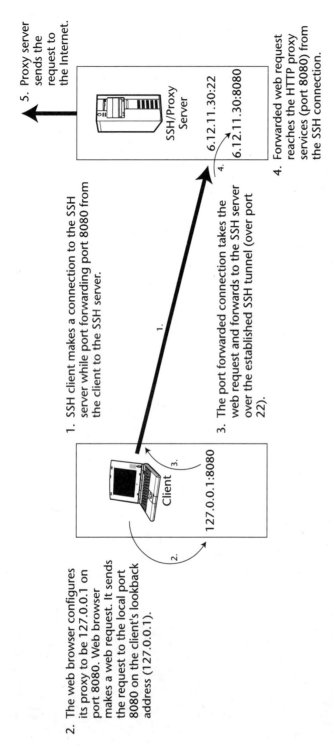

5. Proxy server sends the request to the Internet.

1. SSH client makes a connection to the SSH server while port forwarding port 8080 from the client to the SSH server.

2. The web browser configures its proxy to be 127.0.0.1 on port 8080. Web browser makes a web request. It sends the request to the local port 8080 on the client's lookback address (127.0.0.1).

3. The port forwarded connection takes the web request and forwards to the SSH server over the established SSH tunnel (over port 22).

4. Forwarded web request reaches the HTTP proxy services (port 8080) from the SSH connection.

Figure 9.17   Data flow for secure Web communication.

SSH via HTTP Proxies

Thus far, you have examined using SSH with many proxy technologies, such as SOCKS or dynamic port forwarding. But before you proceed to the next section, you need to explore the use of SSH clients in existing networks where HTTP proxy servers may be deployed. For example, many organizations do not allow internal employees to have full outbound access to the Internet on all ports, specifically on SSH. Many organizations allow their employees to access only port 80 (HTTP) and port 443 (HTTPS) to the Internet. Often, these outbound connections are allowed only through an HTTP proxy server. While the use of proxy servers for HTTP access is useful, this may restrict access to your organization's SSH server (port 22). In order to continue to use SSH clients in networks where HTTP proxy servers are deployed and are the only means of accessing the Internet, the HTTP CONNECT command string must be given to the HTTP proxy server on the specific port it is listening on, usually port 80 or 8080, to access the SSH server on the outside.

Using SecureCRT, the following HTTP command, **CONNECT %h:%p HTTP/1.0\r\n\r\n**, where &h is a variable for host and %p is a variable for port, can allow you to use an SSH client though an HTTP proxy server without the need for any modification on the HTTP proxy server itself. To enable SecureCRT to use an HTTP proxy server for outbound access, complete the following steps:

1. Start ⇨ Programs ⇨ SecureCRT ⇨ SecureCRT.
2. Select Options from the menu bar.
3. Select Global Options.
4. Highlight the Firewall section.
5. Select Generic Proxy for the Type field in the right-hand pane.
6. Enter the hostname or IP address of the HTTP proxy server in the Hostname or IP field.
7. Enter the port being used for HTTP proxy connections. This will be the same port the client's Web browser is using to surf the Web. Most likely, the port will be 80 or 8080.
8. Leave the Prompt textbox blank.
9. Enter **CONNECT %h:%p HTTP/1.0\r\n\r\n** for the Command textbox.
10. Select OK. Figure 9.18 shows the configuration in SecureCRT.

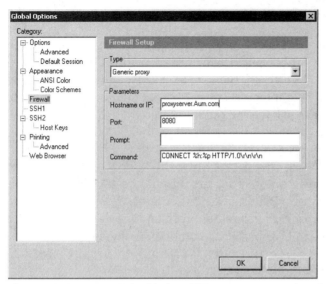

Figure 9.18 SecureCRT with the HTTP proxy command setting.

As with other settings using the Firewall option in SecureCRT, be sure to check the "Use firewall to connect" option for each SSH session that you will use through the proxy server. See Figure 9.19 for the checkbox location.

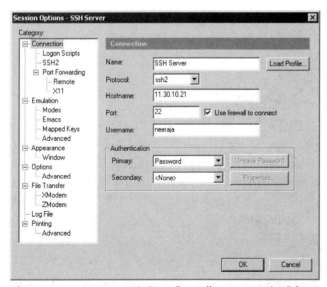

Figure 9.19 SecureCRT's "Use firewall to connection" feature.

Similar to SecureCRT, OpenSSH's command-line client can be used to use SSH via HTTP proxy servers. Unlike with SecureCRT, you will need to download a tool called Corkscrew, written by Pat Padgett, from www.agroman.net/corkscrew. Once you have downloaded the tool to /usr/local/bin, enter the following commands to enable Corkscrew, which will help you use SSH through HTTP proxy servers:

Unzip and install the utility.

```
#gunzip -c corkscrew-2.0.tar.gz | tar xvf -
#cd corkscrew-2.0
#./configure
#make
#make install
```

Edit your ~/.ssh/config file and add the following lines, replacing "http.proxy.server" with the hostname or IP address of your HTTP proxy server and "port" with the port, usually 80 or 8080, that your HTTP proxy server is listening on.

```
ProxyCommand /usr/local/bin/corkscrew http.proxy.server port %h %p
```

Use the –F flag to connect to the remote SSH server.

```
#ssh -F config ip.ssh.server -p 80
```

That's it! You will now be able to use OpenSSH's command-line client through HTTP proxy servers to reach SSH servers.

Securing Wireless Networks with SSH

Wireless connections, specifically 802.11b, have been plagued with security issues almost since their introduction. From serious security issues with WEP, to clear-text communication of management beacons, wireless technology is a key target for attackers. Nevertheless, wireless technology is a "must-have" in many organizations. If your organization will not deploy wireless technology due to its security issues, someone who is unauthorized may deploy it for you, which probably won't be done in a secure fashion. You will be examining how to use your previous SSH and proxy model to secure wireless networks. Keep in mind that you can already secure other protocols, such as mail (POP3 and SMTP) and file transfer (FTP, SMB, NFS), with port forwarding over wireless networks. The following sections discuss how to use port forwarding to secure Web traffic over wireless networks.

Securing Wireless with SSH and HTTP Proxies

Implementation of secure Web communications over insecure wireless networks differs little from other means of implementation in other media, seen in previous examples. As an example, consider an architecture in which an employee is at a coffee shop, using an insecure wireless connection. This architecture is illustrated in Figure 9.20. Guidelines for implementing this type of architecture are as follows:

1. Install an SSH server on 11.17.1.1, listening on port 22.

2. Install a proxy server on 11.17.11, listening on port 8080.

3. Allow port 22 through the perimeter firewalls and routers.

4. Configure an SSH client on "Coffee Shop Client" to port forward port 8080 from the client loopback interface, 127.0.0.1, to the SSH/Proxy server, 11.17.1.1, on port 8080.

5. Configure a Web browser on "Coffee Shop Client" to use 127.0.0.1 on port 8080 for the proxy server.

At this point, "Coffee Shop Client" should be able to use the established SSH connection to make secure connections to the HTTP proxy, giving the client secure Web communication over the insecure wireless network. If port forwarding has been set up for corporate e-mail and file transfer (see Chapters 6 and 7 for more details on how to do so), the client can perform e-mail, file transfer, and Web browsing over a secure connection in an insecure network.

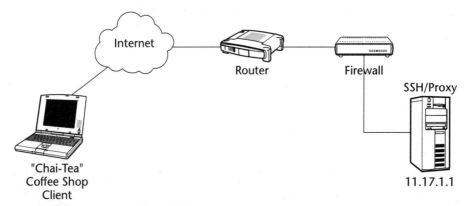

Figure 9.20 External wireless client model.

Securing Wireless with SSH and Dynamic Port Forwarding

Dynamic port forwarding can also be used to secure wireless connections. Instead of requiring the use of a proxy server, dynamic port forwarding needs nothing more than an SSH server and an SSH client. The second example, shown in Figure 9.21, demonstrates an architecture where an employee might also be located at a coffee shop, using an insecure wireless connection. Notice the difference between Figures 9.20 and 9.21. Figure 9.20 shows an SSH server and a proxy server on the same machine, whereas Figure 9.21 requires only an SSH server due to the use of dynamic port forwarding.

To implement secure Web communications over insecure wireless networks, perform the following steps:

1. Install an SSH server on 11.30.6.12, listening on port 22.

2. Allow port 22 through the perimeter firewalls and routers.

3. Configure an SSH client on "Coffee Shop Client" to dynamic port forwarding using SOCKS on the loopback address, 127.0.0.1, on port 8080.

    ```
    OpenSSH      ssh 11.30.6.12 -p 22 -l root -D 1080
    SSH          ssh2 11.30.6.12 -p 22 -l root -L socks/1080
    ```

4. Configure a Web browser on "Coffee Shop Client" to use 127.0.0.1 on port 8080 for their SOCKS server. Select Internet Explorer ➪ Tools ➪ Internet Options ➪ Connections ➪ LAN Settings ➪ Check Use Proxy Server ➪ select Advanced ➪ enter 127.0.0.1 for the SOCKS server on port 1080.

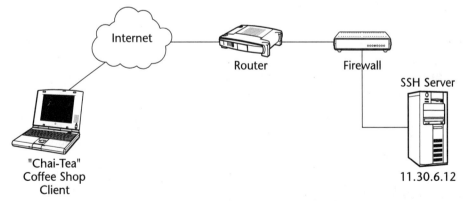

Figure 9.21 Dynamic port forwarding used to secure wireless connections with SSH.

The two preceding approaches provide a fast, easy, inexpensive, and secure solution for wireless networks. While these solutions may not be relevant for all wireless networks or requirements, SSH does solve two of the major requirements for wireless users: secure Web browsing and secure e-mail.

Summary

The combination of SSH and proxy technology, whether it be HTTP proxies, a SOCKS server, or dynamic port forwarding, gives SSH even more powerful capabilities. The combination of these two technologies allows SSH to be used very easily in insecure and inflexible networks, such as 802.11b wireless networks. Also, with the use of Web proxies or SOCKS, protocols that were very difficult to secure unless large investments in security devices were purchased are now easy to set up at a very low cost.

SSH and SOCKS demonstrate how SOCKS servers combined with SSH flexibility can simplify an SSH architecture while providing end-to-end SSH security. The ability to centralize SSH communications to a single destination, which can then be dispersed to several locations, while providing the use of SSH encryption to/from the entire connection, makes SSH and SOCKS an attractive and simple solution in what could be a complex architecture.

Furthermore, the use of dynamic port forwarding, which creates a fully functional SOCKS server on the local SSH client, adds an incredible amount of flexibility to SSH. Since the use of dynamic port forwarding allows SSH clients to have the benefit of SOCKS technology, or even proxy technology, without the use of a secondary proxy or SOCKS server, it is a very attractive solution that is not only easy to implement (with the need for just a single flag on a supporting SSH client), but easy to support as well (by requiring only a default SSH server without extra configuration or plug-ins). The ability to secure Web, FTP, and mail applications with a single port-forwarding rule without changing any aspects of the SSH server or the architecture it resides in makes dynamic port forwarding a very strong feature of SSH.

The ability to use HTTP proxies with SSH allows SSH secure Web communication from insecure networks through a relatively easy process. Many organizations have deployed proxy servers probably for other reasons; however, with the use of local port forwarding, the existing proxy servers can be used to port forward local connections over secure tunnels to an existing (or new) internal proxy server. This combination allows external employees, such as employees who work from home or travel considerably, to use trusted internal servers for sensitive communications, such as financial applications that are only Web enabled.

Lastly, this chapter briefly describes how to use SSH technologies with HTTP proxies and dynamic port forwarding to secure 802.11b wireless networks. The details learned from the previous section of this chapter can be used not only in traditional wired networks but also in newly emerging networks with strong security issues, such as wireless ones. While wireless and SSH do have scalability draw-backs, SSH can secure a wireless network with relatively low overhead, low cost, and high performance without the need to redesign any type of network or network segment.

The next chapter provides a discussion of SSH case studies. This chapter provides various real-world examples on how SSH can be used to solve several critical functionality and security issues within an organization. Furthermore, the chapter will discuss many of the key aspects, features, and functions discussed in the previous chapters, while highlighting the most powerful and useful functions.

## CHAPTER 10

SSH Case Studies

When Trinity needed to hack into the Zion mainframe in order to save the world in the motion picture *Matrix Reloaded*, what utility does she use? That's right, she uses SSH. If this book has shown you one thing, it should be that not only can SSH be used to save the world; it should be regarded as a gift from the gods. Seriously, while Trinity demonstrates one of the many benefits of SSH, which is secure terminal access to a mainframe system, the most important aim of this book is to demonstrate the flexibility of SSH when properly optimized.

In order to fully demonstrate SSH's flexibility, let's examine three case studies in this chapter. These are real-world situations in which SSH is used to significantly improve the functionality and/or the security of a particular architecture. The following are the three case studies:

- Secure remote access
- Secure wireless connectivity
- Secure file servers

Each case study consists of the following four items:

- A problem
- Business requirements
- Configuration
- Results checklist

Case Study # 1: Secure Remote Access

The following case study involves the Ace Tomato Company. The Ace Tomato Company is a multinational organization headquartered in Mumbai, India, that produces and sells dairy milk all over the world. It has sales, professional services, and technical-support divisions that travel to customer sites 90 percent of the time, which is either outside of the country, primarily in the Nashville, TN, Columbus, OH, Brookings, SD, Minneapolis, MN, and San Francisco, CA, or locally around the country, primarily in Belwa, Beneras, and Bangalore.

The Problem Situation

The Ace Tomato Company needs a secure remote-access solution for its external end-users.

Business Requirements

The business requirements provided by the Ace Tomato Company are as follows:

- Must support strong level on encryption (Triple-DES or above)
- Must be accessible from all types of networks, including NAT'd networks, remote offices, hotel rooms, behind internal proxy servers, and organizations that allow only TCP port 80 and 443 outbound
- Must support two-factor authentication
- Must be able to provide easy access to e-mail and intranet servers from internal networks, DMZ networks, and extranets
- Must be able to provide secure file-sharing access
- Must require only a single action from novice end-users for e-mail
- Must provide stable and consistent performance

Secure remote access is one of the premier reasons to use SSH, especially with its port-forwarding feature. Despite the fact that port forwarding will be used, the type of SSH solution chosen for this particular architecture is very important, since not all SSH solutions can meet all of the preceding requirements with the same level of simplicity.

For your solution, you will choose to use the VShell SSH server due to its ability to provide secure file-sharing access without the need for additional file-system restrictions, such as NTFS or Unix file-system security. Since remote access to e-mail, file sharing, and intranet Web pages are the only requirements, VShell also provides the ability to easily restrict command-line access to the SSH server, a feature that must be enabled for all users to secure the SSH server itself. Furthermore, since your remote-access solution requires access behind internal proxy servers, SecureCRT is a great solution, since it can connect through proxy servers using a CONNECT string, as discussed in Chapter 9. Lastly, SecureCRT also offers the ability to automatically execute other applications, such as e-mail clients, once an SSH connection has been established. This will meet the requirement that states that all novice users should have only one step to access e-mail.

In addition to SecureCRT, SSH Communications' SFTP client will be used to access the SFTP session on the Windows file server, since SecureCRT does not have a built-in SFTP client. This will require an additional step for file-sharing access; however, that does not break any of the preceding requirements. The following list states the utilities that will be used:

- VShell for the SSH servers
- SecureCRT for the SSH client
- SSH Communications for the SFTP client

The key requirements from an architecture perspective will be the ability to access e-mail servers, file sharing, and intranet Web servers from the SSH server. Also, since command-line access to the SSH server is not desired, command-line access will need to be restricted. Furthermore, since the internal file server will need to be accessible remotely, another installation of VShell should be installed on the internal file server for remote SFTP users. Figure 10.1 shows the remote-access architecture.

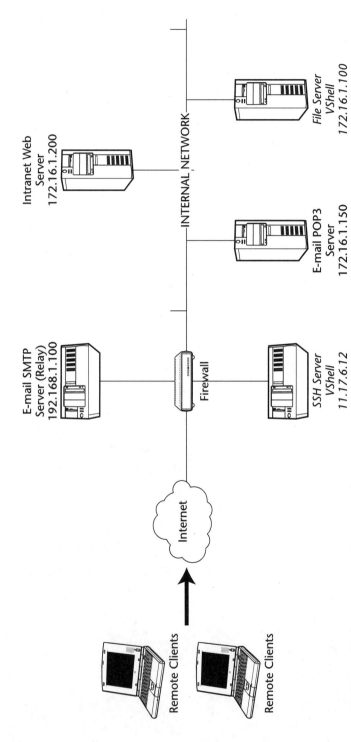

Figure 10.1 SSH architecture for case study #1.

All devices in Figure 10.1 are part of the existing architecture, except for items in italics, which are the VShell SSH server off the perimeter firewall and the installation of VShell on the internal file server. With only the need for two additional items, the architecture for remote access with SSH is quite simple.

In addition to the architecture, the perimeter firewall in Figure 10.1 needs to be modified. The firewall needs to allow external remote clients to access the SSH server on port 443. Why are you choosing port 443 instead of the default port 22? Remember from the requirements lists that the remote-access solutions must be accessible in networks that allow only outbound access on TCP ports 80 and 443. Also, remote clients need to connect through proxy servers that almost always listen on ports 80 and 443 and usually do not allow you to proxy any other ports (These restrictions would eliminate other VPN solutions such as IPSec-based VPNs, which needs UDP 500 to be allowed outbound). Next, the firewall has to allow access from the SSH server, located in a DMZ off one leg of the firewall, to port 25 on the SMTP server (mail relay), port 80 on the internal intranet server, port 110 on the mail server, and port 22 on the Windows file server. Table 10.1 shows the firewall rules that need to be deployed for the remote-access solution.

Table 10.1   Firewall Rules for Case Study #1

RULE	SOURCE	DESTINATION	PORT	ACTION	COMMENT
1	ANY	SSH server	443	Allow	Allow any remote access client to access the SSH server on port 443
2	SSH server	E-mail SMTP server (Relay)	25	Allow	Allow the SSH server to access port 25 on the mail-relay server
3	SSH server	E-mail POP3 server	110	Allow	Allow the SSH server to access port 110 on the E-mail POP3 server

(continued)

Table 10.1 *(continued)*

RULE	SOURCE	DESTINATION	PORT	ACTION	COMMENT
4	SSH server	Intranet Web server	80	Allow	Allow the SSH server to access port 80 on the intranet Web server
5	SSH server	File server	22	Allow	Allow the SSH server to access port 22 (SFTP) on the file server

Rule 1 on the firewall is the most obvious; external remote-access clients need to be able to access the SSH server on port 443. The next four rules are in place for port-forwarding reasons. Since the remote-access SSH clients will be using the SSH server and port forwarding to access the e-mail, file-sharing, and Web servers, the SSH server will need to be allowed to access all of the other servers.

Configuration

Now that the product selection and architecture have been set up for SSH, it's time to examine the configuration options, which are the most important steps.

SSH Client Configuration

SecureCRT, the SSH client, needs to be configured for two items in order to meet the business requirements previously listed, which are password/key-based authentication, in order to meet the two-factor authentication requirement, and port-forwarding configuration, in order to access all necessary servers. SSH Communications' SFTP client also needs to be configured, since that is the client that will be used for file-sharing access. In order to create public and private keys with SecureCRT and upload to the VShell SSH server, complete the following steps (referenced from Chapter 4).

1. Open the SSH Client: Start ⇨ Programs ⇨ SecureCRT 4.0 ⇨ SecureCRT 4.0.

2. From the Menu bar select, Tools ⇨ Create Public Key.

3. The Key Generation Wizard should appear. After reading through the introduction wizard page, select Next.

4. The Key type screen should appear next. This screen gives you the option of selecting a DSA or RSA key type. After selecting your preferred key type, select Next.

5. The Passphrase screen should appear next. This screen allows you to set a passphrase that will protect the private key. The passphrase will need to be entered in order to decrypt the private key. The screen allows you to set a comment, possibly with identification information of the public and private-key pair.

6. The Key length screen should appear next. This screen allows you to set the key length, anywhere between 512 and 2048. Generally, the higher the key length, the stronger the security; however, it will have a greater performance penalty.

7. The Generation screen should appear next. This screen initiates the process of actually creating the key. Move the mouse around in order to create the key. Once the process is completed, select Next.

8. The location screen should appear next. Unless you have a particular area to store the keys, it is recommended to key the keys in the default location (C:\Documents and Settings\Administrator\Application Data\VanDyke\Identity); however, make sure to place NTFS permissions on the folder to restrict access to Guests, Everyone, and other unauthorized groups. After you select the location, click Finish.

9. You should see a pop-up box asking if you would like to use the key as your global public key. Select No since you may have multiple keys with one single default global key.

10. VanDyke SecureCRT public and private-key pairs have been generated!

After the creation process has been completed, uploading the public key is next. The following section demonstrates how to upload a SecureCRT client public and private-key pair to a VanDyke VShell SSH server. Using a Secure-CRT public and private-key pair on VanDyke Software's SSH server is quite simple, as the following steps show:

1. Open up SecureCRT (Start ➪ Programs ➪ Secure CRT ➪ Secure CRT).

2. Make a valid connection to the VShell SSH server using the Quick Connection option.

3. Once a valid connection has been established, go back to the quick connect menu (File ⇨ Quick Connect). Under the authentication section, there should be two drop-down boxes. The Primary method should be Password. For the Secondary methods, choose PublicKey and select the Properties button to the right.

4. The Public Key Properties menu should appear. Make sure the Use Global Public Key Setting radio button is selected and Use identify file radio button is also selected. After you have confirmed this, select the "..." button and browse to the location of your public key; then select the public-key file.

5. After you have selected your public-key file, select the Upload button to upload the public key to the VShell SSH server.

6. When SecureCRT has established a connection, it will ask you to authenticate using your username and password on the VShell SSH server. Enter the valid username and password and select OK.

7. Once the username and password are authenticated, the public key will be uploaded to the VShell SSH server.

8. You should now be able to use your public key to authenticate. To confirm, enable only public-key authentication on the VShell SSH server.

    a. Select Start ⇨ Programs ⇨ VShell ⇨ VShell.

    b. Highlight the Authentication section.

    c. Uncheck Password and check Public key for the required authentication methods. Be sure to uncheck the Allow 3 password attempts checkbox, since the public key is already on the VShell SSH server.

9. On SecureCRT, select PublicKey for the Primary authentication method and <None> for the secondary authentication method. Be sure to browse to the correct public key with the Properties button.

10. Select Connect and you will authenticate with your public key and then receive a VShell SSH session.

Now that username/password and public-key authentication have been configured on SecureCRT, ensure that the VShell server is configured to require both username/password and public-key authentication, as shown in Figure 10.2.

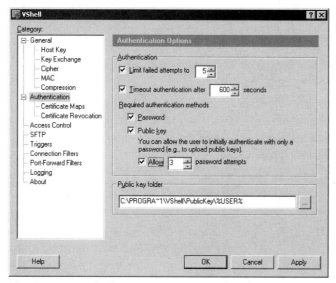

Figure 10.2   VShell SSH server requiring both username/password and public keys for authentication.

Now that the authentication requirement has been completed, you need to ensure that the proper port-forwarding items have been configured. Figure 10.3 shows the correct port-forwarding options to be used in order to meet the requirement to access e-mail, file sharing, and Web servers. Be sure to select the appropriate e-mail client for the application setting in the mail port-forwarding option.

Lastly, ensure that the CONNECT string is configured appropriately if any SecureCRT client ever needs to connect via a proxy server, as shown in Figure 10.4. Remember to remind users to check the "Use firewall to connect" option when they need to access the SSH server via a proxy server.

Now that SecureCRT has been configured for both authentication and port-forwarding requirements, SSH Communications' SFTP client needs to be configured in order to support the file-sharing requirement. Since SFTP will be port forwarding via the SSH connection to/from the file server's SSH server, very little configuration needs to be done on the SFTP client, aside from pointing the IP address to 127.0.0.1 on port 22, as shown in Figure 10.5.

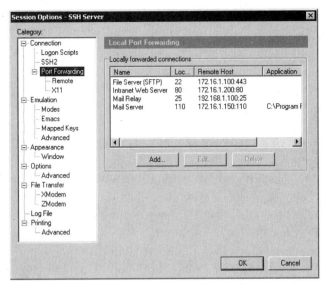

Figure 10.3 SecureCRT port-forwarding options in order to meet the requirements in case- study #1.

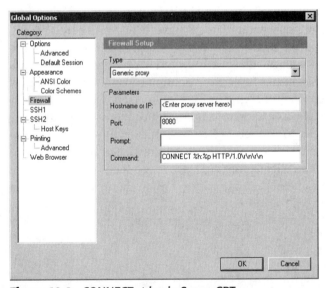

Figure 10.4 CONNECT string in SecureCRT.

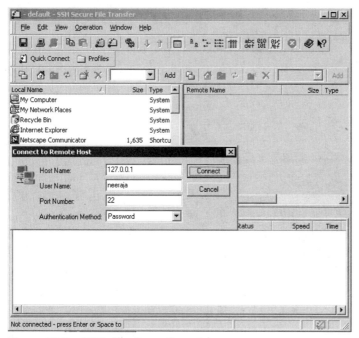

Figure 10.5 SFTP client's configuration.

SSH Server Configuration

I will now shift gears to the SSH servers, specifically the main VShell SSH server (11.17.6.12), which will be used for remote access, and the secondary VShell SSH server on the file server (172.16.1.100), which will be used only for the SFTP subsystem. On the main VShell SSH server (11.17.6.12), you need to configure three items: access control, triple-DES or above cipher options, and port-forwarding filters.

First, set the access-control options for the VShell server. Under VShell's Access Control section, you need to ensure that everyone has access to connect to the SSH sever, but only for port-forwarding reasons, as shown in Figure 10.6.

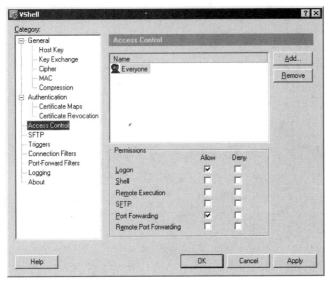

Figure 10.6 Access Control section for VShell.

Second, set the cipher options for the VShell server. Under VShell's General section, there is a subsection called Cipher. Ensure that 3DES has been checked. This will meet the encryption requirement listed previously.

Lastly, set the port-forwarding filters for the VShell server. Under VShell's Port Forwarding section, you will need to ensure that only port forwarding can be allowed to the identified e-mail, Web, and file servers. This setting is optional, since the firewall will block any port-forwarding connections by SSH clients that are not allowed; however, this step adds an extra level of security. The port-forwarding filters are shown in Figure 10.7.

The configuration on the VShell SSH server is minimal when compared with the primary SSH server. Because the VShell SSH server is being used only for its SFTP subsystem on the file server (172.16.1.100), only access control and SFTP need to be configured.

First, set the access-control options for the VShell server on the file server. Under VShell's Access Control section, you will need to ensure that everyone has access to connect to the SSH server, but only for SFTP, as shown in Figure 10.8.

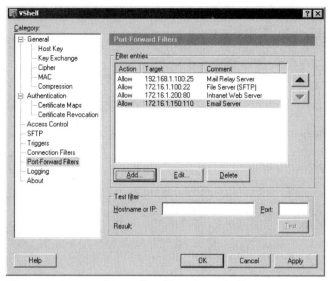

Figure 10.7 Port-forwarding filters for VShell.

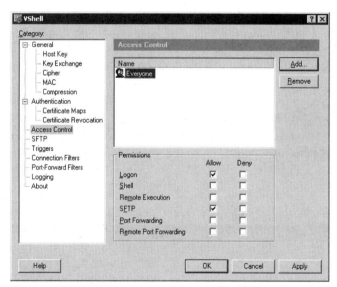

Figure 10.8 Access Control setting on the file server's VShell service.

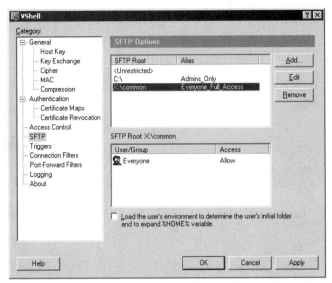

Figure 10.9   SFTP settings on the file server's VShell service.

Next, set the SFTP options for the SFTP subsystem on the file server. The file server's root-file directory is called Common and is located on a separate 500GB hard drive labeled X, which will be the partition (drive) for the SFTP root directory. Using VShell SFTP will limit all remote-access clients to that directory only and any subdirectories and/or files, as shown in Figure 10.9.

The last order of business is to configure the other clients to use the established SSH connection for communication. While limited space does not allow each step to be described in detail (see Chapter 7 for more detailed steps), the basic idea is to use the loopback interface, 127.0.0.1, for each IP address of the desired server and port, as shown in Table 10.2.

Table 10.2   Client Specifications

SERVICE	IP ADDRESS	PORT
Mail Relay	127.0.0.1	25
Mail Server	127.0.0.1	110
SFTP	127.0.0.1	22
Web (http://127.0.0.1)	127.0.0.1	80

Results Checklist

After the client setup has been completed, the requirements of case study # 1 will have all been met, as described in Table 10.3.

Table 10.3 Business Requirements and Results

BUSINESS REQUIREMENT	RESULTS
Must support strong level on encryption (Triple-DES or above)	The VShell SSH server has been configured to use 3DES or above.
Must be accessible from all types of networks, including NAT"d networks, remote offices, hotel rooms, behind internal proxy servers, and organizations that only allow TCP port 80 and 443 outbound	All SSH architecture can always work from NAT'd networks, including remote offices and hotel rooms. VShell SSH server has been configured to listen on port 443, which makes it accessible to clients behind internal proxy servers and organizations that allow only TCP port 443 outbound.
Must support two-factor authentication	VShell has been configured to require a username/password and a public key for authentication, as shown in Figure 10.2.
Must be able to provide easy access to e-mail and intranet servers from internal networks, DMZ networks, and extranets	SecureCRT and VShell have been configured to allow port forwarding to access e-mail and intranet servers. The perimeter firewall allows communication from the SSH server to the appropriate server.
Must be able to provide secure file-sharing access	A separate VShell service has been installed on the file server, limited only for the SFTP subsystem and disabled for other utilities (remote access, port-forwarding, and remote execution).
Must require a single action from novice end-users for e-mail	The application option has been set on SecureCRT's port-forwarding option, which automatically executes the mail client after the SSH session has been established.
Must provide stable and consistent performance	SSH always provides stable and consistent performance after implementation.

Case Study #2: Secure Wireless Connectivity

The following case study examines an organization called Virtucon. Virtucon is a domestic corporation headquartered in Fremont, California. Virtucon is a think-tank organization that generates test questions for the Iowa standard-test program. Any leakage of test questions, whether they are notes, e-mails, chat messages, Web pages, or documents, would undermine the integrity of the Iowa test results. While most Virtucon employees work on the Virtucon campus, employees are often encouraged to work anywhere and anytime on the Virtucon grounds, whether it is in a conference room, a neighbor's cube, or even outside on a box.

The Problem

Virtucon needs to provide secure wireless connectivity for all its internal users. All buildings on the Virtucon campus should be equipped with wireless (802.11) connectivity for all employees, including conference rooms, outdoor lunch areas, and internal cubes and offices.

Business Requirements

The following are the business requirements provided by Virtucon:

- Must support strong level on encryption (Triple-DES or above) and should not expose the internal corporate network to malicious activity
- Must provide complete access for two core-computing aspects of the organization, which are external Web access and internal e-mail
- External visitors, contractors/consultants, and war-drivers should be completely restricted from accessing the wireless network, even for external Web-access purposes
- Must require only a single action from novice end-users for e-mail and external Web access
- Must provide stable and consistent performance

Secure wireless connectivity for internal employees is a must in many organizations. Despite the overwhelming number of security exposures in 802.11 wireless networks, many organizations cannot afford to ignore wireless for much longer. This case study focuses on how to use SSH to secure wireless (802.11) networks.

In order to implement secure wireless connectivity, you need some core requirements from the SSH servers and clients. For this case study, you will be using the flexibility of dynamic port forwarding (local SOCKS proxy), as described in Chapter 9, for the SSH clients. The ability to connect and port forward to the SSH servers, while restricting any type of access to the SSH server itself, will be required. With these two requirements for our SSH servers, the following highlights the utilities you will be using in order to satisfy Virtucon's business requirements:

- SSH Communications' SSH server
- OpenSSH SSH client or SSH Communications' SSH client
- Any SOCKS-enabled e-mail client and Web browser

The key requirements from an architecture perspective will be the ability for the SSH server to access the core Internet connection for Virtucon and the ability to access the e-mail servers. Since command-line access to the SSH server is not desired, command-line access will need to be restricted. Furthermore, since dynamic port forwarding will be used on the SSH clients (port forwarding via SOCKS), you will need to ensure that all Web and e-mail clients have SOCKS support. Figure 10.10 shows the architecture to fulfill the requirements.

All devices in Figure 10.10 are part of the existing architecture, except for SSH Communications' SSH server off the perimeter firewall. Notice that the wireless-access point is not inside the internal network, but segments into another zone. This protects the corporate internal networks by creating a defense in-depth mode. If any compromise were to occur on the wireless network or on the SSH server connected to the wireless network, the internal corporate network would still be protected. The wireless-access points in this architecture are used as bridges to connect the wireless clients to the SSH server. With only the need for one additional item, the architecture for secure wireless access with SSH is quite simple.

In addition to the architecture, the perimeter firewall in Figure 10.10 needs to be slightly modified. The firewall needs to allow the SSH server to access the mail-relay server and the internal e-mail server. The firewall needs to allow the SSH server access to the Internet, since the SSH clients will be using the SSH server to browse the Web. Table 10.4 shows the firewall rules that need to be deployed for the secure wireless solution.

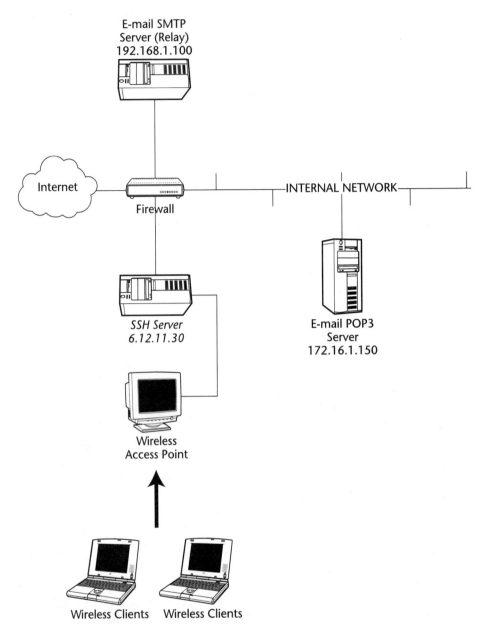

Figure 10.10   SSH architecture for case study #2.

Table 10.4   Firewall Rules for Case Study #2

RULE	SOURCE	DESTINATION	PORT	ACTION	COMMENT
1	SSH Server	Internet	80,443	Allow	Allow the SSH server to access the Internet, using port 80 and 443.
2	SSH server	E-mail SMTP server (Relay)	25	Allow	Allow the SSH server to access port 25 on the mail-relay server.
3	SSH server	E-mail POP3 server	110	Allow	Allow the SSH server to access port 110 on the E-mail POP3 server.

Rule 1 on the firewall is the most obvious; allow the SSH server to access the Internet. (Depending on which firewall you have deployed, make sure you do not allow the SSH server access to the entire network, specifically to the internal network, but full outbound access to the Internet only). The next two rules are in place for port-forwarding reasons. Since the wireless SSH clients will be using the SSH server and port forwarding to access the e-mail, the SSH server will need to be allowed access to all of the other servers.

Configuration

Now that the architecture and firewall rules have been set up for SSH, the configuration options need to be examined.

SSH Client Configuration

OpenSSH and SSH Communications' command-line SSH client can both be used in this situation, since they both support dynamic port forwarding. In order to enable dynamic port forwarding to forward e-mail and Web communication via the SSH server, according to Figure 10.10, complete the following steps:

1. For OpenSSH, enter the following command:

   ```
   ssh 6.12.11.30 -p 22 -l <username> -D 1080
   ```

2. For SSH Communications' SSH server, enter the following command:

   ```
   ssh2 6.12.11.30 -p 22 -l <username> -L socks/1080
   ```

3. On the SSH client, configure any relevant applications to use a SOCKS server for outbound connections. Enter the loopback address (127.0.0.1) for the IP address and port number 1080. Figures 10.11 and 10.12 show a sample SOCKS configuration of Internet Explorer and Netscape Messenger, respectively.

NOTE Netscape Communicator, Mozilla, Eudora, Outlook, and Outlook Express also support SOCKS.

To reach the SOCKS configuration screen on Internet Explorer, shown in Figure 10.11, open Internet Explorer ➪ Tools ➪ Internet Options ➪ Connections ➪ LAN Settings. Make sure that Use Proxy Server is checked. Then select Advanced and enter the SOCKS information.

Figure 10.12 shows SOCKS configuration on Netscape Messenger. To reach this SOCKS configuration screen for Netscape Messenger, shown in Figure 10.12, open Netscape Messenger ➪ Edit ➪ Properties ➪ Advanced ➪ Proxies ➪ Manual Proxy Configuration. Select View and enter SOCKS information.

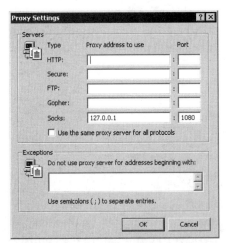

Figure 10.11 SOCKS configuration on Internet Explorer.

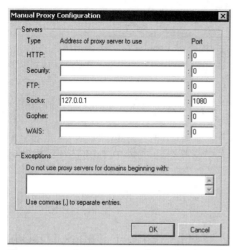

Figure 10.12 SOCKS configuration on Netscape Messenger.

All communication between the wireless SSH client to the SSH server, through the wireless-access point, is encrypted with SSH. This allows the flexibility of a local SOCKS server port (dynamic port forwarding) to be used with any applications that support SOCKS, while gaining the benefit of secure communications on any applications to and from the SSH server.

In addition to setting up SOCKS for Web and e-mail clients, be sure to keep in mind that the basic idea is to use the loopback interface, 127.0.0.1, for the SOCKS address, shown in the preceding example, and to use the server's real address for the regular client configurations. Table 10.5 shows the configurations for SSH clients according to Figure 10.10.

Table 10.5 Mail and Web-Client Specifications

SERVICE	IP ADDRESS	SOCKS IP ADDRESS: PORT
Mail Relay	192.168.1.100	127.0.0.1:1080
Mail Server	172.16.1.150	127.0.0.1:1080
Web	Any	127.0.0.1:1080

To support the requirement that novice users have one-step access to e-mail and Web browsing, the two preceding SSH commands can be scripted quite easily into a Windows batch file or a Unix shell script. This will allow novice Windows users to double-click the batch file (.bat) and be prompted for a password only for access. Similarly, novice Unix users will have to single-click or simply execute the shell script from the command line. To create the two scripts, copy and paste the preceding SSH syntax and paste it into a blank file. In Windows, save the file as ssh.bat; in Unix, save the file as ssh.sh. Then you are done. Once novice users execute that script, the SSH command will be executed, and the end-user will be prompted only for a password.

SSH Server Configuration

The next and last focus in this case study will be to configure the SSH server itself. Since dynamic port forwarding requires nothing from the SSH server in order to work, the only items to configure on the SSH server are to ensure that strong encryption is used, from the business requirements, and that terminal access to the SSH server is restricted.

First, set the encryption settings for the SSH Communications' SSH server. Under the SSH server's encryption section, which is under the SSH Server Settings, ensure that 3DES or AnyStdCipher (any standard cipher) is selected. This will enforce the level of encryption the meets the business requirement previously stated, as shown in Figure 10.13.

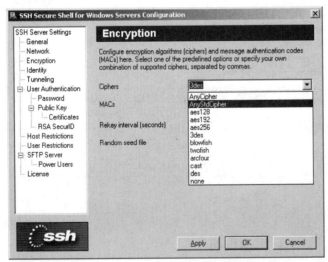

Figure 10.13 Encryption section for SSH Communications' SSH server.

Second, set the user settings for the SSH server. Under the SSH server's User Restrictions section, under User Authentication, ensure that Allow login for users states the domain, a forward slash, and an asterisk, such as Virtucon/* (described further in Chapter 2). This will enable all users that belong to the Virtucon domain to authenticate. Also, ensure that Permit user terminal is set to No or Admin, which will restrict terminal access to all users or allow only admin users to gain terminal access, as shown in Figure 10.14. This will allow wireless clients to port forward with the SSH server but restrict the clients to terminal access.

Results Checklist

After the server setup has been completed, the requirements of case study #2 will have all been met, as described in Table 10.6.

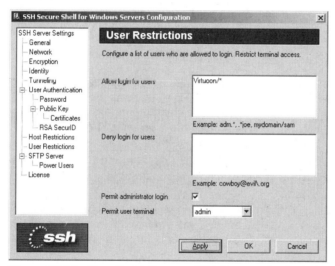

Figure 10.14   User Restrictions on SSH Communication's SSH server.

Table 10.6 Business Requirements and Results

BUSINESS REQUIREMENT	RESULTS
Must support strong level on encryption (3DES or above) and should not expose the internal corporate network to malicious activity.	The SSH Communications' SSH server has been configured to use 3DES or above, as shown in Figure 10.13. The wireless network is segmented from the internal corporate network into its own zone of the permitted firewall, as shown in Figure 10.10.
Must provide complete access for two core-computing aspects of the organization, which are external Web access and internal e-mail.	All SSH clients have been configured to use dynamic port forwarding, allowing e-mail and Web communication to use a local SOCKS server, running on 127.0.0.1, to port-forward HTTP, SMTP, and POP3 through the SSH server. The SSH server has been granted access to the Internet, mail relay, and mail server.
External visitors, contractors/ consultants, and war-drivers should be completely restricted from accessing the wireless network, even for external Web-access purposes.	All users are required to have valid accounts on the SSH server, or the domain, or access will be denied to unauthorized users, including free Web access. Since all traffic on the wireless network is encrypted, no Web or e-mail information can be sniffed from passive wireless machines.
Must require only a single action from novice end-users for e-mail and external Web access.	The command-line SSH clients can be easily scripted so that novice end-users, either on Windows or Unix, need only to execute an SSH script file, which holds the one-line command syntax for the SSH connection, and enter the correct password to log in.
Must provide stable and consistent performance.	SSH always provides stable and consistent performance after implementation.

Case Study #3: Secure File Servers

The following case study examines an organization called MicroHat. Micro-Hat is a pharmaceutical organization that engineers medicine to help victims of epilepsy. There is a great deal of collaboration among engineers at Micro-Hat; therefore, secure access to file servers, where hundreds of medical documents can be shared among co-workers, is provided to all employees.

The Problem

MicroHat needs to provide secure access to the corporate Microsoft Windows file server to the engineering department, while using only Linux Red Hat workstations.

Business Requirements

The business requirements provided by MicroHat are as follows:

- SSH client must only support Red Hat Linux.
- Windows server can only support SMB.
- All SMB traffic must be encrypted with 3DES or above.

One of the major advantages of SSH, aside from its port-forwarding options, is its SFTP subsystem. Many, if not all organizations, need, have, and support file servers. Many of these file servers contain sensitive information used to support and fuel organizations. This case study focuses on how to use SSH for a secure file server for organizations that use the Windows operating system for file servers and use Unix, or more specifically Linux, for client workstations.

To implement a secure file server, you need one core requirement from the SSH server: to encrypt all file-transfer connections that use SMB. The following lists the utilities you will be using in order to satisfy MicroHat's business requirements:

- OpenSSH for the SSH server
- OpenSSH's SSH client
- smbclient for the SMB client

The key requirements from an architectural perspective will be quite minor. Since the engineering department belongs in the internal network, where the Windows file server also resides, each client will be able to access the server by default. All clients will require the OpenSSH SFTP client to access the SFTP subsystem on the SSH server or smbclient to access the port-forwarding SMB connections. Figure 10.15 shows the architecture to fulfill the requirements.

All devices in Figure 10.15 are part of the existing architecture, except for the OpenSSH server that has been installed on the Windows file server. All clients are Red Hat Linux and will have access to the SSH servers, which includes the SFTP subsystem, on the Windows file server.

Configuration

The paragraphs that follow examine two types of configuration: SSH server configuration and SSH client configuration.

SSH Server Configuration

The first order of business is to configure OpenSSH on the Windows file server. (For more information on the installation process, see Chapter 1.) The Windows file server basically has two partitions with two separate disk drives. Partition 1 is for the operating system's files, including binaries, libraries, and support files, to keep the operating system running. Partition 2 is a separate 100GB disk that is mounted as drive D. After the OpenSSH server has been installed from the Windows file server, you will need to mount the D partition for all SSH clients on the Linux workstations. To mount the D partition, complete the following steps:

1. Open the passwd file from c:\Program Files\OpenSSH\etc\.

2. Change the default directory for each user in the passwd file on the Windows file server. Enter **/cgydrive/d**, as shown in the following syntax:

```
administrator:::::administrator-account:/cygdrive/d:/ssh/switch.exe
kusum::520::Kusum's-Account:/cygdrive/d:/ssh/switch.exe
sudhanshu::521::Sudhanshu's-Account:/cygdrive/d:/ssh/switch.exe
neeraja::522::Neeraja's-Account:/cygdrive/d:/ssh/switch.exe
kanchan::523::Kanchan's-Account:/cygdrive/d:/ssh/switch.exe
jignesh::524::Jignesh's-Account:/cygdrive/d:/ssh/switch.exe
anand::525::Anand's-Account:/cygdrive/d:/ssh/switch.exe
```

```
amiee::526::Amiee's-Account:/cygdrive/d:/ssh/switch.exe
amit::527::Amit's-Account:/cygdrive/d:/ssh/switch.exe
katie::528::Katie's-Account:/cygdrive/d:/ssh/switch.exe
rohan::529::Rohan's-Account:/cygdrive/d:/ssh/switch.exe
shreya::530::Shreya's-Account:/cygdrive/d:/ssh/switch.exe
shashi::531::Shashi's-Account:/cygdrive/d:/ssh/switch.exe
prabha::532::Prabha's-Account:/cygdrive/d:/ssh/switch.exe
chandradhar::533::Chandradhar's-Account:/cygdrive/d:/ssh/switch.exe
```

3. Stop and restart the OpenSSH service using the following commands:

```
c:\net stop "OpenSSH Server"
c:\net start "OpenSSH Server"
```

Now the Windows file server has an OpenSSH server running on the system, with all users in the engineering group having access to the D partition.

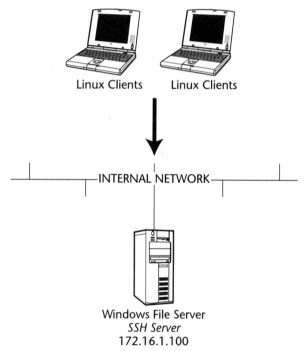

Figure 10.15   SSH architecture for case study #3.

SSH Client Configuration

The second order of business is to configure the smbclient and OpenSSH clients on the Red Hat Linux workstations. Since both the smbclient and OpenSSH client are included by default on the RedHat Linux 8.0 operating system, no special installation is required. For the Linux clients to access the Windows file server in a secure fashion, two separate methods can be used: SFTP or SMB with port forwarding. To connect to the Windows file server using SFTP on the Linux clients, complete the following steps:

1. Change directories to /usr/bin, where the SFTP client is located, shown with the following syntax:

   ```
   #cd /usr/bin
   ```

2. Type the appropriate SFTP command to connect to the SSH server on port 22. Enter the password when prompted, as shown in the following syntax:

   ```
   #sftp administrator@172.16.1.100
   administrator@172.16.1.100's password:
   ```

3. After the correct password is entered, you will have SFTP prompt to upload and download files from the Windows file server over a secure channel, as shown in the following syntax:

   ```
   sftp>
   ```

To connect to the Windows file server using smbclient and port forwarding on the Linux clients, complete the following steps:

1. Change directories to /usr/bin, where the SSH client is located, shown with the following syntax:

   ```
   #cd /usr/bin
   ```

2. Type the appropriate SSH command to connect to the SSH server on port 22. Be sure to port forward the required SMB ports, which would be port 445 on both the local workstation and remote host (or 139 if NT 4.0 or lower is being used). Enter the password when prompted, as shown in the following syntax:

   ```
   #ssh administrator@172.16.1.100 -L 445:172.16.1.100:445
   administrator@172.16.1.100's password:
   ```

3. After the correct password has been entered, you will have a valid SSH prompt on the Window file server, which would be the d:\ prompt from the cygdrive entered earlier. Furthermore, you will have a port-forwarding session enabled on your local Linux workstation, using port 445, to the remote Windows file server, also using port 445.

4. After the SSH session and port-forwarding entries have been enabled, open a different shell on the Linux client. Type the appropriate smb-client syntax that connects to your loopback interface (127.0.0.1), which will then be port forwarded to the remote SMB service (the Windows file server's protocol for file transfer) over the encrypted SSH tunnel:

```
#smbclient \\\\127.0.0.1\\D -U administrator -p 445
```

5. After entering in the correct password, you will be given an SMB prompt to transfer files to and from the Windows file server over an encrypted SSH tunnel, as shown in the following syntax:

```
smb: \>
```

Now all engineering users can use SSH port forwarding to use smbclient, which allows access to the Windows file server in a secure and encrypted manner.

Results Checklist

After the setup has been completed, the requirements of case study #3 will have all been met, as described in Table 10.7.

Table 10.7   Business Requirements and Results

BUSINESS REQUIREMENT	RESULTS
All SMB traffic must be encrypted with 3DES or above.	OpenSSH server and client can always support 3DES or above encryption.
The SSH client must support only RedHat Linux.	All RedHat Linux workstations have OpenSSH installed, which holds utilities such as SSH and SFTP by default. Also, smbclient is available on all RedHat Linux machines.
Windows server can support only SMB.	The Windows file server was not modified, except for the fact that OpenSSH was installed on the file server, which does not affect the SMB networking protocol.

Summary

This chapter presents three case studies that describe several of the key items discussed in this book. The chapter begins with secure remote access, one of the strongest and most powerful uses of SSH. SSH has provided the ability for secure remote access since SSH version 2 was developed. The chapter then shifts to a more recent problem that SSH has been able to solve. Insecure wireless (802.11) connectivity is a new issue that many organizations are unprepared for. Wireless networks brought so much ease and flexibility to end-users, but devastated corporate security architecture and policies. Even though SSH was developed long before wireless networks were introduced, due to SSH's flexibility, secure wireless connectivity with SSH has become relatively easy. Lastly, the third case study focuses on a very straightforward feature of SSH, which is providing secure file access among different operating systems. The key idea behind this case study is to demonstrate that SSH is not a Unix-only tool, although most of its history resides in the Unix world, but a utility that can work in both the Windows world and the Unix world. While different operating systems provide different types of file-sharing protocols, such as SMB and NFS, without a lot of security, SSH is not only able to bridge the gap between different systems when it comes to dependable file sharing, but is also able to offer such functionality in a secure manner.

Epilogue

In many types of competitive events, certain groups, teams, and organizations receive awards and recognitions based on their outstanding capabilities and accomplishments. Some of the awards are called All-American, All-state, All-conference, All-academic, All-star, All-first-team, All-region, or All-pro. Because SSH can do so much and can do it all very well, the perfect name for it would be All-everything. SSH can offer secure remote access; secure SOCKS; secure Telnet; secure RSH/Rlogin; secure backups; secure FTP; secure file transfer (SMB/NFS); secure authentication; secure management; secure wireless; secure e-mail; and secure Web browsing. With so much to offer, there is no comparison between SSH and any other utility.

This book has taken a methodical approach toward describing SSH, even though it feels as though I have just hit the tip of the iceberg. I introduce some of the basics of SSH in Chapter 1, describing its features and popular uses. While Chapter 1 discusses why you should use SSH, the focus of the rest of the book is to show you how to use SSH. Chapters 2 and 3 discuss some of the major SSH servers and clients to make you aware of all the basics of these products. Then the book turns to the details of how to optimize SSH. Chapter 4 describes the authentication advances of SSH, such as username/password, public-key authentication, server-side authentication, and host-based authentication. Chapter 4 shows how to implement the various authentication features of SSH, while making the process seemly for the end-user. Chapter 5 shifts gears and shows how SSH can be used with other products for secure management. While many organizations secure many aspects of their architecture, some architects forget how important management security becomes, especially when considering that management connections hold advanced privileges. Chapters 6 and 7 are dedicated to one of the strongest features of SSH: port forwarding. SSH's ability to port forward any TCP port gives it the ability to provide security to many insecure entities such as mail, file transfer, management, and so on. Chapter 8 shows how to use SSH in some of the typical means, such as an RSH or Rlogin replacement, and then demonstrates how to use it with file transfer and secure backups. Lastly, Chapter 9 discusses the use of SSH and SOCKS and dynamic port forwarding. This chapter shows how to use two existing features of SSH and how to make SSH architecture more streamlined with the use of SOCKS or how to apply SSH architecture to new dangerous technologies such as wireless networks.

To best summarize SSH, I have to refer to the opening paragraph of this book, which states that SSH can be described in many different ways. It can be described as a protocol, an encryption tool, a client/server application, or a command interface. Along with its various descriptions, SSH provides various functions with a single package. SSH's diverse set of services, and the ability to provide those services in a secure manner, have allowed it to become a staple in many enterprise networks.

All in all, I have discussed a lot of faces of SSH in this book, each of which can add, establish, or support functionally and security requirements in any architecture. Whether SSH will be used as a Telnet replacement or as a utility to secure 90 percent of your network architecture, it has the ability to be deployed so that it is flexible and optimal to your organization.

Mahatma Gandhi once said, "I have nothing new to teach the world, truth and non-violence are as old as the hills." Although Gandhi was always ahead of his time, you probably never thought his words would be applied to SSH. Gandhi showed the world how an old idea can be used to overcome the biggest challenges when it is applied in an optimal way. Similarly, all the core encryption features, flexibility techniques, functionality methods, and security utilities discussed in this book are not new to SSH but have always existed. This book is just a tool to help both novice and expert SSH users familiarize themselves with SSH and to demonstrate the many ways to optimize it.

Index